Enterprise Risk Analysis

for Property & Liability Insurance Companies

A PRACTICAL GUIDE TO STANDARD MODELS
AND EMERGING SOLUTIONS

Guy Carpenter & Company, LLC, New York 10010

© 2007 by Guy Carpenter & Company, LLC. All rights reserved. Published 2007. Printed in the United States of America
ISBN 0-615-13356-8

Section 2.5 of the present work appeared in a modified format in *Casualty Actuarial Society Forum* (Summer 2001) pp. 179-199.
© 2001 by Casualty Actuarial Society.

FOREWORD BY

David Spiller

CONTRIBUTING AUTHORS

Paul J. Brehm, FCAS, MAAA

Spencer M. Gluck, FCAS, MAAA

Rodney E. Kreps, FCAS

John A. Major, ASA, MAAA

Donald F. Mango, FCAS, MAAA

Richard Shaw, FIA

Gary G. Venter, FCAS, MAAA

Steven B. White, FCAS, MAAA

Susan E. Witcraft, FCAS, MAAA

EDITORS

Paul J. Brehm, FCAS, MAAA

Geoffrey R. Perry, CEng MIET

Gary G. Venter, FCAS, MAAA

Susan E. Witcraft, FCAS, MAAA

Table of Contents

FOREWORD

1. Introduction
1.1 Historical Context — 2
1.2 Overview of Enterprise Risk Management — 4
1.3 Enterprise Risk Modeling Overview — 8

2. Applications of Models in ERM
2.1 Corporate Decision Making Using an Enterprise Risk Model — 24
2.2 Risk Measures and Capital Allocation — 31
2.3 Regulatory and Rating Agency Capital Adequacy Models — 42
2.4 Asset-Liability Management — 49
2.5 Measuring Value in Reinsurance — 55
2.6 Measuring the Market Value of Risk Management: An Introduction to FLAVORED Models — 80

3. General Modeling Considerations
3.1 Considerations on Implementing Internal Risk Models — 102
3.2 Modeling Parameter Uncertainty — 108
3.3 Modeling Dependency: Correlations and Copulas — 117
3.4 Timeline Simulation — 130

4. Operational and Strategic Risk
4.1 Operational Risk — 144
4.2 Strategic Risk — 161

5. Insurance Hazard Modeling
5.1 Severity and Frequency Distributions — 176
5.2 Overview of Loss Reserve Risk Models — 197
5.3 Reducing the Variance of Reserve Estimates — 211
5.4 Approaches to Modeling the Underwriting Cycle — 226

6. Financial Risk Models
6.1 Reinsurance Receivable Risk: Willingness to Pay — 244
6.2 Investment Market Risk — 247

CHAPTER REFERENCES — 256
INDEX — 276

Foreword

By David Spiller, Chief Executive Officer
Guy Carpenter & Company, LLC

The insurance industry is being both pushed and pulled toward Enterprise Risk Management (ERM). On one hand, regulators and rating agencies are pushing insurers and reinsurers for ERM analysis to verify solvency and effective risk management. On the other hand, ERM is increasingly being recognized by management as simply a good idea. Industry leaders are recognizing that an integrated basis can add value to a corporation.

While the concept of ERM makes perfect sense, implementing enterprise-wide measurement, analysis and risk management practices is not an easy task. It is particularly difficult for companies who assume portfolios of risk that originate with others. For insurers and reinsurers, it is complex, broad in scope, rapidly evolving and ultimately requires knowledge of advanced risk modeling techniques.

So how do you get started? What are the best practices? Where are the pitfalls?

Within this book, we have assembled years of research and practical applications in ERM — from leading specialists in the field — to help our insurers and reinsurers address this important issue. It is a "practical" guide to ERM — a "how-to" book on risk modeling techniques.

Even if you are not planning to adopt a comprehensive Enterprise Risk Management program, risk managers can still draw on approaches from the ERM world. Here are a few lessons that we believe are helpful to the overall management of a company:

- First, "experience the future." If you have already considered scenarios other than what is "expected" in the firm's strategic plan and budget, you will be better prepared to address the "unexpected" when the real world does not conform according to plan.

- Second, follow through with ERM-generated contingency plans and avoid being a slave to the budget plan. Regulators and rating agencies are looking for active use of ERM in planning and management decisions. When the world does not behave as planned, poor decisions may be made if management feels obligated to "make a budget" that is unreasonable given environmental changes.

- If ERM is to drive real action, the need for quality data to underpin risk models is an obvious third lesson. Without accurate, detailed data, we cannot have confidence in our models, no matter how sophisticated they might be. And without confidence, it would be difficult to justify decisions with any conviction about the outcomes.

- Finally, recognize the need to identify and manage correlated risks. Large events, economic scenarios and industry shifts can have a "knock-on" effect that magnifies loss. ERM can help reveal relationships between lines of business and categories of risk that might otherwise be overlooked.

While these are but a few of the useful lessons discussed within these pages, we are confident that readers will find numerous practical examples for managing their business using ERM methodologies.

Given the fast-growing field of ERM, our hope is that the depth and comprehensive nature of the modeling techniques contained herein will prove to be a timely and valuable resource for those working in this field.

While the key audience for this book is expected to be actuaries requiring technical assistance in creating ERM-type models for their companies, those in top management can gain a fuller appreciation of the topic by reading Section 1, the early sections of Sections 2 and 3, and Section 4. A perusal of the other chapters, while daunting to the mathematically challenged, nevertheless provide some sense of the process and tasks involved in creating workable models for ERM decision making.

Introduction

1.1 Historical Context

In the early 1990s, the National Association of Insurance Commissioners (NAIC) proclaimed that the newly minted risk-based capital (RBC) framework was just a necessary first step and that scenario testing and dynamic models were to follow. If this proclamation wasn't the germination of dynamic financial analysis (DFA) in the U.S. property-casualty insurance industry, it was at least a potent fertilizer. DFA became the rage throughout the balance of the 1990s, especially in consulting circles.

The NAIC has yet to compel anything beyond RBC. Within the walls of insurance companies, developing financial models of the entire enterprise, and then managing accordingly, required crossing traditional silos, such as underwriting and investments. Furthermore, DFA models focused on volatilities, as well as on expected results. The combination of internal factors often meant there was no natural champion for DFA within the company. Lacking an external impetus and internal champions, the promise of DFA was never realized.

Contrast the brief history of DFA with that of catastrophe (cat) models. Cat models existed in the 1980s but were primitive by today's standards. Also, by today's standards, these models were not widely used. Following Hurricane Andrew in 1992, however, there were both internal and external pressures that led to the increased use, and eventual acceptance, of cat models to measure and manage risk accordingly. Indeed, cat models have now become so entrenched in the operations of an insurance company that the inability to speak to a company's modeled loss exposure at benchmark return periods (PML) in today's environment would be seen as *de facto* evidence of mismanagement by rating agencies.

Where in this spectrum of acceptance – both internal and external to a company – is enterprise risk management (ERM) today? Truthfully, it's probably somewhere in between the near-universal acceptance enjoyed by cat models and the lack of traction suffered by DFA models. But the world is changing.

Externally, pressure is certainly increasing on companies to develop internal enterprise-wide risk models and make use of them in the management of the business. In 1998 and 1999, the Basel Committee established a three-pillar regulatory framework (quantification, risk management or supervision and transparency or disclosure) for assessing the capital requirements for banks, called Basel II[1]. Since then, there has been a flurry of activity in accounting and regulatory circles relating to the insurance industry. These developments include:

---

1   In simplest terms, Basel II added operational risk to the previous banking regulations of Basel I, which assessed credit and market risk.

- In 1999, the International Association of Insurance Supervision (IAIS) began the development of an approach to the rating of an insurer based on its unique risks, relying heavily on the Basel II three-pillar approach. The IAIS documented this approach in a paper published in 2004. Included in the quantification pillar is a solvency capital requirement (SCR), based, in part, on a company's internal risk model. The European Union (EU) is expected to adopt this framework through the Capital Requirements Directive (CRD).

- Both Canada (Canadian Dynamic Capital Adequacy Test) and Australia (Australia Internal Model Based Method) have developed and implemented regulatory requirements regarding the construction and use of internal risk models in the management of an insurance enterprise.

- The Financial Services Authority (FSA) in the UK implemented Individual Capital Adequacy Standards (ICAS) in 2004. Under ICAS, "a firm is required to undertake regular assessments of the amount and quality of capital which in their view is adequate for the size and nature of their business…"

- The NAIC is moving toward a new audit paradigm called CARRMEL – capital adequacy, asset quality, reserves, reinsurance, management, earnings and liquidity.

- In 2005, Standard & Poor's stated that an insurer's ERM program will become a critical component in its rating methodology. Other rating agencies – Moody's, A.M. Best's and Fitch – are similarly adjusting their methodologies. In fact, Moody's and Fitch[2] are developing their own ERM models for application to insurers, based primarily on statutory annual statement data in the United States.

If external pressures are building, the problem of finding the internal champion still remains. Enterprise-wide risk assessment and management will require quantitative skills, operational experience and, last but not least, political skills (or executive rank) to transcend organizational silos. Clearly, the natural champion would be the Chief Risk Officer (CRO). However, the CRO is not a position that many insurers currently have.

We believe external pressure will grow to a level in which internal politics will give way to external pressures and a new paradigm of running an insurance company. Much like their integration of cat models in analyzing and managing risk, well-managed insurance companies will, in our view, establish and execute internal, enterprise-wide risk models and use such models to understand and manage the risks and opportunities faced by the company.

---

2   Fitch released an exposure draft of its proposed methodology on June 6, 2006.

It is with this backdrop that we offer this book on topics in enterprise risk analysis. ERM is an evolving subject with evolving methods. This book is an anthology of works from the Guy Carpenter & Company, LLC, Instrat® professionals who describe an approach to ERM today. Guy Carpenter has been a pioneer in the insurance industry in the modeling of risk and its treatment. In the sections that follow, we present models and management frameworks that are the result of years of research and practical application for insurance clients. We hope you find this book to be a valuable resource.

1.2 Overview of Enterprise Risk Management

We start by defining Enterprise Risk Management (ERM).
"Enterprise risk management is the process of systematically and comprehensively identifying critical risks, quantifying their impacts and implementing integrated strategies to maximize enterprise value."

There are several key aspects to the above definition, including:

1. An effective ERM program should be a regular process, not just a one-time event.
2. Risks should be considered on an enterprise-wide basis. We have developed a risk taxonomy (see Figure 1.2.1) for insurers that considers insurance hazard risk, financial risk, strategic risk and operational risk.
3. Not all risks are material. The focus of ERM is on those risks that represent the most significant impact to the value of the firm.
4. Risk exists due to actual outcomes that may differ from expected outcomes. Risk is not confined to only adverse departures from expectations.
5. Risks must be quantified to the extent possible. Their impacts must be evaluated on a portfolio basis to gauge significance. Correlations among risks must be evaluated and quantified.
6. Strategies and plans must be developed and implemented to avoid, mitigate or possibly exploit significant risk factors.
7. To maximize the firm's value, risk management strategies are evaluated for trade off between risk and return.

An insurer is unique in that it faces the same business risks borne by any and all businesses – financial, strategic and operational – but it also purposely assumes an additional risk (insurance hazard) as its core purpose for being. We have organized company risk according to the categories shown in Figure 1.2.1.

FIGURE 1.2.1: RISK TAXONOMY

In the above taxonomy, risk factors are defined as follows:

- Insurance hazard risk, in our context, is the risk assumed by the insurance enterprise from outside parties in exchange for a premium.

    We split the insurance risk between currently in-force exposures and past exposures. Current insurance exposure is further split between catastrophic (or accumulation – affecting multiple insureds in a single event) and noncatastrophic (labeled "underwriting" above).

    Insurance hazard risk is not to be confused with the various hazards faced by the firm in its own operations. Whereas "insurance hazard" risk is that *assumed* by the company, the operational risk subcategory "hazard" includes the company's own exposure to such risks as fire, weather, liability, etc. For the company's own exposure, hazard represents only down-side risk. But for an insurance company, insurance hazard risk is two-sided (a "speculative risk"), as it represents the firm's reason for being.

- Financial risk includes risk in the insurer's asset portfolio related to the volatility in interest rates, foreign exchange rates, equity prices, credit quality and liquidity. Though all companies have some degree of financial risk, insurers are somewhat unique in this regard, as well, given the preponderance of invested assets on the balance sheet relative to the company's equity.

- Operational risks are the execution risks of the company. We are in the business of accepting the insurance risk of others, so we understand and accept that insurance hazard, and even financial performance, is random. However, beyond the obvious randomness in the business, insurance companies face the same risk as do all businesses: Despite the best of intentions, things don't always turn out as planned.

- Strategic risk is about choices – making the right or wrong strategic choices, refusing to choose or even failing to recognize that choices needed to be made. Operational risk relates to threats to company value from actions, where either the action itself or its consequences departed from plan. By contrast, strategic risk is the inherent threat to the company in choosing the wrong plan, given the current and expected market conditions.

The categories of operational and strategic risk are less amenable to quantitative modeling and have been a source of frustration for enterprise risk practitioners, at least the quantitative ones. Perhaps ongoing research will prove fruitful in these areas. However, regardless of the inability to precisely quantify some risk factors, the discipline of ERM still adds value to the firm.

We view the ERM process as a sequence of steps that runs the gamut from diagnosis to treatment and is then repeated. The diagram in Figure 1.2.2 illustrates our framework.

FIGURE 1.2.2: ENTERPRISE RISK MANAGEMENT PROCESS

At the outset of the process, in the diagnostic stage, the company must conduct a high-level risk assessment. What are those factors that pose a potentially serious threat to the value of the firm? While every potential risk is fair game at this point, this phase should include a preliminary assessment of a critical threshold value that the company considers a material or significant risk.

In his seminal paper on integrated risk management, Kent Miller [1], offered a categorization of uncertainties for the sake of their systematic consideration. Miller's list (below) serves as a structured way to analyze the pillars of the risk taxonomy.

1. General environment
    a. Political uncertainties (democratic changes, war, revolution...)
    b. Government policy (fiscal, monetary changes, regulation...)
    c. Macroeconomic (inflation, interest rates...)
    d. Social (terrorism...)
    e. Natural (hurricane, earthquake, flood, drought...)
2. Industry
    a. Input market (supply, quality...)
    b. Product market (demand...)
    c. Competitive uncertainties (new entrants, rivalry...)
3. Firm specific
    a. Operating (labor, supply, production...)
    b. Liability (products, pollution, employment...)
    c. R&D
    d. Credit
    e. Behavioral

After risks have been identified, they are subjected to an analytical process. Critical risks – those that have the potential to exceed the company's threshold – are modeled to the extent possible. Analysis begins along the lines of the taxonomy outlined above. Risks are quantified, preferably by creating probability distributions of potential outcomes.

Correlations among risk factors must be recognized, and distributions must be integrated across the various risk silos. Using the combined distribution of outcomes, risk metrics are calculated to establish a measure of the degree of risk. The selected risk measures must be consistent with management's views toward risk. Those risk factors that contribute to the adverse scenarios or risk metrics above the critical threshold must be prioritized.

The "M" in ERM does not stand for "modeling," but rather "management." Therefore, the process is not complete when the analysis is done. The next step is implementation of the activities identified in the preceding analysis. Traditional forms of risk management include:

1. Avoidance of the risk
2. Reduction in the chance of occurrence
3. Mitigation of the effect of given occurrence
4. Elimination or transference of the consequences, and/or
5. Retention, and assumption internally of (by design or by default) some or all of the risk.

If a risk factor is speculative (chances of gain as well as loss), there can be an opportunity to capitalize on the risk rather than manage it away. Analysis is required in this step as well, since choosing between various options will often come down to a cost/benefit analysis or a risk/return trade-off.

Finally, it is perhaps true in all management contexts that, having executed a plan or implemented an activity, it is incumbent upon management to monitor the process vis-à-vis expectations. Furthermore, ERM should not be viewed as a "project" to be completed. As the company, market or competitors change, the company will frequently update plans and expectations and will continually have new risks to address, new ways to control them, new options for treating them and new ways of transferring them.

1.3 Enterprise Risk Modeling Overview

The aim of enterprise risk modeling is to understand and quantify the relationships among the risks to the business that arise from its assets, liabilities and ongoing underwriting, all of which are affected by internal decisions and external factors. Such models combine submodels of the many contributing elements to produce an overall risk profile of the business. This modeling can help the insurer with important management functions and strategic decisions, such as:

- Determining capital needed to support risk, maintain ratings, etc.
- Identifying the sources of significant risk and the cost of capital to support them
- Setting reinsurance strategies
- Planning growth

- Managing asset mix
- Valuing companies for mergers and acquisitions

Enterprise risk models are data-hungry, complex programs underpinned by very sophisticated mathematical arguments. While they don't produce any magic answers, there are differences between better models and weaker models.

A good model will show, as realistically as possible, the balance between risk and reward from a range of different strategies, such as changing the asset mix or reinsurance program, or choosing which lines of business to grow. A weaker model may exaggerate certain aspects of risk while underestimating others. If so, it will give a misleading impression that may result in an overly aggressive or overly cautious approach, which in turn may lead to less-than-optimal financial performance.

A good model also recognizes and reflects its own inevitable imperfection. The structure of the model only approximates the insurer's reality, and the parameters of the model are uncertain. As a simple example, annual inflation over the next three years could be 3 percent or 5 percent, and the difference is likely to be material to both sides of the insurer's balance sheet.

In every model, a variety of different risk elements are represented – each with its own set of issues and pitfalls. The extent and quality of the data may vary, and there are numerous choices to be made regarding assumptions and mathematical methods. All can affect the suitability and usefulness of the model.

Ultimately, for ERM to be truly effective, the insurer needs to have confidence in the model maker. We believe that the most important elements that differentiate model quality are:

- The model reflects the relative importance of various risks to business decisions.
- The modelers have a deep knowledge of the fundamentals of those risks.
- The model includes mathematical techniques to reflect the relationships among risks (dependencies).
- The modelers have a trusted relationship with senior management of the company.

The enterprise risk model may incorporate the output of other models. Likely examples are catastrophe models, macroeconomic models and credit risk models. When the results of other models are incorporated, it is essential that the enterprise risk model take into account the uncertainty associated with those other models.

There are significant business risks and issues that are less amenable to detailed representation in an enterprise risk model. For example, operational risks such as IT hardware and software exposures, pension funding inadequacy, loss of key executives, rogue traders or fraud can be extremely important to the success of a business. In fact, these types of risks have more often been the cause of defaults by seemingly sound insurers than the specific financial risks of the business.

Operational risks require specialized management processes and are difficult to incorporate into an overall risk model. Operational risk can be modeled in bulk using informed judgments, but only with a high degree of associated uncertainty. Often, the most reasonable approach is to use the model to manage the risks for which the modeling process is effective, while recognizing that there are some operational risks that are at best weakly represented in such a model, requiring other management methods.

Essential elements of the enterprise risk model are thus:

- Underwriting risk
- Reserving risk
- Asset risk
- Dependencies (correlation)

The remainder of this chapter discusses additional details of these model elements. We then conclude with a discussion of using such a model to evaluate capital requirements.

Each of the topics is developed in greater detail in later chapters.

Underwriting Risk

Some of the issues that must be addressed to properly model underwriting risks include:

- Loss frequency and severity distributions
- Pricing risk
- Parameter risk
- Catastrophe modeling uncertainty

Loss frequency and severity distributions are used to quantify loss potential, an essential element of modeling underwriting risk. Pricing risk is also crucial and can arise from misestimation of projected losses, as well as competitive market pressures. Parameter risk is a critical area of focus and competes with catastrophes as the largest risk to which an insurer is exposed. In fact, net of reinsurance, parameter risk may exceed catastrophe exposure. Catastrophe modeling uncertainty is a special case of parameter risk, meriting specific discussion.

Loss Frequency and Severity Distributions

A variety of frequency and severity distributions that fit the unique characteristics of insurance loss data are now available, based on Gary Venter's *Transformed Beta and Gamma Distributions and Aggregate Losses* [2], and reformulated by Rodney Kreps in the Instrat® working paper, *Continuous Distributions*[3] [1]. Modern statistics also provides good methods of estimating parameters, testing the quality of fit and understanding the uncertainties that remain. Good control of these issues, however, is still a differentiating feature of the best modelers. The topic of distribution modeling is taken up in Section 5.1.

Pricing Risk

Instability in underwriting results arises from variations in the premiums as well as the losses. Sometimes underpricing is difficult to ascertain for a number of years, creating an accumulation of losses that is subsequently recognized as a reserve deficiency.

Insurance pricing is notoriously cyclical. The underwriting cycle contributes significantly to pricing risk. Any multiperiod model of an insurance company will have to model the underwriting cycle and management's responses to it. Section 5.4 offers some insights into models of the underwriting cycle.

Parameter Risk

The frequency and severity distributions discussed previously reflect random uncertainty to which the insurer is exposed, given the form and parameters of those distributions. But the form and parameters of those distributions are only estimated. Parameter risk reflects the imperfection of the model itself: misestimated parameters, imperfect form and risk not modeled. Aspects of parameter risk include:

- Estimation risk
- Projection risk
- Event risk
- Systematic risk

---

3 Kreps' "Continuous Distributions" is available at http://ERMBook.guycarp.com.

Estimation Risk
Estimating the form and parameters of frequency and severity distributions requires data. However, by definition, there is never enough data to know the true form and parameters. More data and better data quality reduces this risk, but never eliminates it.

Statistical methods quantify how far the estimated parameters may be from the true parameters. This information can then be used in scenario generation, by modeling the probability that any given set of parameters is the correct one.

Projection Risk
Projection risks refer to changes over time and the uncertainty in the projections of these changes. The most common of such projections are:

- Trends in frequency and severity from the time of the data to the current and future underwriting periods, and
- Development of immature loss experience from recent underwriting periods to its ultimate value.

Each of these projections is itself based on a model, subject to uncertainty in its form and parameters.

Trend and development are also likely to be affected by macroeconomic factors, most notably inflation, and the corresponding dependencies should be reflected in the model.

Unexpected changes in risk conditions also add to projection risk. For example:

- Driving increases because fuel is cheaper.
- Criminals attack security vehicles because banks are more secure.
- A long-term shift to more extreme weather events aggravates property damage.

Event Risk
Event-related risk describes situations in which there is a causal link between a large unpredicted event and losses to the insurer. We refer to events outside of the company's control that affect the frequency or severity of losses. For example:

- A court finding favors a large group of policyholders (class action).
- An exposure that existed, unknown, for many years comes to light (asbestos).
- A new cause of loss emerges that was previously regarded as not covered (environmental losses, mold, construction defects).
- A regulator or court bars an important exclusion in the policy wording.
- A new entrant into the market reduces rates to grab market share.

These risks can occasionally be so large that they dwarf others, as the continuing asbestos saga demonstrates. They are hard to predict, but the possibility of such events needs to be included in the range of potential scenarios.

Systematic Risk
Systematic risks operate simultaneously on a large number of individual policies. They are, therefore, nondiversifying. They do not improve with added volume. Some of these are macroeconomic factors, of which inflation is the most important, affecting most liability and many asset classes. All of the previously discussed parameter risks are nondiversifying.

Consider, as an example, an automobile insurer with 200,000 expected claims. Even with a heavy-tailed severity distribution (standard deviation seven times the mean), the loss ratio would be quite stable in the absence of parameter uncertainty. Given an expected loss ratio of 65 percent, the 1-in-10-year loss ratio would be 66.3 percent and the 1-in-100 would be 67.4 percent. This is unrealistically stable. Modeling parameter risk at 10 percent increases the 1-in-10 loss ratio to 72.1 percent and the 1-in-100 to 78.3 percent, which may be somewhat more reflective of real insurance company experience.

Parameter risk is treated in more detail in Section 3.2.

Catastrophe Modeling Uncertainty

The insurer's exposure to natural and man-made catastrophes will most likely be reflected in the enterprise risk model by incorporating one or several proprietary catastrophe models. These catastrophe models are a further source of uncertainty. The providers' models differ not only from each other but also from themselves over time, as the modeling companies frequently release updates. Within these models, there is considerable uncertainty relating to the probabilities of various events and even more uncertainty in the amount of insured damage that will result from a specific event. Further uncertainty in the output results from data quality, including mismatches of company data fields and cat model assumptions. An enterprise risk model, therefore, needs to incorporate the uncertainties in catastrophe model results, which can in part be quantified by the use of more than one model for each peril.

The subject of natural catastrophe modeling is not specifically treated further in this book. From a modeling standpoint, incorporating natural catastrophes into an enterprise risk model requires only specific frequency and severity distributions (covered in general in Section 5.1). Catastrophe distributions are subject to the same considerations of parameter risk (Section 3.2) and correlation (Section 3.3) as other risk distributions. The difference with natural catastrophes, of course, is that the frequency and severity distributions are generally produced by widely accepted third-party models. In that regard, we have little to add to what vendors have already published.

Reserving Risk

The risk of reserves developing other than as anticipated is significant for property-casualty insurers, especially for business subject to a long development "tail." Both the reserve estimate and the reserve uncertainty can easily be understated. Reserve uncertainty affects both the amount of required capital and the time for which that capital must be held.

The discussion that follows focuses on reserves for losses and loss expenses (loss reserves for short). Unearned premium reserves also create risk exposure, but that exposure is more naturally modeled in conjunction with underwriting risk.

Traditional actuarial methods for loss reserve analysis are deterministic – a series of calculations that lead to a single number. The most common approaches are based on development factors, supplemented with additional calculations such as the Bornheutter-Ferguson method. However, some authors have been studying reserve variability and developing stochastic methods for a number of years. More recently, there has been an increasing interest in these approaches.

A model of reserve uncertainty is an essential part of the enterprise risk model. As for all previously described modeling, the uncertainty in the form and parameters of the reserve model must be accounted for. Specifying the reserve runoff model and testing it with quality-of-fit measures are key aspects of the risk modeling process.

Reserve risk models are discussed in additional detail in Sections 5.2 and 5.3.

Asset Risk

Companies in different segments of insurance in different regions take diverse approaches to investing. Modeling of asset risk needs to emphasize the correct issues in each market. The main asset classes are equities and bonds, but real estate-linked investments are important in some markets. Different types of bonds are important in different regions. Modeling of foreign exchange risk and inflation risk are closely related to asset modeling.

A key aspect of asset modeling is probabilistic reality; that is, modeling scenarios consistent with historical patterns. Asset modelers try to generate a large variety of scenarios against which to test the insurer's strategy, but variety alone is not enough for proper risk assessment. The more probable scenarios should be given more weight, while the less likely ones should be present according to their probability of occurring. The reasonableness of the scenarios and their probabilities can be evaluated to some degree by looking at historical patterns.

An enterprise risk model can also address the balancing of asset and underwriting risk. Because insurers have different risk profiles on the liability and asset sides of their balance sheets, it is possible for them to optimize the use of capital by offsetting insurance risks with investment risk. This strategy works especially well for life insurance companies, in that the matching investments often have high returns. Some studies have shown that property-liability companies can lose out on potential return by perfect matching, and that they can adopt a longer-duration strategy with better return characteristics while overall risk is still at manageable levels. However, these studies did not incorporate inflation-sensitive liabilities, which could lead to different conclusions. Liabilities carried at present values, marked to current interest rates, would also change the dynamic. In any case, a good enterprise risk model will create new opportunities for determining optimal strategies.

A traditional tool for asset risk analysis is the mean-variance efficient investment frontier, which should be supplemented with ranges of return around the means. Enterprise risk modeling also allows analysis of how the efficient frontier of total return changes with different reinsurance programs. The reinsurance program can be adjusted to fit best with the investment portfolio, or the asset mix itself can be altered according to conditions in the reinsurance and financial markets.

Asset-liability modeling and management is covered in Section 2.4.

Bonds

One way to eliminate unlikely scenarios in the bond market is to use arbitrage-free models. Although some arbitrage is often possible with published yield curves, these possibilities tend to be fleeting and hard to exploit. Having such scenarios in a bond model could misdirect choices toward strategies that ostensibly make arbitrage profits but which would fail in practice. The model should also capture historical features of the bond markets, like high autocorrelations and distributions of yield spreads. Bond models are discussed in detail in Section 6.2.

Equities

There is a degree of correlation between bond and equity returns that should be incorporated into the scenario generation. A starting point for equity modeling is the geometric Brownian motion model underlying the famous Black-Scholes options pricing model. However, the implied volatilities of options in the market do not relate to each other as this model predicts. Models that allow for more extreme motion of equity prices, or even discontinuities, are more realistic.

Foreign Exchange

There are historical relationships between a country's interest and exchange rates, and these relationships can be used to formulate a foreign exchange model. Economists have found that changes in actual and anticipated interest rates in two countries lead to changes in the exchange rates. However, to model this effect accurately, it is not enough to separately model the interest rates in the two economies and then forecast exchange rates. The interest rate movements across different economies are themselves correlated, and the model should build this in before creating the resulting exchange rate scenarios.

Dependencies (Correlation)

Modeling of dependencies and their effects is fundamental to the enterprise risk model. This is a difficult aspect of the modeling, and inadequate treatment is a dangerous pitfall and an easy trap to fall into. Without a realistic model of dependencies, the individual elements of the enterprise risk model may each be realistic, but when they are combined, the enterprise as a whole is unrealistically stable. Often, actual circumstances that have happened to real companies are modeled as highly improbable.

We begin with a general discussion of the sources and causes of dependency and follow with a discussion of a crucial issue in dependency modeling.

Sources of Dependency

Some aspects of dependency may be caused by the simultaneous impact of macroeconomic conditions on many risks. A good macroeconomic model will generate scenarios of inflation rates, interest rates, equity values, etc., all of which are interrelated (mutually dependent). For the insurer, asset values are directly affected. Inflation rates influence underwriting losses and loss reserve development simultaneously. Interest rates may influence the underwriting cycle.

Other dependencies are not specifically related to macroeconomic causes. Underwriting cycles, insurance loss trends and reserve developments correlate across lines of business and with each other. Catastrophes and other kinds of event risks can cross lines, and extreme events can have macroeconomic effects.

These dependencies are not easily quantified. An insurer's own data is rarely adequate in and of itself. The modeler may reference studies of multiple insurers, public insurance industry information and macroeconomic data. Inevitably, a good deal of professional judgment will be required.

Modeling Dependency

A statistical dependency is most often described by a single number, the correlation coefficient, and correlation is often used as a synonym for dependency. We have avoided that usage to emphasize that a dependency relationship is more complex than a single number. This is far more than a technical distinction – it can significantly impact the output of your enterprise risk model.

We focus on the crucial issue of tail dependency – the degree of dependency in extreme events. An insurance example might be the following: A large earthquake causes simultaneous large losses for property, workers compensation and automobile lines. Absent severe circumstances, the correlations among these lines are low.

An economic example might be the following: Inflation rates for medical services and automobile parts can be quite different, but when general inflation is extremely high, inflation will be high in both sectors. High tail dependency is characteristic of many of the types of risks we will be modeling. And yet, the most common practice is to reflect correlation through the multivariate normal distribution, which has relatively low tail dependency.

Figure 1.3.1, below, compares joint probability distributions for dependent random variables. The colored bands represent levels of probability. The dependency is illustrated with two different dependency functions, known as copulas. The two graphs represent the Heavy Right Tailed (HRT) copula and the normal copula, respectively. The overall correlations are identical for the normal and HRT copulas.

FIGURE 1.3.1: VARIATIONS IN THE CORRELATION OF EXTREME EVENTS

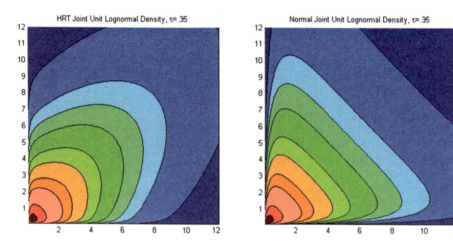

In each graph, the upper right corner is the region where losses are large for both lines. In this region, the normal copula is more similar to the uncorrelated case, while the HRT shows a more elevated probability.

Copulas provide a mathematical tool for expressing different forms of dependency. There are different types of copulas, and the choice of copula is critical in determining how well the model describes the likely impact of an extreme event on a portfolio. Venter's *Tails of Copulas* [3] and *Fit to a t – Estimation, Application and Limitations of the t-copula* [4] develops methodology for using copulas.

The topics of correlations and copulas are covered in greater detail in Section 3.3.

Setting Capital Requirements

Insurers sell promises and capital makes those promises valuable. Capital must be sufficient to sustain current underwriting, provide for adverse reserve changes or declines in assets and support growth. While the need for adequate capital comes from policyholders, the specific demands come from their surrogates: regulators and rating agencies. At the same time, shareholders require that capital be used efficiently. One of the key uses of the enterprise risk model is to help the insurer find the optimum level of capital that balances the competing requirements of efficiency and prudence.

A common approach for setting capital requirements is default avoidance: setting the capital so that the probability of default – total loss of capital – is appropriately remote. However, default is not necessarily the most germane reference point. Default is strictly about protecting current policyholders. To protect shareholder value, avoiding significant partial losses of capital may be a more important place to focus.

An insurer's value is more than its balance sheet. Its franchise value includes its customer base, agency relationships, reputation, infrastructure and expertise, all of which create its ability to produce profitable business. For an insurer, financial strength is inevitably a key component of its franchise value. When an insurer suffers financial losses large enough to damage its franchise value, its total loss of value exceeds the financial loss. For example, ratings downgrades beyond certain levels can be devastating for some insurers, and the amount of financial loss that would create such a downgrade may be a more meaningful reference point than a total default.

Setting capital to maximize the insurer's value creates a conceptual framework that unifies the seemingly competing requirements of efficiency and prudence. Section 2.2 presents historical and current developments in this theory that can lead to useful applications.

Other meaningful reference points that are less severe than default could include:

- Maintaining sufficient capital to continue to service renewals. The renewal book is typically significantly more profitable than new business. If writing the renewal business requires 80 percent of current capital levels, the relevant reference point would be a loss of 20 percent of capital.
- Maintaining sufficient capital so that the insurer not only survives a major catastrophe but thrives in its aftermath.

There is also an important practical consideration in focusing too heavily on extreme reference points – this is where the model is least reliable. Exhausting all capital is an extreme outcome that is difficult to model accurately. Events far in the tail of the risk distributions are poorly understood. There is little data in the tail, and the results are sensitive to assumptions about the form of the distributions.

Thus, in defining capital requirements, it is both more feasible to measure, and more relevant to business needs to refer to probability levels that are not nearly as remote as the probability of default. Management may also choose to monitor a number of key reference points.

The next step is to use the enterprise risk model to associate the selected probability levels with amounts of financial loss. A common value is the corresponding point of the cumulative distribution, also called the value at risk (V@R). Thus, the 99th percentile is the V@R-99[4]. However, the V@R-99 does not represent the amount the insurer loses 1 percent of the time, only the smallest amount the insurer loses 1 percent of the time. The average amount the insurer loses 1 percent of the time is called the tail value at risk, or TV@R-99. Increasingly, the TV@R is considered the more appropriate value to associate with a given probability level.

Combining the above concepts, an insurer might want to set its capital so that its 1-in-50-year result was a loss of no more than 20 percent of its capital. In that case, its minimum capital requirement would be five times TV@R-98.

In the end, the determination of optimal capital levels is not purely a risk measurement exercise. Having sufficient financial strength to attract business is essential for insurers. This has to be balanced against the requirements of the shareholders to achieve attractive returns. The place for risk measurement is in quantifying the risk the company is exposed to in relationship to the capital so established. Strategic risk decisions can then be made in the framework created. Capital is not set by risk measures, but analyzed by them to understand the sources of risk and for further strategic decision making.

---

4 In the insurance industry, the 99th percentile is typically the 99th worst outcome out of 100. In banking, the opposite convention is used, as this same outcome would be described as the 1st percentile.

Another important application of risk modeling is risk-adjusted performance measurement to identify business segments with higher (and lower) returns. Some companies allocate capital to each line or unit and then compare rates of return on the allocated capital. There are also other approaches to address the issue of risk-adjusted profitability, however. Several alternative approaches are outlined in Venter's *A Survey of Capital Allocation Methods with Commentary* [5].

Some companies allocate risk capital to the investment function as well. It can be useful to compare the riskiness of investments versus underwriting. The validity of such a comparison will depend on the consistency of the risk measures that are developed.

The topics of risk measures, capital and capital allocation are discussed in further detail in Section 2.2.

In the pages that follow, we offer models for the analysis of risk, tools and processes for the management of risk and examples of the marriage between analytics and execution.

Applications of Models in ERM

2.1 Corporate Decision Making Using an Enterprise Risk Model

BY DONALD F. MANGO, FCAS, MAAA

Evolution of Corporate Decision Making Under Uncertainty
Simulation modeling is widely used in all forms of corporate and organizational decision making under uncertainty. A science has developed around this topic and is known as decision analysis. In the seminal decision analysis reference, Spetzler [7] outlines this three-step evolutionary process, illustrated below in Figure 2.1.1.

FIGURE 2.1.1 EVOLUTION OF CORPORATE DECISION MAKING

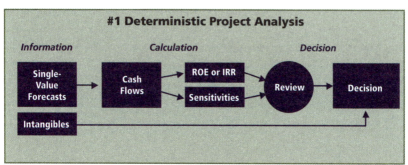

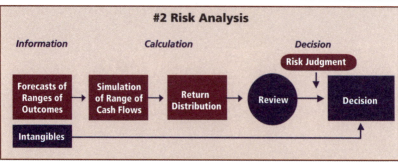

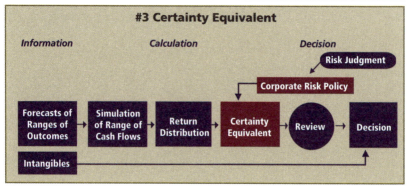

1. Deterministic Project Analysis – Using a single deterministic forecast for project cash flows, an objective function such as present value or internal rate of return is produced. Sensitivities to critical variables may be shown. Uncertainty (along with other intangibles) is handled judgmentally (i.e., intuitively) by decision makers.

2. Risk Analysis – Forecasts of distributions of critical variables are fed into a Monte Carlo simulation engine to produce a distribution of present value of cash flows. Risk judgment is still applied intuitively.

3. Certainty Equivalent – Certainty equivalent is an extension of risk analysis that quantifies the intuitive risk judgment by means of a corporate risk preference or utility function. The utility function does not replace judgment but simply formalizes the judgment so it can be consistently applied.

Best practice in actuarial risk modeling has evolved to Step 2, the risk analysis stage. Indeed, that is what actuaries call DFA. There is not yet consensus that the next evolutionary leap from Step 2 to Step 3 is proper or even meaningful. The debate centers on the role of corporate risk preference[5] in an efficient market/modern portfolio theory world.[6] An attempt to summarize the debate might go as follows:

- Diversified investors, with many small holdings of all available securities (the market portfolio) are concerned only with nondiversifiable (i.e., systematic) risk.
- Diversifiable (i.e., firm-specific) risk does not command any risk premium (additional return above the risk-free rate) in the market, since it can be diversified away by simply holding the market portfolio.
- Investors require a risk premium as compensation for bearing systematic risk.
- Firm managers should focus on maximizing shareholder value.
- Since their shareholders can diversify away firm-specific risk, the shareholders are indifferent (risk neutral) towards it.
- Therefore, firm managers ought to be indifferent to firm-specific risk as well.

Within such a theoretical framework, there is no apparent place for the Step 3 certainty equivalent approach, with its mathematical formulation of corporate risk preferences. Managers should care only about the wealth, risk preferences and other investment opportunities of the firm's owners. Absent a real-time survey system, the best proxy for this information is the record of stock prices – both their own stock and other comparable stocks. Firm managers and equity analysts perform these (admittedly complex) analyses in an attempt to discern the probable impact of major firm decisions on the stock price.

---

5 See Walls [16] for discussions of corporate risk attitudes and preferences.
6 There are numerous references on efficient markets and modern portfolio theory – for example, Bodie and Merton [1].

While this theory is appealing and has many advocates, it is short on practical advice for use in risk management decision making within the firm itself. For example:

- Those managing the firm have no way to identify which of the risks they face are firm specific and which are systematic. Finance theory offers no assistance beyond the aforementioned attempts to discern which decisions produced a noticeable impact on stock price and which did not.
- One of the more common market-based risk signals – the risk-adjusted discount rate – reflects risk only if there is a time lag. For many kinds of risks, the time aspect is unimportant – the risk is essentially instantaneous (what is called a jump risk).
- Market-based risk signals often lack the refinement and discriminatory power that managers need to make cost-benefit and tradeoff decisions for mitigation or hedging efforts.

Neither external (market) nor internal (company) perspectives appear sufficient on their own. However, there may be a perspective from which both approaches are seen as complementary parts of a single whole. Shareholders want market value maximized. Market value consists of book value – the recorded value of held assets – plus franchise value – the present value of future earnings growth. Risk management aims to both facilitate future earnings growth and prevent loss of future earnings – that is, to protect franchise value. So it appears that shareholders and managers may be aligned in this regard. Both want risk management in place to protect the franchise value (see Section 2.6 for a further discussion of modeling the market value of risk management). Therefore, both camps should support an internal corporate risk policy to help the firm make its risk management decisions in a more objective, consistent, repeatable and transparent manner. This provides some degree of support for the evolution to Step 3.

Decision Making with an Internal Risk Model (IRM)

Now we will discuss how corporate risk management decision making might be done with an internal risk model (IRM), a DFA model of the organization itself. Figure 2.1.2 shows the major elements in the process.

FIGURE 2.1.2: INTERNAL RISK MODELING MAJOR COMPONENTS

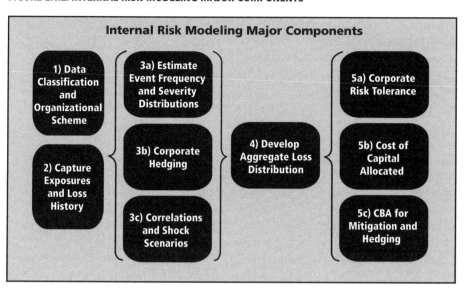

Elements 1 through 4 have been covered in depth elsewhere in this book. Elements 5a and 5b will be the focus in this chapter. Element 5c is covered in depth in the following section. We will begin with corporate risk tolerance.

Element 5a – Corporate Risk Tolerance

We seek a mechanism that:

1. Takes an aggregate loss distribution, with many sources of risk (e.g., lines of business);
2. Assesses (quantifies) the impact of the possible aggregate loss outcomes on the corporation;
3. Assigns a cost to each amount of impact; and
4. Attributes the cost back to the risk sources.

Corporate risk tolerance is needed in Steps 2 and 3. The impact (effect) of a loss depends on the organization's size, financial resources, ability and willingness to tolerate volatility. We will call this combination of factors the corporation's risk tolerance.

Alternatively, the translation of impact into cost requires a risk preference function of some form, either implicitly taken from an outside source (e.g., the capital markets), or explicitly derived from firm management attitudes. The key point is that any selected method implies some type of translation from impact to cost.

Some questions facing practitioners include: Should the choice be yours or someone else's (i.e., adopted by default)? Should it be implicit or explicit?

If a firm would like to develop its own explicit risk preferences, there are methods available. Spetzler [7] shows how to identify the parameters of a normative[7] corporate risk policy using a series of experiments involving indifference. One of the outputs of such a process is the transparent, objective, mathematical expression of the corporation's acceptable risk-reward tradeoffs. Such a function can improve cost-benefit analyses by quantifying, for example, the minimum decrease in risk (measured by any number of possible metrics) sufficient to justify a certain mitigation cost. Without such a function, cost-benefit analysis (CBA) decisions will still be made; however, the criteria will be inconsistent and opaque, driven in large part by the individual decision makers' intuitions and preferences.

Walls [10] demonstrates this in the context of energy exploration and production (E&P). He applies modern portfolio concepts to a set of available E&P opportunities. He identifies an efficient frontier of possible portfolios (i.e., those minimizing risk for a given return, subject to a constraint on total investment funds) and plots risk (measured as standard deviation of NPV) against return. In his example, the firm's existing portfolio is suboptimal, measured in terms of either risk (i.e., there are efficient frontier portfolios with the same return at lower risk) or return (i.e., there are efficient frontier portfolios with higher return at the same risk). So far, his approach is consistent with "standard" modern portfolio theory.

Walls' innovation is the notion that in order to select one of the efficient frontier portfolios, the firm must be able to answer the following questions:

- How much risk (standard deviation) are we willing to tolerate?
- How much reward are we willing to give up for a given reduction in risk, and vice versa?
- Are the risk-reward tradeoffs available along the efficient frontier acceptable to us?

The first question requires an answer to the firm's risk tolerance. The answer will indicate the riskiest portfolio choice that is tolerable. The second question requires the firm to express its risk preferences. The answer will allow the firm to select among available returns for given risk levels.

Once the first two answers are known, the third question can be answered.[8] Walls shows how, by using a corporate utility function, "decision makers can incorporate their firm's financial risk propensity into their choices among alternative portfolios"

---

7 Decision analysis differentiates among three possible purposes for a corporate utility function: descriptive, describing the subject's current risk attitude; predictive, predicting the subject's future behavior in risk situations; and normative, as a tool for improving future decisions involving risk. See Spetzler [13].
8 If the *market price of risk* is currently too low, the firm could opt to hold off and not tie up any capital at that time.

[10]. Of particular importance is the idea that modern portfolio theory presents a set of choices among possible portfolios. Which of those portfolios to choose is still a firm-specific decision, requiring explicit expression of firm risk preferences.

Element 5b – Cost of Capital Allocated

Capital allocation is among the most significant open questions in actuarial science. A thorough treatment is well beyond the scope of this paper. Some references include Mango ([2], [3]), Meyers, Klinker and Lalonde [5], Myers and Read [6], Venter [8] and Merton and Perold [4].

There appears to be general agreement that what is really allocated is the cost of risk capital as opposed to capital itself. This is in contrast to the capital allocations that occur in manufacturers. Those allocations involve actual cash transfers of retained earnings and the investment of that capital in the operation of the business – in salaries, materials, power, marketing, etc. Risk capital allocations, on the other hand, are completely theoretical. When an insurer writes an automobile policy, no risk capital is transferred to that policy.

Perhaps by an unfortunate turn of history, the same manufacturing capital language was used to describe risk capital. This reinforced the adoption of capital decision analysis techniques based on manufacturing analogies, such as internal rate of return.

Risk capital for financial intermediaries provides a buffer that secures a certain counterparty status for the firm in total. In this regard, risk capital is a measure of the firm's total risk-bearing capacity. Because of the portfolio phenomena of diversification and accumulation, however, this capacity is solely an aggregate measure, only having meaning for the portfolio in total. In the case of a generic firm, the "portfolio" is the accumulation of risk exposures from all sources – operational, credit, market, etc. Because the elements of portfolios may have nonlinear interdependence, the impact of any one element on the portfolio can also be nonlinear. This makes a linear, proportional allocation of a total amount back to individual elements quite complicated. There are many possible ways this problem can be solved, each having its own compromises and limitations. Some examples of current research include Kalkbrener [1], Venter, Major and Kreps [9] and Mango [3].

Many researchers continue to allocate risk capital but use it as an interim step in assigning the cost of that risk capital to portfolio elements. The cost is the product of a risk-adjusted capital amount and a hurdle rate. Since the capital is risk-adjusted, this goes by the acronym RORAC=Return on Risk-Adjusted Capital[9].

---

9   Many authors are imprecise in their use of the acronyms RAROC and RORAC interchangeably. RAROC, Risk-Adjusted Return on Capital, is a method of arriving at a cost of risk capital by using simplistic (non risk-adjusted) capital amounts and risk adjusting the hurdle rates. See Mango [6].

Merton and Perold [4] tried to address this by taking a fundamentally different tack altogether. They define risk capital for a financial intermediary as the amount needed to guarantee the performance of that intermediary's contractual obligations at the default-free level. Under this framework, the notion of return on risk capital has no meaning, since they have bypassed the two-step RORAC process and leapt straight to a cost. Mango [3] extended Merton and Perold to insurance, further clarifying the true nature of insurance capital usage. The fundamental innovation is the recognition and treatment of the entire pool of risk capital as a shared asset or common pool resource.

Given cost of risk capital, with no allocated capital amount, a good candidate decision variable is economic value added (EVA®[10]). The formula for EVA is:

$$EVA = NPV\ Return - Cost\ of\ Capital$$

EVA is typically expressed as an amount. An activity with a positive EVA is said to "add value," while one with a negative EVA "destroys value."

Element 5c – Cost-Benefit Analysis (CBA) for Mitigation
Once the corporate risk tolerance and capital cost allocation are completed, the CBA is straightforward. For example, under the EVA approach, any mitigation effort resulting in a positive incremental EVA is worth doing. Under capital allocation, any mitigation project where benefit (reduced capital cost) exceeds costs should be undertaken.

Risk management in an organization with multiple business units and risk sources involves analysis of a complex, multidimensional space. Effective decision making in that space will be challenging, based solely on a single risk metric. Statistical theory would recommend a suite of decision metrics that are (as much as possible) distinct and independent, reflecting different dimensions of the space, and responsive to different dynamics. However, corporate realities often mandate that a compromise be struck in the interest of parsimony. Corporations must make decisions, and effective decision making often simplifies complex situations as much as possible, but no more so.

Section 2.2 goes into further detail on risk measures and capital, and serves as a natural extension to this section on decision making, using an enterprise risk model.

---

10 EVA is a registered trademark of Stern Stewart & Co. (www.sternstewart.com).

2.2 Risk Measures and Capital Allocation

By Gary G. Venter, FCAS, MAAA

Introduction

Capital consideration in the ERM framework for noninsurers typically starts with the notion of economic capital, which is typically measured using V@R at a fairly remote probability, such as 1-in-3000. This approach is probably too simplistic for insurers, which tend to use a number of risk measures, many of which are more informative than V@R.

The advantages attributed to economic capital typically include:

- It provides a unifying measure for all risks across an organization.
- It is more meaningful to management than risk-based capital or capital adequacy ratios.
- It forces the firm to quantify the risks it faces and combine them into a probability distribution.
- It provides a framework for setting acceptable risk levels for the organization as a whole and for individual business units.

The same could be said for many other risk measures. Insurers often like to see how decisions sort out under a few different measures to see if a consistent picture emerges. Labeling one of these measures as "economic capital" is more likely to confuse this process than to clarify it.

It should also be pointed out that V@R is not calculated by summing up the contributions of the different business units. It is more likely to be calculated from the distribution of all risks and then allocated down to individual units. It is this allocation that provides a consistent measurement of risk across units.

For an insurance company, probability levels like 1-in-3000 are not within the range of current modeling. There are so many approximations involved that a wide range of loss amounts could be assigned that probability with equal plausibility.

Also, the choice of probability level itself is questionable. Analysts often cite default probabilities for bonds of different grades as target probability levels. But bond rating is not done by computing the default probability. It uses a factor approach along the lines of risk-based capital and assigns probability levels only retrospectively, after observing rated bonds for many organizations for many years. Further, the target level for a given company is often selected so that a round number is used for probability, but the economic capital is somewhat less than the actual capital. Thus, if the current capital is the 1-in-3467 V@R, economic capital might be set at the 1-in-3333 V@R. While it is nice to have round numbers, making them the basis of the risk measurement is fairly artificial.

All in all, most companies would be better off focusing on their actual capital and expressing that through several different risk measures. The modeling difficulties can be circumvented by using impairment rather than insolvency levels. Impairment means losing a significant amount, but not all, of capital. Thus, the current capital might be expressed as a multiple of the capital that would be lost at different levels (e.g., perhaps one-quarter of capital would be lost at the 98 percent probability level).

Risk Measures

Most risk measures can be classified as moment-based, tail-based or probability transforms. There is actually some overlap among these classifications.

Moment-based Measures

Moment-based measures start with probabilistic expectations of random variables. For an insurance company, the decrease in capital (negative if capital increases) from operations for an accounting period would be a typical random variable being measured. The variance of this variable is an example of a moment-based measure. A variance of change in capital would have units of (currency)^2. Often it works out better to use risk measures in actual currency units, thus standard deviation is sometimes preferred. A disadvantage of either measure is that favorable deviations are treated the same as unfavorable ones. Semistandard deviation uses only the unfavorable deviations.

There is some evidence that quadratic risk measures like variance and standard deviation are not enough to capture market attitudes to risk. Measures like skewness, which use higher moments, address these attitudes. Another approach is to use exponential moments, which in some sense encapsulate all moments. The risk measure $E[Ye^{cY/EY}]$ is scaled to currency units but captures the effect of large losses on the risk exponentially. Usually this moment will not exist unless there are policy limits, however, or unless there is a maximum possible loss, as in catastrophe models.

Tail-based Measures

Tail-based measures emphasize large losses only. This focus is popular but not necessarily appropriate. Losses do not have to be extreme to be uncomfortable, and management cannot always ignore intermediate-valued losses. The advantage of measures like the exponential moment above is that they reflect all losses but still respond more to larger losses.

Some tail measures are:
- V@R (value at risk)
- TV@R (tail value at risk)
- XTV@R (excess tail value at risk)
- EPD (expected policyholder deficit)
- Value of default option

As mentioned above, V@R is just a percentile of the probability distribution. The probability level has to be defined to fully specify V@R and, in fact, any of the tail measures.

TV@R is the expected loss at the specified probability level and beyond. XTV@R is simply TV@R less the mean. When the mean is financed by other funding, capital is needed for losses above the mean, so subtracting the mean can capture this need.

EPD is calculated by multiplying TV@R minus V@R by the probability level. This is easiest to interpret if the probability is chosen so that capital is V@R at that level. Then TV@R minus V@R is the expected value of defaulted losses if there is default. Multiplying this quantity by the complement of the probability level yields the unconditional expected value of defaulted losses. This result is the origin of the name, but the calculation can be done at any probability level.

The insurer is unlikely to be able to reinsure all default possibility away by paying the EPD. The market value of that risk is called the value of the default option. It is typically estimated by options pricing methods. It could also be calculated at other probability levels.

Probability Transforms

Probability transforms measure risk by shifting the probability towards the unfavorable outcomes and then computing a risk measure with the transformed probabilities. The prime example of a transformed measure is just the expected loss under the transformed probabilities. Most of the usual asset pricing formulas, like the capital asset pricing model and the Black-Scholes options pricing formula, can be expressed as transformed means. It would be useful for a risk measure to provide the market value of the risk it is measuring, so transformed means are a promising type of risk measure.

The theory of pricing in incomplete markets favors two transforms in particular, called the minimum martingale transform and the minimum entropy martingale transform. Their application to the compound Poisson process of risk theory has been worked out and gives reasonable approximations to market prices of reinsurance (see, e.g., Venter, Barnett and Owen). The mean under the Wang transform has also been found to closely approximate market prices, in this case of bonds and catastrophe bonds.

Transformed probabilities can be used with other risk measures as well. For instance, most approximations of the value of the default put option are based on transformed expected values of the EPD. TV@R has been criticized for its linear treatment of all large losses, which is contrary to most ideas of risk preferences. Calculating TV@R with transformed probabilities overcomes this objection. Usually a "W" for "weighted" is added to a tail risk measure to indicate that it is calculated with transformed probabilities, hence WV@R, WTV@R, WXTV@R, etc.

Generalized Moments

Generalized moments can include all of the above measures. These moments are expectations that are not simply of powers of the variable. For instance, TV@R at probability level α can be written as $E[Y(Y>F_Y(\alpha))]$, where $(Y>X)$ is the logical function that takes on the value 1 if $Y>X$ and zero otherwise. One class of generalized moment measures that includes many tail measures is the spectral measures. These are risk measures that can be written in the form $\rho = E[Y \cdot \eta(F(Y))]$ for non-negative scalar functions η. We have just shown, in fact, that TV@R is a spectral measure. There are many other possibilities, however. For instance, a blurred V@R can be defined by taking the distance from the target percentile as the weighting function (e.g., $\eta(\rho) = e^{-\theta(p-0.99)^2}$).

Which risk measures to use is an open problem. It is not uncommon to use TV@R at a high probability level. However, as noted, this metric ignores important risks. If TV@R is favored, perhaps the probability level where any capital is lost should be the target. This threshold is meaningful economically and captures all risk beyond that level.

Trying to get closer to the market value of the risk also would be useful. WTV@R with the minimum entropy transform is promising here. The exponential moment risk is similar.

Required Capital

The capital an insurance company should hold arises from a number of practical considerations. The actual capital can be compared to risk measures once they are established, but choosing a risk measure and a probability level is usually not enough to get to the capital needed in practice.

Foremost for capital requirements is customer reaction. Some insurance buyers are particularly price sensitive and not too focused on capital. But others are concerned about the quality of the insurance guarantee. Different insurers can thus find different niches in the industry, targeting different client bases. Therefore, there is no single most efficient capital or rating level.

Research has indicated that increasing an insurer's rating level can slowly increase growth, while dropping a level can produce a more rapid decline in business. These findings may be observed because customers that want a higher level can quickly leave when the rating drops. A higher rating just provides an opportunity to compete with other insurers who already have the business.

To assess capital needs from this point of view requires keeping in touch with customers. Knowing whether pricing or security is a bigger issue when winning and losing bids would be a part of this process.

Capital requirements of rating agencies are a part of this process as well. Modeling may help convince an agency of the adequacy of capital. However, making this case is not likely to rely on a single risk measure.

Another perspective is the comparative profitability of new and renewal business. Many companies have noted that renewal business tends to be more profitable. This difference could be due to improved information for pricing and underwriting accruing over time. Thus, there is imbedded value in the renewal book, and it is especially worthwhile to maintain the ability to keep this business. If renewals typically compose 80 percent of the book, then the insurer would like to be able to maintain 80 percent of its capital even in a bad year. In this case, it would like to have enough capital so that 20 percent of its capital could cover a fairly adverse scenario.

Once the capital level is established, there are any number of risk measures against which it can be compared. For instance, the percentage of capital lost at various probability levels would be relevant. TV@R is useful, as it represents the average loss at any given probability level and beyond. TV@R better represents return time than does V@R – there is not a 90th percentile loss every 10 years; it is more accurate to act as if there is a random draw once every 10 years from the 90th percentile and beyond. Thus, TV@R at 90 percent represents the average loss for the 10-year return period. WTV@R, etc., could also be used in this context.

Capital Allocation

Allocation of risk measures can show the contribution of each business unit to the company risk. Risk allocation can be used for setting capacity controls like premiums and limits by line and can also be a basis for computing risk-adjusted profitability.

Allocating capital in proportion to one or more risk measures can provide the denominator for return on capital by line. Alternatively, allocating the cost of capital can provide a minimum target profit for each business unit, with any profit above that considered economic value added.

Estimating the contributions of the business units to the overall risk is conceptually a bit different from allocating the risk to business units. It is more akin to seeing where the risk comes from, rather than sending it out, and thus, more like decomposition of the risk measure than allocation of it.

A typical method of allocating a risk measure is first calculating the risk measure separately on each business unit, then spreading the overall risk measure proportionally. Analyzing the risk measure into component contributions is also a two-step process. The risk measure first has to be definable as an average of company results under certain conditions (a conditional general moment). Many, but not all, risk measures can be so defined. Then the contribution from each business unit is the average of the business unit results under the same conditions.

Other risk measures, such as TV@R (the average loss when the loss is above a selected probability level), are easily amenable to determining each business unit's contribution. Each business unit's contribution to TV@R is the business unit's average loss when the company loss exceeds that threshold. Similarly, the components of V@R from the business units are the units' average losses when the company loss is at that probability level. Thus, under risk decomposition, V@R is additive – the business units' contributions to V@R add up to company V@R. However, these contributions are unstable when simulation is used to compute the distribution, because there is only one simulation exactly at that probability level for each run of the simulation model.

Variance $E[(Y-EY)(Y-EY)]$ is the average squared deviation of a variable from its mean. Denoting Y, the total company negative profit, as the sum of the business units' negative profits $X_1 + \ldots + X_n$ allows expressing the contribution of the jth unit to the variance as $E[(X_j - EX_j)(Y- EY)]$. This formula is the definition of the covariance of X_j with Y, and these covariances add up over the Xs to the variance. Because of this terminology, the contributions of business units to other risk measures described above are called co-measures, like co-TV@R, co-V@R, etc.

Co-measures
Co-measures define r(X) when ρ(Y) is expressed as a conditional expected value:

$$\rho(Y) = E[h(Y)L(Y)|g(Y)], \qquad [2.2.1]$$

where g is some condition about Y, h is an additive function (i.e., h(V+W) = h(V)+h(W)) and L is any function for which this conditional expected value exists. It turns out that many risk measures can be expressed in this general conditional mean form. The co-measure for component j for such a risk measure is the same formula but with Y replaced by X_j in the argument of the h function, which is the linear part of the formula.

That is, the co-measure r is defined by:

$$r(X_j) = E[h(X_j)L(Y)|g(Y)] \quad [2.2.2]$$

By the additivity of h, this satisfies $\rho(Y) = \Sigma r(X_j)$.

As an example of a co-measure, excess tail value at risk (XTV@R) excess of level b can be defined as:

$$\rho(Y) = E[(Y - EY)|Y>b]. \quad [2.2.3]$$

Now h(X) is $X - EX$, $L(Y) = 1$, the condition is $Y>b$ and $r(X_j) = E[(X_j - EX_j)|Y>b]$.

There may be more than one set of conditions and h and L functions that define the same risk measure, each one leading to a different co-measure. In fact, given a risk measure defined by L and h functions L_1, h_1, and given another additive function h_2, if we set $L_2 = L_1 h_1/h_2$, then $L_2 h_2 = L_1 h_1$, which defines the same risk measure. Also note that making the definition a conditional expectation is for convenience only. It could be simply an expectation, with the conditioning being done with indicator functions put into L(Y).

Having a Marginal Method

Having a marginal method is a desirable feature of a risk decomposition methodology. That is, the change in overall company risk due to a small change in a business unit's volume should be attributed to that business unit. This marginal property links to the standard financial theory of pricing proportionally to marginal cost. It also leads to consistent strategic implications. Under a marginal decomposition of risk, if a business unit with an above-average ratio of profit to risk increases its volume, then the overall company ratio of profit to risk will increase.

So how is marginal risk attribution method developed? Addressing this issue is easier when the business units can change volume in a homogeneous fashion. An example would be business units that buy quota share reinsurance and so can change their volume uniformly just by changing the quota share percentages.

For such a company, if the risk measure is also scalable (or homogeneous of degree one, i.e., multiplying the random variable by a factor multiplies the risk measure by the same factor), then there is a marginal risk attribution method. Under these conditions, the marginal attribution is just the proportional change in the company risk measure due to a small change in the volume of the business unit. This result is a co-measure as well. And the marginal attributions sum up to the company risk measure, which is a direct consequence of a theorem of Euler about derivatives of homogeneous functions.

Common risk measures expressed in monetary units, like standard deviation, TV@R, etc., are scalable. However, other measures are not, such as variance (square dollars) and probability of insolvency (unit-less).

For many companies and business units, growth in exposure units can approximate homogeneous growth; so the same procedure would apply. However, it can happen that exposure units come in large enough lumps compared to overall volume that adding one changes the shape of the distribution so that the marginal changes in risk measure will not add up to the overall risk even for some homogeneous risk measures. For this case, transformed probability risk measures will still be marginal and additive.

The Marginal Impact

The marginal impact of the jth business component can be formalized by the jth directional derivative, defined as:

$$r(X_j) = \lim_{\varepsilon \to 0} \frac{\rho(Y + \varepsilon X_j) - \rho(Y)}{\varepsilon}$$

The strategic decision of growing a unit that has higher-than-average profit/risk can be more formally treated in this framework. Say P is the overall expected profit and P_j is that of the jth unit, and suppose $P/\rho(Y) < P_j/r(X_j)$, so $Pr(X_j) < P_j\rho(Y)$. Multiplying this by ε and adding $P\rho(Y)$ gives $P\varepsilon r(X_j) + P\rho(Y) < \varepsilon P_j\rho(Y) + P\rho(Y)$. But the left-hand side is $P\rho(Y+\varepsilon X_j)$ in the limit, so $P/\rho(Y) < [P+\varepsilon P_j]/\rho(Y+\varepsilon X_j)$. Thus, comparative to risk, the total company is more profitable with the incremental business.

Our approach to allocation is to find marginal decompositions of scalable risk measures by the directional derivative. (Only one co-measure is marginal as derivatives are unique.) This co-measure is still a decomposition under non-homogeneous growth and is often still close to marginal.

For XTV@R, $\rho(Y) = E[(Y - EY)|Y>b]$ is not scalable if b is a fixed constant amount. But if b is a fixed percentile of Y, say the αth percentile, then it is. That is because multiplying Y by a constant increases EY and every percentile of Y by the same factor. XTV@R can be written as $\rho(Y) = E[(Y - EY)|F(Y) > 1- \alpha]$. Then, the directional derivative is given by:

$\rho(Y+\varepsilon X_j) = E[(Y+\varepsilon X_j-EY-\varepsilon EX_j)/F(Y+\varepsilon X_j)>1-\alpha]$ and
$\rho'(Y+\varepsilon X_j)/0 = E[X_j-EX_j/F(Y)>1-\alpha]$, which is the unique marginal co-measure. (The derivative is not obvious.)

Variance and V@R

For variance and V@R, co-measures can be defined quite easily:

$\rho(Y) = Variance(Y) = E[(Y-EY)^2]$, so taking $L(Y) = h(Y) = Y-EY$ gives
$r(X_j) = Cov(X_j,Y) = E[(X-EX_j)(Y-EY)]$ and defining

$\rho(Y) = V@R_\alpha(Y) = E[(Y/F(Y) = 1-\alpha]$ gives the co-measure,
$r(X_j) = Co-V@R_\alpha(X_j,Y) = E[X_j/F(Y) = 1-\alpha]$

In both cases, r(X) can be plausibly interpreted as the contribution of X to $\rho(Y)$. Variance does not meet the scalability criterion for decomposition by directional derivative, as Variance $(aY) = a^2 Variance(Y)$, but V@R does; and the directional derivative gives the same decomposition as the co-measure shown.

Standard Deviation

When there are alternative intuitively reasonable definitions of a risk measure as a conditional expected value, then the derivative could help determine the preferred decomposition. For instance, there are different ways to use co-measures to express standard deviation. Taking $h(X) = X$ and $L(Y) = Std(Y)/EY$, with the condition Y=Y, results in:

$\rho(Y) = E[YStd(Y)/EY] = Std(Y)$
Then, $r(X_j) = E[X_j Std(Y)/EY] = Std(Y)EX_j/EY$

This just spreads the standard deviation in proportion to the mean of the components. Or, taking $h(X) = X - EX$ and $L(Y) = (Y - EY)/Std(Y)$, the result would be:

$\rho(Y) = E[(Y-EY)^2/Std(Y)] = Std(Y)$ and
$r(X_j) = Cov(X_j,Y)/Std(Y)$

This decomposes the standard deviation in proportion to the covariance of the component with the total.

The standard deviation is scalable, so there should be a marginal decomposition. Taking the derivative of $\mathrm{Std}(Y+\varepsilon X_j) = [\mathrm{Var}Y + 2\varepsilon\mathrm{Cov}(X_j,Y) + \varepsilon^2\mathrm{Var}(X_j)]^{1/2}$ gives at $\varepsilon = 0$ $r(X_j) = \mathrm{Cov}(X_j,Y)/\mathrm{Std}(Y)$.

This agrees with the second form of the co-measure, so that is the one which provides h and L functions that lead to marginal decomposition. Thus, the total change in $\mathrm{Std}(Y)$ brought about by a small change in X_j can be attributed to j by this procedure.

Exponential Moment

The measure $\rho(Y) = E(Ye^{cY/EY})$ is scalable, since $\rho(aY) = a\rho(Y)$. Thus, it should have a marginal decomposition. The simplest co-measure is $r_1(X_j) = E(X_j e^{cY/EY})$. Although these add up to $\rho(Y)$, this is not a marginal decomposition. Taking the directional derivative (straightforward, if messy) yields the marginal decomposition $r(X_j) = r_1(X_j) + c(EX_j/EY)E[Ye^{cY/EY}(X_j/EX_j - Y/EY)]$.

Without the excess ratio factor $(X_j/EX_j - Y/EY)$, the second term is an allocation of $c\rho(Y)$ by the ratio of means EX_j/EY. The $c\rho(Y)$ term is dominated by the large values of Y. When Y is large, the components of the company that are contributing most to the large losses would have $X_j/EX_j > Y/EY$; so the excess ratio factor gives them an increase in allocation. The other components would have a decrease in allocation.

A Scalable Form of EPD

A scalable form of EPD can be obtained by making it excess of a quantile of Y. That is, $B = F_Y^{-1}(1 - \alpha)$ and

$$r(Y) = aE[Y - B | F(Y) > 1 - a]$$

In this case, the directional derivative gives: $r(X_j) = \alpha[E(X_j|Y>B) - E(X_j|Y=B)]$, which is $\alpha[\text{co-TV@R} - \text{co-V@R}]$.

That sums up to $\alpha[E(Y|Y>B) - E(Y|Y=B)] = \alpha[E(Y|Y>B) - B] = \alpha E(Y - B|Y>B) = \rho(Y)$. This r can be formulated as a co-measure by taking $h(X) = X - E(X|Y=B)$, $L(Y) = \Pr(Y>B)$ and the condition Y>B.

Using Decomposition

Using decomposition of a risk measure to measure risk-adjusted profitability of business units works particularly well if the risk measure is proportional to the market value of the risk. Then, the ratio of the profit of a unit to its risk measure would be proportional to the ratio of the profit to the market value of the risk. Thus, business units with higher ratios would have more profit relative to the value of the risk they are taking.

Although there are various theories of how to measure the market value of risk, at this point it is not a settled question. Thus, it makes sense to compare several risk measures, in the hope that market value will be close to proportional to one of them and that the indicated strategic directions will not be too different among them.

Thus, some transformed probability risk measure is likely to exist that is proportional to the market value of the risk being measured, and it will have an attribution to business unit that is marginal.

Allocating the Cost of Capital

Allocating the cost of capital instead of capital itself as an alternative method of comparing profitability of business units was suggested by Merton and Perold [2]. This approach has a lot in common with what Mango [1] calls capital consumption (see also, Section 2.1). The general idea is to set the minimum profit target of a business unit to the value of its right to call upon the capital of the firm. The excess of the unit's profits over this cost of capital is added value for the firm. Since the company is carrying the risk of the unit's right to access the insurer's entire capital, the value of accessing capital is an implicit cost of carrying the unit, as viewed by Merton and Perold.

The value of the right to access capital and the value of the profits, if positive, are options and so can be computed using the theory of pricing of contingent claims. However, these options are not simple. If the unit requires a capital call, its timing is not fixed in advance, and it is likely that a sequence of cash flows would be needed over time. The timing of the realization of profit is not predetermined either.

A starting point for computing this capital cost is to calculate its expected value as the expected value of a stop-loss for the business unit at the break-even point. The company is essentially using its capital to provide such a stop-loss to each unit.

The economic value of the implicit stop-loss is more than its expected value, however. If the entire distribution of results for the unit is modeled, then the theory of pricing in incomplete markets could be applied, which would involve a probability transform of the profit stochastic process. The minimum entropy martingale transform would be a good starting point. This calculation could be done for a business unit in isolation if the whole company has not yet been modeled. However, any practical risk-pricing methodology would give a reasonable risk load to the expected value of the implicit stop-loss cover. Something as simple as the mean plus 30 percent of standard deviation would provide a consistent methodology.

Summary: Comparing Allocating the Cost of Capital to Allocating Capital

Allocating capital, even using marginal decomposition, is still arbitrary and artificial. It is arbitrary because different risk measures give different allocations, and artificial because a business unit has access to the entire capital of the firm – the allocated capital is not walled off. Using the value-added approach (i.e., allocating the cost of capital) is more economically realistic.

2.3 Regulatory and Rating Agency Capital Adequacy Models

By Susan E. Witcraft, FCAS, MAAA

Prior to the early 1990s, regulators and rating agencies relied primarily on leverage ratios to monitor capital adequacy. The introduction of RBC in the United States began a movement toward more complex capital adequacy measurement. Not much later, Canadian regulators introduced stress testing of financial statements through their Dynamic Capital Adequacy Test, and New York State insurance regulators introduced seven interest rate scenarios for testing capital adequacy of life insurers. More recently, there is a movement towards stochastic modeling for evaluating capital adequacy.

This section will first review these three types of tools used by regulators and rating agencies for evaluating capital adequacy and will provide comparisons of the models currently in use. It will then demonstrate a way in which risk-based capital models[11] can be used in a less-than-theoretically rigorous, but quite practical, manner for comparing different sources of capital.

---

[11] The term "risk-based capital model" has different meanings in different parts of the world. In the United States, the term is commonly used to refer to a model in which factors are multiplied by various accounting balances (such as premium, reserves and receivables), and the resulting risk charges are combined to determine the amount of required capital. In many other areas of the world, a risk-based capital model is any model that evaluates capital adequacy but with particular focus on stochastic models, such as dynamic financial analysis models. This section will use the U.S. definition of the term.

Leverage Ratios

Leverage ratios were used for many years for evaluating capital adequacy. The first commonly used ratio was the ratio of net written premium to surplus. In the United States, property-casualty insurers needed to maintain a premium-to-surplus ratio of less than 3.00 to avoid regulatory scrutiny of capital adequacy. As the insurance business became more diverse and there was increased writing of long-tailed business, regulators began to also look at the ratio of net reserves to surplus. Both premium-to-surplus and reserve-to-surplus ratios were generally compared to a single value, such as 3.00, for all companies regardless of the nature of the risks to which a company was exposed.

In the European Union, solvency monitoring still relies primarily on a variation of leverage ratios. Solvency I essentially estimates required capital as the greater of fixed fractions of net premium and incurred claims. Although Solvency I differs in structure from the leverage ratio approach, it is equivalent to what is sometimes referred to as net leverage (the sum of the premium-to-surplus ratio and the reserve-to-surplus ratio) in that it does not distinguish among classes of business and does not incorporate risks other than underwriting risks.

In the early 1970s, the Insurance Regulatory Information System (IRIS) tests were introduced in the United States. The IRIS tests are now a set of 12 ratios used to evaluate capital adequacy. The list of ratios is shown in Figure 2.3.1.

FIGURE 2.3.1: IRIS TESTS

1a. Gross written premium to surplus
1b. Net written premium to surplus
2. Change in writings
3. Surplus aid to surplus
4. Two-year operating ratio
5. Investment yield
6. Change in surplus
7. Liabilities to liquid assets
8. Agents' balances to surplus
9. One-year reserve development to surplus
10. Two-year reserve development to surplus
11. Estimated current reserve deficiency to surplus

For each ratio, a range of reasonable values was determined. Any company that had four or more ratios that did not fall within their corresponding reasonable ranges was considered to be at risk and generally merited regulatory scrutiny. The IRIS tests are still in use in the United States today but are given less weight than other regulatory capital adequacy measures.

Many rating agencies and regulators continue to use some form of leverage ratios in evaluating capital adequacy, although they are generally not the only tool used.

Risk-Based Capital Models

Risk-based capital models differ from leverage ratio approaches to capital adequacy monitoring in that they combine measures of several different aspects of risk of an insurance company into a single number. Currently, risk-based capital models are used by regulators in many jurisdictions and by at least two of the major rating agencies. A partial list of the risk-based capital models currently in use is included in Figure 2.3.2. Also, German regulators have introduced a proposal for a Solvency II-compatible standard approach.

Most risk-based capital models have similar structures and incorporate generally the same types of risk. The aspects of an insurer's risk typically included are: invested asset risk, credit risk, premium risk and reserve risk. Each of these risks is usually measured by multiplying factors by accounting values. The magnitude of the factors varies by the quality and type of asset or the line of business. The way in which specific company characteristics are reflected and the manner in which the various risk charges are combined varies across models.

FIGURE 2.3.2: RISK-BASED CAPITAL MODELS

REGULATORS
US Risk-Based Capital
Canadian Minimum Capital Test
Australian Minimum Capital Requirement
UK Enhanced Capital Requirement
Japanese Solvency Margin Ratio

RATING AGENCIES
Best's Capital Adequacy Ratio
Standard & Poor's Capital Adequacy Ratio

In addition, many risk-based capital models include explicit recognition of accumulation risk. This aspect of risk-based capital models is evolving rapidly, through stress tests of the impact of a second severe event, as well as the use of annual aggregate loss amounts rather than per-occurrence losses. At present, most models focus on return periods of between 1-in-100 years and 1-in-250 years for evaluating solvency, though Canada is moving to a 1-in-500-year return period for earthquake and A.M. Best is moving toward what is effectively a 1-in-10,000-year return period in its stress test.

Figure 2.3.3 compares key features of several models currently in use.[12] As can be seen, all of the models contain risk factors for invested asset risk, credit risk and premium risk. Figure 2.3.4 shows a comparison of the premium risk factors across these models for several lines of business. These factors are generally multiplied by the net earned premium by line reported in the insurer's financial statements.[13]

FIGURE: 2.3.3: KEY MODEL FEATURES

Model	Invested Asset Risk	Credit Risk	Reinsurance Dependence	Reinsurance Diversification	Premium Risk	Reserve Risk	Accumulation Risk	Covariance Adjustment
UK	Yes	Yes	No	No	Yes	Yes	No	No
Aus	Yes	Yes	No	No	Yes	Yes	Yes	No
US	Yes	Yes	No	No	Yes	Yes	No	Yes
Canada	Yes	Yes	No	No	Yes	Yes	Yes	No
Japan	Yes	Yes	No	No	Yes	No	Yes	Yes
Best	Yes	Yes	Yes	No	Yes	Yes	Yes	Yes
S&P	Yes	Yes	No	No	Yes	Yes	No	No

FIGURE 2.3.4: COMPARISON OF PREMIUM RISK FACTORS

Line	UK	Aus	US	Canada	Japan	Best (US)	S&P (EU)
Health	5%	16.5%	12%	12% - 40%	9%	33%	12% - 18%
Motor	10%	13.5%	24%	8%	8%	36%	12%
Marine	22%	16.5%	26%	8%	21% - 56%	48%	17%
Property	10%	13.5%	26%	8%	12%	47%	19%
Liability	14%	22.5%	17%	8%	17%	39%	27%

12 The characteristics of the BCAR model described relate to its US model, whereas the characteristics of the S&P model relate to its European model.
13 The Australian and Canadian factors are applied to the unearned premium reserve rather than to the net written premium.

As can be seen, some models, such as the Canadian Minimum Capital Test, use the same or similar factors for each line of business, whereas other models show much greater disparity among the lines. One example is the UK Enhanced Capital Ratio, for which the largest factor is more than four times the smallest factor.

There are also significant differences among the models in the levels of the factors. For example, the A.M. Best factors used in the United States are in the range of 40 percent, whereas the factors used in most of the regulatory models are almost all less than 20 percent. These differences can be explained in part by:

1. The use of the models. The A.M. Best and S&P models[14] are used to determine whether the company will be viable in the long term. By comparison, the regulatory models are used to evaluate one-year likelihood of insolvency. As such, the higher factors observed for the rating agency models are expected in light of the different purposes.
2. The presence of a covariance adjustment.[15] As shown in Figure 2.3.3, several models have covariance adjustments. Covariance adjustments are intended to reflect the independence of the various risk components in the risk-based capital models. Their practical impact is that the required capital after covariance is somewhat, to substantially, less than the sum of the individual risk charges. The amount of reduction depends on the relative magnitudes of the risk charges, with greater reductions occurring when the risk charges are relatively similar in size. As such, the higher factors in the A.M. Best model are reduced in the covariance calculation, bringing them more closely in line with the S&P factors for many companies.

The largest component of credit risk usually emanates from reinsurance recoverables. Several of the models, including both rating agency models, include risk factors that vary with the credit quality of the reinsurers. In addition, A.M. Best increases the credit risk charge for companies that it perceives to be heavily dependent on reinsurance. Dependence on reinsurance is determined based on the ratio of reinsurance recoverables to surplus. None of the models explicitly reflects the spread of the recoverables among reinsurers, though there are statutory limits on the percentage of recoverables that can emanate from any one reinsurance group in the UK. Specifically, annual premiums ceded to one reinsurer (group) cannot exceed 20 percent of gross inward premium, and total recoverables from any one insurance group cannot exceed 100 percent of capital resources.

---

14 The factors shown for these models correspond to the minimum capital requirement for a secure rating.
15 The covariance adjustment discussed here relates to how the major risk components are combined. Some models include adjustments for diversification among lines of business. In Australia, the reported loss reserves include a risk margin that reflects correlation among lines. In the UK, the risk factors themselves were calibrated to reflect diversification among the major risk components.

All of the models, except the one used in Japan, include reserve risk. Reserve risk is incorporated in the models in a manner similar to that used for premium risk, with factors that generally vary by line applied to reported reserves, net of reinsurance. In Japan, loss reserves tend to be a much less significant liability than in other countries. As such, the factors are multiplied by net loss payments rather than by reserves.

The component of risk-based capital models that shows the largest differences across models is accumulation risk (i.e., exposure to catastrophic events affecting a large number of insureds). As this book is being written, this component is being reviewed in all of the models used in the United States. As can be seen in Figure 2.3.3, the UK, US regulatory and S&P models do not include accumulation risk components at the time of this writing; although S&P has announced that it will be including such a component using annual aggregate exposures and the NAIC has opened the subject for discussion. As indicated previously, most models use return periods of 1-in-100 to 1-in-250 for accumulation risk and include natural perils, such as wind, hail and earthquake.

Scenario Testing

Solvency monitoring through the use of either static or stochastic scenario testing is emerging. In the late 1990s, Canada introduced its Dynamic Capital Adequacy Test, under which insurance companies demonstrate the impact on capital of a list of static scenarios. More recently, Australia and Great Britain have introduced stochastic scenario testing for regulatory capital management, and Moody's and Fitch have developed stochastic models for use in their rating processes. It is also anticipated that some form of scenario testing will be included in the European Solvency II initiative.

In the more recent regulatory regimes, the risk-based capital formula is used as a base metric. Each insurer then performs its own assessment of its risk-based capital needs based on certain underlying principles and rules. Such assessments generally involve scenario testing and/or stochastic modeling. The regulator subsequently will review the company's analysis and can provide an alternate capital requirement. In the UK, the typical ratio of the internal capital requirement to the formula-based results is between 120 percent and 150 percent, depending on the size of the company and other factors.

Whether the scenarios are determined from a list or generated stochastically, scenario testing for measuring capital adequacy usually involves preparation of a one- to five-year financial projection model and incorporation of probability distributions for as many sources of uncertainty as can be modeled. Critical features of these models are incorporation of the correlations among risks and, for multiyear models, reflection of management responses to adverse financial results. The thresholds for evaluating regulatory capital adequacy in use today are:

- Great Britain — no more than 2.5 percent probability of ruin over 5 years, 1.5 percent probability of ruin over 3 years or 0.5 percent probability of ruin in 1 year.
- Australia — no more than 0.5 percent probability of ruin in 1 year.

Although measured over different time periods, these criteria appear to be reasonably consistent with each other.

Evaluating Capital Structure Strategies

Risk-based capital models can be used to perform simplistic comparisons of different capitalization strategies. Consider, for example, a company that needs to increase its A.M. Best's Capital Adequacy Ratio (BCAR) to maintain its rating. Although the company has an A rating, it is projected to have a BCAR that is in the B++ range one year hence. While investigating the issuance of surplus notes or increased use of reinsurance, the company determined that it can achieve an expected BCAR in the A range by issuing a $120 million surplus note or by ceding 15 percent of premium ($135 million) to a quota share contract.

By issuing the surplus note, the company increases its adjusted surplus. However, this increase is on less than a dollar-for-dollar basis, because the interest on the surplus note is higher than Best's estimate of its annual return on capital and because the amount of the surplus note exceeds 20 percent of capital. A.M. Best reduces the benefit of surplus notes for both of these factors. In addition, required capital is increased slightly, as the amounts of invested assets – and therefore asset risk – increase.

By purchasing reinsurance, the company reduces required capital. Both net written premium and net loss reserves are reduced by the cession. Reinsurance recoverables are increased, but the risk factor applied to reinsurance recoverables is about one-quarter of the risk factors applied to loss reserves and net written premium. In addition, because of the covariance adjustment in the BCAR calculation, a dollar increase in the credit risk charge has a smaller impact on total required capital than does a dollar reduction in either the premium or reserve risk charges. Adjusted surplus is reduced by the reinsurer's margin on the contract.

The pre-tax coupon on the surplus note is 8 percent in an environment when bond yields are 4 percent, so the annual cost of the surplus note is $3 million. By comparison, the economic margin on the quota share contract is 12 percent of ceded premium, or $16 million. Thus, viewed on a one-year basis, reinsurance is a more expensive source of capital than the surplus note.

However, the company's profits are projected to increase surplus by enough that the quota share cession can be reduced to 10 percent in the second year, 5 percent in the third year and eliminated in the fourth year. The surplus note cannot be repaid for a minimum of 10 years. Thus, the long-term cost, discounted at 4 percent, is approximately $38 million for the surplus notes and $30 million for the quota share reinsurance option. And, with the flexibility of the quota share option, it is less expensive in the long term.

2.4 Asset-Liability Management

By Paul J. Brehm, FCAS, MAAA

Introduction

In insurance, asset-liability management is often treated as synonymous with asset-liability matching. Matching refers to establishing and maintaining an investment portfolio – typically fixed income – that has the same duration characteristics or even the same cash flow patterns as the liability portfolio it supports. A matching strategy may be prudent, but it protects the net value of the firm only from the next interest rate change. Modern enterprise risk analysis and management provides the tools to achieve much more than interest rate hedging.

We define asset-liability management (ALM) as a comprehensive analysis and management of the asset portfolio in light of current liabilities and future cash flows of a going concern company, incorporating existing asset and liability portfolios as well as future premium flows. Asset-liability management beyond duration matching considers additional risk factors beyond interest rate changes, such as inflation risk, credit risk and market risk. ALM also considers actions beyond the characteristics of a fixed-income portfolio and seeks to identify and exploit hedges of any sort. For example, equities may prove an effective hedge against inflation-sensitive liabilities. Reinsurance, in this context, is a form of hedge.

Insurance companies can benefit from the discipline of a more integrated analysis of the asset and liability portfolios in seeking better risk-return decisions. An enterprise-wide analysis of potential risks and rewards affords an ideal opportunity to analyze the company's investment portfolio and underwriting portfolio in concert. Since insurance liabilities are far less liquid than assets, such analysis and management activity tends to focus on adjustments to the investment portfolio, given the constraints of the loss reserves and underwriting portfolio, to improve the risk-return characteristics of, say, annual earnings or a terminal (future) value of surplus. In this respect, assets can be thought of as a way to hedge liability risk.

However, management activity need not be confined to fine-tuning investment strategy. Future underwriting considerations, along with other hedges such as reinsurance, are risk management variables at their disposal.

Venter et al. [2], presented a series of simple numerical examples illustrating that the optimal risk-return portfolio decisions are very different as the asset and liability considerations become more realistic and complex. The authors started with a stand-alone asset portfolio, then, in a series of adjustments, added a constant fixed duration liability, a liability that varied as to time and amount, and then added consideration of cash flows from current underwriting. As the various layers of complexity are added to the illustration, the nature of the inherent risks changes, as does the optimal investment portfolio:

- Looking at assets in isolation, short-term treasuries are considered risk-free, while higher-yielding assets – stocks and bonds – are considered riskier. Modern portfolio analysis would look at combinations of assets and measure their expected mean and variance, plotting return versus risk and searching out alternatives on an efficient frontier.

- Venter et al., point out that when fixed liabilities are considered, holding shorter-term (that is, shorter than the liabilities) assets creates a new risk – a reinvestment risk. If interest rates drop, total investment income may prove insufficient to cover the liabilities. If interest rates increase, longer-term investments, too, present a new risk, if depressed assets need to be liquidated to fund liabilities. The risk to net assets, or surplus, can be reduced by duration matching. That said, the risks and conclusions are somewhat different still if the liabilities are discounted at current interest rates.

- Adding in the complexity of liabilities that are variable as to amount and timing of cash flows makes precise duration matching impossible or transitory at best. Inflation-sensitive liabilities add even more complexity. A model incorporating both asset and liability fluctuations over time is required at this point to seek out optimal investment strategies.

- To make matters more difficult still, Venter et al., introduce the notion of a company that is a going concern, with variable (positive or negative) cash flow from underwriting. Going concerns have greater flexibility. If, for example, conditions for liquidation are unfavorable, the company could pay claims from premium cash flows. At this level of complexity, an enterprise-wide model is truly needed, because, in addition to asset and liability models, a model of the current business operation is needed, including premium income, losses (including catastrophic losses), expenses, etc.

Venter et al., did not address tax considerations, which can also have a profound impact on investment decisions. Recent studies have found that insurers consider cyclical changes in the investment portfolio between tax-exempt and taxable fixed income securities over the course of the underwriting cycle to be one of the principal drivers in investment strategy (as underwriting losses absorb taxable investment income). In addition to the integration of underwriting and investment results, such strategies rely on reallocation of assets to maximize income while avoiding alternative minimum taxes (AMTs).

Little has been said up to this point about equity investments, but consideration of equities, too, adds some complexity and richness to the asset-liability analysis. Equities are considered risky in their own right and will imply a potentially worse downside risk to capital. Some believe that equities may provide a better inflation hedge for liabilities in an increasing loss cost environment. This proposition may be tested through the enterprise risk model, although the conclusion will be sensitive to input assumptions of the incorporated macroeconomic model.

In 2002, the Casualty Actuarial Society's Valuation, Finance and Investment Committee (VFIC) published a report [1] testing the optimality of duration matching (between assets and liabilities) investment strategies for insurance companies. To address this question, VFIC applied a simulation model to a variety of scenarios – long-tailed business versus short-tailed (with catastrophe exposure), profitable versus unprofitable and growing versus shrinking. In doing so, VFIC attempted to tackle Venter's most complex scenario, above.

Where Venter et al., focused on changes in GAAP pre-tax surplus as the risk measure, VFIC looked at several different risk measures on both a statutory and a GAAP basis. Return, too, was considered on both accounting bases. In doing so, VFIC's conclusion as to optimality was what one might expect in the real world: It depends. In fact, duration matching was among a family of optimal strategies. However, the choice of specific investment strategies was dependent on the company's choice of risk metrics, return metrics and risk-return tolerances or preferences:

- Statutory accounting-based metrics implied little hedge from duration matching, as bonds were amortized and liabilities were not discounted.

- GAAP accounting-based metrics resulted in similar conclusions: Though bonds were marked to market, there was no hedge to the liabilities.

- If metrics are calculated based on "true economics," that is, with bonds marked to market and liabilities discounted at current market rates, matching produces a low interest rate risk. In this case, a short investment strategy increases risk (creates mismatch in duration) and decreases return. Longer-duration investment strategies increase risk and increase return, making the tradeoff more of a value judgment. In the economic case, the introduction of cash flows from operations greatly complicated the analysis and conclusions.

An Asset-Liability Modeling Approach

It has been asserted above that an enterprise-wide model is the ideal, perhaps the only, way to model and ultimately manage an insurance company investment portfolio. The preceding sections of this chapter have provided many of the building blocks for such an analysis, and asset-liability management makes for an excellent application of such an integrated model.

The comments below highlight a series of modeling steps and management considerations that supply the necessary structure to an analysis of an insurer's investment portfolio, given the liabilities it supports.

1. Start with models of asset classes (stocks, bonds), existing liabilities (loss reserves, receivables) and current business operations.

2. Define risk metric(s) for the analysis. Consideration should be given to accounting basis – statutory, GAAP or economic. Risk can be defined based on the volatility of periodic income or of ending surplus or equity. Decisions are, therefore, also necessary as to the time frames of the analysis. Examples of risk metrics – either income-based or balance-sheet-based – include the standard deviation and the probability of falling below a predetermined threshold. Balance sheet (surplus or equity) measures are more amenable to other metrics as well, such as V@R, TV@R, probability of ruin or probability of impairment.

3. Similarly, management must define what constitutes "return." Again, consideration must be given to accounting basis, and clearly risk and return must be defined in a compatible fashion. Additionally, return can be income-based or balance-sheet-based. For example, return can be return on equity (ROE) or periodic earnings (income measures), or it can be a terminal value of surplus (balance sheet).

4. Consideration must be given to the time horizon of the analysis and the relevant metrics. Single-period models are perhaps simpler but may not adequately reflect the true nature of the business throughout a cycle. Multiperiod models can be more sophisticated – but also more difficult and complicated – especially if cycles and serial correlations are incorporated throughout.

5. The model will have to consider relevant constraints. For example, constraints might include limits on asset classes imposed by state regulators, or investments that drive required capital calculations too high in RBC or BCAR scores or restrictions based on the company's own investment policy.

6. The model should be run for a variety of investment strategies, underwriting strategies and reinsurance options under consideration. For each combination of scenarios, there will be thousands of realizations. The selected risk and return metrics are calculated over these simulations.

7. An efficient frontier, illustrated in Figure 2.4.1, can be constructed across the various portfolio scenarios. The point in the risk-return space that defines the current portfolio should be represented. Portfolio moves should be explored where risk can be decreased without sacrificing return (A), where return can be increased without increasing risk (B) and at points in between (C).

FIGURE 2.4.1: EFFICIENT FRONTIER

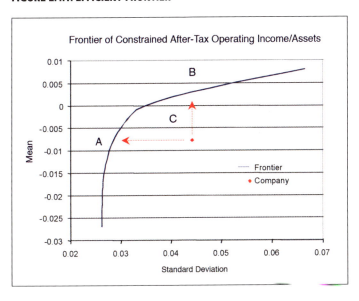

8. It was noted at the outset of the process description that since liabilities are more illiquid, the asset-liability analysis and management can be largely asset-centric given the existing liabilities. The nature of the liabilities, however, can be adjusted – risks can be hedged – through reinsurance purchases. The effects of such purchases can have profound impacts on an ALM analysis, especially in a multiperiod model.

Various reinsurance structures should be modeled with the alternative asset portfolio options, and the results compared. For example, Figure 2.4.2 compares the results of reinsurance and asset allocation decisions in the worst 1 percent of the simulations over time.

FIGURE 2.4.2: REINSURANCE AND ASSET ALLOCATION METRICS

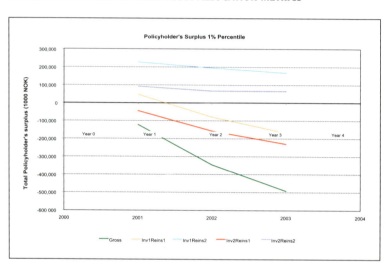

9. Given indications on asset and reinsurance movements, the simulations should be reviewed to identify those situations where even the preferred portfolio(s) performed poorly. It is possible that an asset hedging strategy can be employed to reduce downside risks. It may also be the case that further investigation will highlight the type of prevailing conditions that can lead to substandard performance, for example, a large catastrophe that forces liquidation of assets or a persistent soft market. Management can establish policy and monitoring mechanisms to identify the existence or the likelihood of such conditions and make appropriate adjustments.

Future Research

While enterprise-wide modeling is perhaps the only way to adequately address asset-liability management issues, there are a number of real-world issues that are the subject of continuing research. For example:

- Correlations between lines of insurance (either in current business or in past reserves), between assets and liabilities, and over time are poorly understood today. And yet correlations can materially alter one's view of the optimal portfolio.

■ Models of unpaid losses, while they can derive expected values and distributions, have not been developed as explanatory models. That is, unlike asset models, reserving models do not predict future loss payments with parameters linking losses to economic indices. Inflation sensitivity is often hypothesized on an accident-year, a calendar-year or a payment-year basis but is rarely explicitly developed from historic economic data and projected based on, say, an economic scenario generator.

If parameterized models are not up to the task, one alternative is to treat such variables as correlations and inflation sensitivity as random variables themselves. Models can then be created with parameter estimates but with appropriate reflection of the fact that the true parameters (and perhaps even the process) are unknown.

2.5 Measuring Value in Reinsurance[16]

By Gary G. Venter, FCAS, MAAA, Spencer M. Gluck, FCAS, MAAA and
Paul J. Brehm, FCAS, MAAA

Introduction

On one hand, investment portfolio managers have a wide variety of tools available to manage the risks in their portfolios, largely facilitated by fairly efficient and liquid markets. On the other hand, insurance portfolios, though risky, are fairly illiquid and have limited means to mitigate the assumed hazard risk. Reinsurance is, of course, the most readily available tool to transfer assumed hazard risk. Enterprise risk analysis can greatly facilitate effective use of reinsurance in hedging an insurance portfolio.

When asked to complete a cost-benefit analysis of their reinsurance purchases, cedents sometimes use the following calculation: First, they add up all the ceded premiums for the past several years, which they call the cost. Then, they add up all the recoveries and ceding commissions received, which they identify as the benefit. Subtracting cost from benefit gives the net benefit. Completion of this calculation is usually followed by a lament that the net benefit has been negative. Sometimes, one or two treaties have had a positive net benefit, but these are usually canceled or repriced soon after. Occasionally, some treaties return more than they cost over a long period but pay losses several years after the premium has been received, so that premium plus loss investment income exceeds recoveries. The cedent decides that reinsurance has been a losing proposition for the company for some time.

---

16 Venter [5] previously published a paper on this topic dealing primarily with measuring value in reinsurance based on cost versus stability achieved. His paper is reproduced in large part here, augmented with new sections.

A moment's reflection, though, will reveal that this result was almost a foregone conclusion. Reinsurers are in business to make money, and some have succeeded at it. There are expenses involved. Thus, over time, total payouts by reinsurers have to be less than the premium they receive plus its related investment income. A given client can beat these odds in the short run, but probability eventually wins out – at least for the vast majority. And the exceptions usually are cedents with such poor results that they envy the rest.

So what's wrong with the analysis? Is reinsurance just a bad deal that should be shut down as soon as possible, or are there some other benefits that this calculation misses? We offer the following three related paradigms for measuring the value in a reinsurance structure.

1. Reinsurance provides stability. In the simplest terms, the benefit of reinsurance is that it provides stability of results. "Stability" includes protection of surplus against erosion from adverse fluctuations, improved predictability of earnings growth and customers' assured recovery of their insured losses. There is a cost to gaining this benefit, but the cost is not simply ceded premiums. Premiums less recoveries (including expense recoveries) would be a better measure of the cost to the cedent for gaining stability. In fact, this cost measure is what the naïve analyst receives as the net benefit.

2. Reinsurance frees up capital. Going one step further, the incremental stability gained by purchasing reinsurance frees up risk capital that would otherwise be required of the ceding company. That is, reinsurance can be a substitute for required capital. The value of reinsurance, then, could be gauged by the amount of income foregone to purchase the cover versus the amount of capital freed up. In accounting terms, both numbers would be negative for an insurer, so the ratio of the two will be positive. This ratio can be thought of as the ROE cost of the reinsurance purchase. If this ROE cost is less than the firm's target returns, the purchase is a good financial decision.

3. Reinsurance adds to the value of the firm. In the end, the activities undertaken by the firm in the course of business are meant to add value to the firm. If the company is publicly traded, we are speaking directly of adding market value. It would perhaps be ideal if we could measure the value in a reinsurance purchase as the incremental market value added to the company.

The next three sections cover the three paradigms, above, in turn.

Quantifying Stability and Its Value

There are a few measures of stability that can be used – standard deviation and related quantities, percentiles or value at risk and excess aggregates – to name a few. Measures can be applied to surplus, earnings or related accounts. Some companies prefer to look at more than one measure.

Perhaps the best way to illustrate these concepts is through an example. Consider ABCD, a small company or department that writes $33 million of excess property and liability insurance. This consists of $14 million in casualty insurance, with an expected loss ratio of 78 percent, and $19 million in property insurance, with an expected loss ratio of 63 percent. Total expected losses are $22.9 million, and there is an expense ratio of 23 percent for a total expected combined ratio of 92 percent.

FIGURE 2.5.1: ABCD COVERAGE CHART

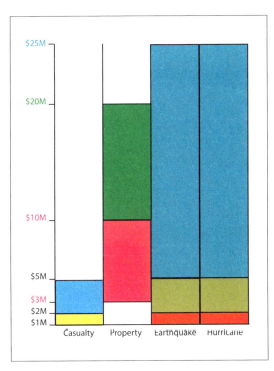

As shown in Figure 2.5.1, ABCD currently purchases a reinsurance program in several layers, providing 4 million x 1 million of casualty cover for $4.41 million, 17 million x 3 million of per-risk property cover for $2.36 million and a catastrophe program covering 95 percent of 24 million x 1 million for $1.53 million, with one reinstatement at 100 percent. This totals $8.3 million in ceded premiums prior to any reinstatement premiums. The catastrophe program is designed to cover at least up to the 1-in-250-year catastrophe event.

ABCD has been offered, as an alternative, a stop-loss program of 20 million x 30 million for a premium of $1.98 million. Is this a better option? Cost-benefit analysis addresses such issues.

Doing a cost-benefit analysis requires first establishing cost and benefit measures. A reasonable cost measure, as discussed above, is the net excess of ceded premiums over expected recoveries. Results can be estimated using a simulation study of financial results before and after reinsurance. Some of the technical issues of doing such a study are discussed below.

Based on a simulation of 25,000 possible realizations of the underwriting results, average net recoveries after reinstatement premiums are $5.08 million for the current program and $0.98 million for the alternative. The ratio of these recoveries to ceded premium is 61 percent for the current program and 49 percent for the alternative, which makes the current program sound more favorable. The proposed cost measure, however, is not ceded loss ratio but premium less expected recoveries. This is $3.2 million for the current program and $1 million for the alternative. This difference is significant for ABCD, as its expected pre-tax income prior to ceded reinsurance is just $6 million ($2.5 million underwriting + $3.5 million investment).

The stop-loss program thus has a lower ceded loss ratio but costs less than the current program. Can it possibly provide enough protection? An analysis of the probability of adverse deviations from expected results is needed.

FIGURE: 2.5.2: ABCD SIMULATION OUTPUT

Statistic	<BARE>	Current	Stop-Loss
Mean	$10.1M	$6.9M	$9.12M
Standard Deviation	$8.09M	$5M	$6.24M
Skewness	-0.8619	-0.4235	0.0945
Safety Level, Percent	99.0%	99.0%	99.0%
Safety Level, Value	$24.3M	$17M	$22.3M
Smallest Simulated	-$49.3M	-$23.2M	-$32.2M
Largest Simulated	$30.9M	$22.7M	$29M
Number of Simulations	25,000	25,000	25,000

Figure 2.5.2, which is the ABCD simulation output, shows some summary statistics for net premiums minus losses (gross less ceded) prior to any expenses or investment income. The difference in the means is the relative net cost differential between two programs.

The safety level shown in this case is the best result at the 1-in-100 level. It shows that the stop-loss program is more than $5 million better in this very good year. However, the stop-loss has a higher standard deviation, and its worst result in 25,000 years is $9 million more adverse than the current program. Thus, under some measures, the current program provides more protection than the stop-loss.

Most companies do not manage to a 25,000-year event, so a comparison is needed at more realistic probability levels. Figure 2.5.3 shows the simulated probability densities for the net premium less net losses. It shows that the current program does produce a compression of results, but much of this compression comes by cutting off the profitability of the good years.

FIGURE: 2.5.3: ABCD COVERAGE OPTION PROBABILITY DENSITIES

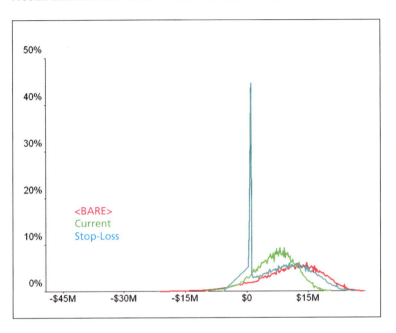

This is also a problem with using standard deviation as a measure of volatility: Standard deviation measures upward and downward deviations and can be reduced by eliminating the favorable deviations. Measures that capture only unfavorable deviations are more useful and will be discussed below.

Also apparent in Figure 2.5.3 is the concentration of events at the retention of the stop-loss program and the similarity of the stop-loss and the gross or bare positions in good years.

The cumulative probability distributions in Figure 2.5.4 (here truncated at the 1-in-500 levels, good and bad) give another perspective on the relative performance of the alternative programs. The upper right part shows that the stop-loss is indeed more profitable in the good years. But in the 1-in-10 to 1-in-4 range, the current program provides more protection. For the years beyond 1-in-10, the stop-loss gives a considerably more favorable result.

FIGURE 2.5.4: ABCD COVERAGE OPTION CUMULATIVE DISTRIBUTION

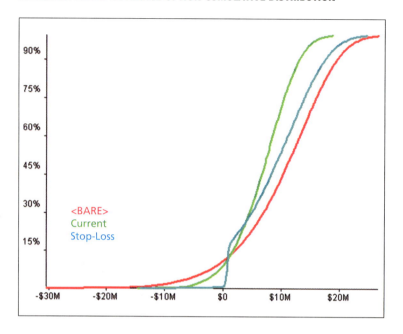

These distributions are shown in Figure 2.5.5. The current program better protects the worst-case event; but by the 0.25 percent level (worst case in 400 trials), the stop-loss is better. From the 12 percent to 26 percent levels, the current program is better, by as much as $1,100,000. But in the worst years, the stop-loss could be more than $6,000,000 better than the current program, and the median result is almost $2,000,000 better. As the stop-loss is less costly and usually provides a better result, sometimes dramatically so, it would have to be considered a more useful program for ABCD.

A more careful use of vocabulary is actually appropriate here. Even though we would use Figure 2.5.5 to say that the stop-loss is $6,350,000 better at the 1-in-100 level, the 99th percentile loss event is unlikely to be the same event for the two programs. Thus, the difference between the programs in the 1-in-100-year gross loss event could be more or less than $6,350,000, as could the 99th percentile of the distribution of the difference between the programs. What the table actually allows us to calculate is the difference in the 99th percentiles of the net result under the two programs (or in this example the 1st percentile, since we are looking at earnings).

FIGURE 2.5.5: ABCD CDF OUTPUT

PROBABILITY	<BARE>	CURRENT	STOP-LOSS
0.00%	-$49,263,333	-$23,198,963	-$32,243,333
0.25%	-$25,817,548	-$12,416,243	-$9,439,234
0.50%	-$21,827,529	-$10,377,108	-$6,311,695
0.75%	-$17,837,510	-$8,337,973	-$3,184,156
1.00%	-$13,847,491	-$6,298,838	-$56,618
1.25%	-$12,641,527	-$5,703,459	$237,924
1.50%	-$11,677,654	-$5,290,176	$286,117
1.75%	-$10,713,781	-$4,876,893	$334,311
2.00%	-$9,749,908	-$4,463,610	$382,505
4.00%	-$5,892,701	-$2,551,287	$575,365
6.00%	-$3,602,653	-$1,315,561	$689,867
8.00%	-$2,008,347	-$409,204	$769,583
10.00%	-$686,845	$284,986	$835,658
12.00%	$416,042	$951,819	$890,802
14.00%	$1,448,699	$1,464,523	$942,435
16.00%	$2,415,661	$1,919,933	$990,783
18.00%	$3,226,822	$2,388,329	$1,251,605
20.00%	$3,905,868	$2,802,539	$1,925,868
22.00%	$4,554,807	$3,190,684	$2,574,807
24.00%	$5,209,039	$3,549,185	$3,229,039
25.00%	$5,513,974	$3,713,920	$3,533,974
26.00%	$5,832,081	$3,880,394	$3,852,081
28.00%	$6,371,517	$4,205,322	$4,391,517
30.00%	$6,891,421	$4,514,526	$4,911,421
32.00%	$7,401,904	$4,827,688	$5,421,904
34.00%	$7,856,716	$5,146,708	$5,876,716
36.00%	$8,321,687	$5,428,461	$6,341,687
38.00%	$8,761,854	$5,694,960	$6,781,854
40.00%	$9,208,534	$5,962,559	$7,228,534
42.00%	$9,639,097	$6,244,632	$7,659,097
44.00%	$10,021,333	$6,495,969	$8,041,333
46.00%	$10,439,457	$6,780,995	$8,459,457
48.00%	$10,823,625	$7,026,301	$8,843,625
50.00%	$11,191,515	$7,269,232	$9,211,515

In the end, the company is going to select a single program, and it will end up with the probability distribution produced by that program. Thus, the necessary decision is which probability distribution it desires. The decision is facilitated by comparing the ending probability distributions of the various programs, not by looking at the distribution of differences between programs. The company may gain a psychological benefit from thinking that its program is better more often than others. However, if that program does not produce a better final distribution of net results, that psychological benefit will not translate into a better financial position for the company.

The figure shows the general features of a cost-benefit comparison of alternative reinsurance programs. The cost is the expected income foregone by buying the program, and the benefit is the protection against adverse deviation.

Other Comparisons

Once financial risk can be simulated, a variety of methods are available to compare reinsurance programs. Different analysts and decision makers will find different methods more intuitive. Some of these are illustrated using the data from the ABCD example. Figure 2.5.6, known as the box or space needle view, shows probability in ranges. The area of each box is proportional to the probability of being in the range from the bottom to the top of the box. The middle box shows the interquartile range, that is, from 25 percent to 75 percent. The two boxes on either side show the range from 1-in-4 to 1-in-20. Thus, the outside of the middle three boxes is the range from 5 percent to 95 percent. The next range is from 1 percent to 99 percent, and the outer boxes get to the 1-in-500 levels: favorable and unfavorable.

FIGURE 2.5.6: ABCD COVERAGE OPTION BOX OR SPACE NEEDLE VIEW

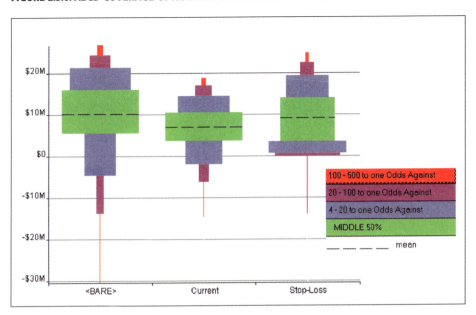

The current program can be seen at a glance to be most compressed, but achieves this compression by sacrificing profitability in the good years. The stop-loss program shows more protection in the 1-in-20 and 1-in-100 years, but is about the same as current at 1-in-500.

Figure 2.5.7 is a cost-benefit diagram at selected probability levels. Each point shows the cost of a program versus its loss amount (net premium less net loss) at a given probability level. To be efficient at a selected probability, a more expensive program has to have a lower loss level at that probability. In this example, the current program is not efficient at any of the levels shown, although it is at a few other levels, as discussed above. The choice of programs becomes more difficult when programs of different costs are all efficient – that is, the more expensive programs provided more benefit at most probability levels.

FIGURE 2.5.7: ABCD COVERAGE OPTION COST BENEFIT

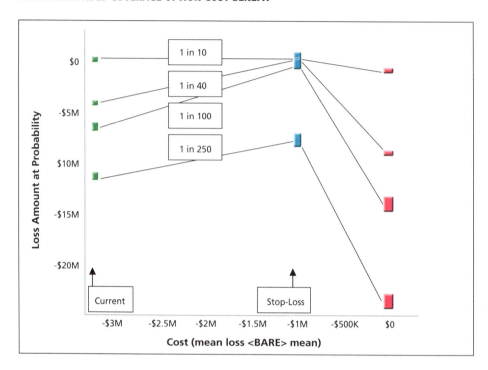

Other financial measures can also be compared. Figure 2.5.8 shows the probability distribution for pre-tax income net of each reinsurance structure. The comparison and the decision processes are very similar to those for premium less loss, but the monetary values include expenses and investment income. For ABCD, this shows a 20 percent probability of a loss with no reinsurance, 28 percent with the current program and 26 percent for the stop-loss. Besides giving a reinsurance comparison, these figures give ABCD management perspective on their prospects of overall profitability.

FIGURE 2.5.8: ABCD PRE-TAX NET INCOME

PROBABILITY	<BARE>	CURRENT	STOP-LOSS
0.00%	-$55,178,595	-$28,306,230	-$37,630,975
0.25%	-$31,005,991	-$17,189,245	-$14,119,948
0.50%	-$26,892,281	-$15,086,897	-$10,895,456
0.75%	-$22,778,572	-$12,984,549	-$7,670,964
1.00%	-$18,664,862	-$10,882,200	-$4,446,471
1.25%	-$17,421,513	-$10,268,365	-$4,142,799
1.50%	-$16,427,760	-$9,842,270	-$4,093,112
1.75%	-$15,434,007	-$9,416,175	-$4,043,424
2.00%	-$14,440,254	-$8,990,080	-$3,993,736
4.00%	-$10,463,474	-$7,018,476	-$3,794,897
6.00%	-$8,102,434	-$5,744,442	-$3,676,845
8.00%	-$6,458,705	-$4,809,988	-$3,594,659
10.00%	-$5,096,235	-$4,094,278	-$3,526,536
12.00%	-$3,959,159	-$3,406,773	-$3,469,682
14.00%	-$2,894,490	-$2,878,175	-$3,416,448
16.00%	-$1,897,552	-$2,408,648	-$3,366,601
18.00%	-$1,061,245	-$1,925,731	-$3,097,694
20.00%	-$361,149	-$1,498,681	-$2,402,529
22.00%	$307,908	-$1,098,503	-$1,733,472
24.00%	$982,421	-$728,889	-$1,058,959
25.00%	$1,296,808	-$559,048	-$744,572
26.00%	$1,624,777	-$387,412	-$416,603
28.00%	$2,180,935	-$52,412	$139,555
30.00%	$2,716,957	$266,377	$675,577
32.00%	$3,243,264	$589,248	$1,201,884
34.00%	$3,712,176	$918,157	$1,670,796
36.00%	$4,191,560	$1,208,645	$2,150,180
38.00%	$4,645,373	$1,483,405	$2,603,993
40.00%	$5,105,900	$1,759,300	$3,064,520
42.00%	$5,549,810	$2,050,117	$3,508,430
44.00%	$5,943,890	$2,309,246	$3,902,516
46.00%	$6,374,982	$2,603,107	$4,333,602
48.00%	$6,771,059	$2,856,018	$4,729,679
50.00%	$7,150,354	$3,106,480	$5,108,974

Financial ratios, on the other hand, may give considerably different comparisons of net results. The combined ratio, for example, combines premium, loss and expense in a fairly different way than does net underwriting income. Underwriting income subtracts direct losses and expenses and ceded premium from direct premium and adds in loss and expense recoveries. The combined ratio subtracts loss and expense recoveries from direct loss and expense and divides by direct less ceded premium. This can give a misleading result, especially if there are minimal ceded expenses, as part of the ratio is direct expense divided by net premium. Figure 2.5.9 illustrates this for ABCD's reinsurance alternatives.

FIGURE 2.5.9: ABCD COVERAGE OPTION COST BENEFIT

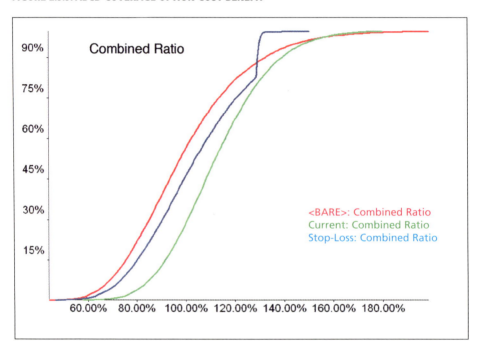

Here, the current program shows up as not better than the stop-loss at any probability level, and rarely better than the option of no reinsurance, even though in many adverse cases it provides considerable income benefit over the direct position and is sometimes better than the stop-loss. This distortion is due to this program's relatively high ceded cost impacting the expense ratio.

Efficient frontier charts, like the one shown in Figure 2.5.10, that graph a scattering of alternative scenarios according to their risk (by some measure) and return (by some measure) are a common way of assimilating and summarizing the vast amount of data and information from the modeling of reinsurance structures. Efficient frontier analyses can explicitly show the tradeoff between cost and benefit. Such analyses can help identify programs that are clearly inefficient and point the analyst in the direction of a structure that could be more advantageous. The efficient frontier can also illustrate that competing programs may not be inherently better or worse but rather alternative points on an optimal curve that can be distinguished only based on company preferences or budgetary constraints.

FIGURE 2.5.10: ABCD COVERAGE OPTION

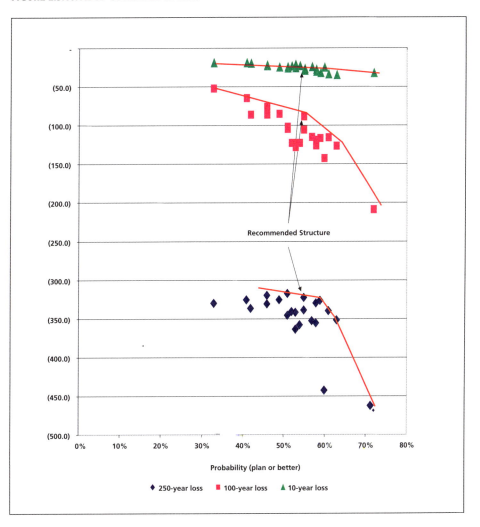

Efficient frontiers are often reviewed at several probability levels, as shown above. Here, the 1-in-10, 1-in-100 and 1-in-250 levels are shown for a number of alternative programs. In this case, the comparison of risk and return is between loss at the probability level and the probability of the combined ratio being at plan or better (scale at top). Each possible program is at the same point on the horizontal scale but is shown three times to represent its loss at each probability level on the vertical scale.

The more expensive programs make meeting plan less likely, due to the cost of the reinsurance. Thus, even though they have less possibility for adverse loss, they are not recommended. In fact, the most expensive programs are not efficient at the 1-in-250 level, as they are low-attaching programs that also run out of limit too soon.

There are a variety of ways stability can be measured and portrayed, in efficient frontier graphs or otherwise, depending on management criteria. Emphasis on rating agency or regulatory requirements and constraints (see also Section 2.3) or market expectations suggests some common, real-world options that might include the probability:

- Of surplus dropping below 2x RBC,
- Of surplus dropping below a BCAR score supporting a target rating,
- That an expected loss in a 10-year return period exceeds a threshold level of surplus or
- Of an x percent drop in quarterly earnings per share.

The paradigm of measuring value in reinsurance in the tradeoff between the net costs of the reinsurance cover versus the stability gained in the purchase is superior to a more simple dollars-out-against-dollars-in analysis. In the end, however, significant judgment is still required to evaluate the efficacy of the cost-benefit tradeoff. The next sections take this analysis further by essentially trying to quantify the value of stability.

Reinsurance as Capital

Insurers hold capital or surplus in part as a contingency fund to pay claims and expenses even in those scenarios where actual losses and expenses exceed available revenues. It stands to reason that the more volatile a company's results, the more surplus ought to be held. Stated in the context of the previous section, the more stable the company's results, the less surplus is required. The relationship between stability and surplus (or equity or required capital) forms the basis for the second paradigm for measuring value in reinsurance.

The second paradigm adds the step of translating the measure of stability into a measure of required capital or surplus. Since reinsurance is meant to stabilize results, the directional change in required capital should be negative. Since capital – either debt capital or equity capital – carries a cost, the reduction in required capital translates into a reduction in capital costs. In the cost-benefit considerations of the previous section, the reduced cost of capital is the benefit of the reinsurance. The cost of the reinsurance is still the net amount foregone in the reinsurance transaction on a present-value basis.

In this second paradigm, then, an explicit dollar benefit can be compared to an explicit dollar cost. This cost-benefit comparison allows for direct and unambiguous comparisons of reinsurance structures. Presumably, the only role for non-numeric preferences would come in those instances where the net monetary benefits of competing structures were the same.

Alternatively, the cost of reinsurance (a negative value, as it is outflow) can be divided by the change in required capital (also a negative amount, since capital is released) to calculate what amounts to a marginal ROE measure. Reinsurance structures with the better ROEs would be preferred. Furthermore, reinsurance structures with marginal ROEs above the company's cost of capital would be preferable to going bare.

While the numerator in our marginal ROE is straightforward, the denominator is more of a challenge. In general, we divide models of required capital into two classes:

1. "Theoretical models" – those that derive required capital and changes in it based on the calculated risk metrics from an enterprise risk model and
2. "Practical models" – those that derive required capital for the company by concession to the reality of various rating agency formulas (e.g., BCAR, S&P CAR), regulatory requirements (e.g., RBC, ICAR) or actual capital.

The more theoretical models would establish a level of required capital based on a risk metric consistent with management's views towards risk. Some of the usual suspects include V@R, TV@R, XTV@R, WXTV@R and more. Each has its advantages and its disadvantages and is further discussed in Section 2.2. Having selected the appropriate risk measure and threshold value that define the required capital, the methodology is simple. Required capital is calculated as the threshold value of the selected risk metric using the risk distributions produced for the company for each of the competing reinsurance structures. Using the current structure (or perhaps the scenario where the company is bare) as the base case, the marginal changes in required capital can be easily calculated.

Calculation with the "practical" models proceeds in a similar fashion. However, the analyst need not be concerned with risk metrics. A threshold value is still required, such as BCAR = 175 percent, or RBC = 4x authorized control level. The company's current or prospective model score is calculated as the basis. The model score is then recalculated for each reinsurance program under consideration and compared to the basis case. The models in question are all relatively similar – capital factors are applied to premiums, reserves, assets, etc. Capital requirements are reduced by reinsurance because premiums and possibly current or expected reserves are reduced. There is, however, typically a small corresponding increase in required capital due to a factor applied to reinsurance receivables.

While the practical method is, in some sense, easier to implement, it suffers from the disadvantage that it measures capital based on risk-producing proxies (e.g., premiums), rather than explicitly modeling the risks themselves. So, in the previous example of the stop-loss contract versus the current structure, the stop-loss would likely show little effect on rating agency or regulatory required capital, as it would have little impact on premiums and no prospective impact on reserves.

One way to compensate for the above disadvantage is to build the various rating agency and regulatory required capital models into the enterprise risk model. A capital score can then be calculated for each scenario and with each iteration. Rather than rely on the marginal differences as described above, required capital can be set at predetermined levels based on the probability distributions of the regulatory scores. For example, a company may define required capital at that level where there is less than a 10 percent probability that BCAR drops below 130 percent (the level typically associated with an A-).

Consider an example of a company deliberating changing the retention and/or the limits of an excess of loss reinsurance contract. The sample loss distributions of the alternatives are shown in Figure 2.5.11.

FIGURE 2.5.11: RETENTION/LIMIT COVERAGE OPTION CDFs

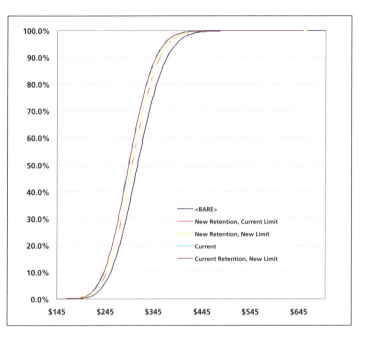

In this example, the cost or benefit was measured as the net present value of the alternative's ceded premiums less the net present value of ceded losses as compared to the current program. Current capital was based on management's view of minimum capital required to retain existing ratings, which coincided with the V@R at the 99.98^{th} percentile. This V@R value was then used as the proxy for required capital for each of the options, and capital was read off of the curves above.

FIGURE 2.5.12: COMPARISON OF ALTERNATIVE REINSURANCE STRUCTURES WITH MARGINAL ROE

		<BARE>	Option 1	Option 2	Current	Option 3
	Retention	0	New	New	Current	Current
	Limit	Unlimited	Current	New	Current	New
△ NPV Ceded Premium - (less)/more		-39.6	-8.9	-10.1	0.0	-0.2
△ NPV Ceded Loss - (less)/more		-23.3	-9.1	-9.2	0.0	-1.5
△ NPV Net Benefit/(cost)		16.2	-0.2	1.0	0.0	-1.4
Capital Consumed/(released)		51.6	1.5	1.8	0.0	0.3
After Tax Marginal ROE		20%	-8%	35%	0.0	-339%

Option 2, above, was deemed superior, as it had the highest marginal ROE. Alternatively, one could have compared the increased capital required (1.8) with its associated cost of capital (say, 10 percent) to the benefit achieved (1.8 x 0.1 = 0.18 vs. 1.0).

The above example is illustrative, but the specific algorithm is not necessarily recommended. The use of higher percentile V@R estimates to gauge required capital can be very volatile. And V@R itself, while intuitive, restricts the definition of risk to a single point on the loss distribution. We generally recommend using a risk metric such as XTV@R at a lower percentile. Figure 2.5.13 shows the XTV@R calculation, by peril, for a variety of thresholds for three different reinsurance options. The capital consideration would be expressed as a multiple of these XTV@Rs, for example, six times the 90th percentile (1,182 for Option A and 1,218 for Option B) or 4.5 times the 95th percentile (1,193 for Option A and 1,220 for Option B).

FIGURE 2.5.13: COMPARISON USING XTV@R RISK METRIC

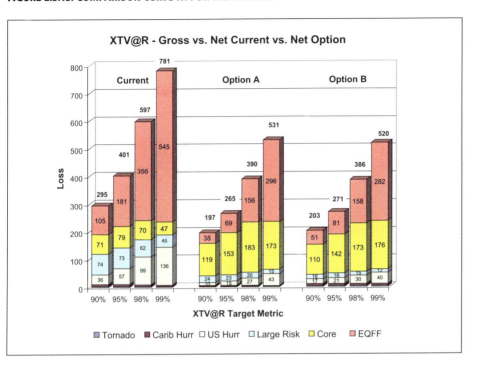

In summary, the second paradigm attempts to judge the value in the reinsurance program based on a comparison of the marginal cost of capital implied for each program to the respective marginal cost of the reinsurance. The company can use the results of the analysis to select the best reinsurance program from among alternatives or choose to retain the risk, perhaps with additional capital.

Reinsurance, Capital and Accumulated Risk

Whether capital requirements are defined by enterprise risk models, rating agency formulas or regulatory ratios, loss reserve risk requires capital. In the prior section, the ROEs are based on capital for a single year, but business that contributes loss reserves absorbs capital for more than one year. For long tailed business, the difference is highly significant and should be considered when analyzing the value of reinsurance.

Accumulated loss reserves create accumulated risks. The accumulation of risk is exacerbated by aspects of risk that are correlated across accident years. As a convenient mechanism for modeling capital absorbed for many future years, we introduce the notion of *as-if* loss reserves. For an accident (or underwriting) year of new business, the as-if loss reserves are the loss reserves that would exist at the beginning of the accident year, if that business had been written in a steady state (except for trend) in all prior years. The capital absorbed in the current year by the combination of the accident year and the as-if loss reserves is a surrogate for the present value of the capital absorbed by the accident year over time.

The as-if reserves mechanism provides two practical advantages:

1. It can measure the impact of accumulated risk caused by correlated risk factors.
2. The reinsurance being analyzed or considered can be applied to the accident year and the as-if reserves, providing a more valid measure of the impact of the reinsurance on accumulated risk and on capital absorbed over the full life of the accident year.

The results of an analysis of accumulated risk will be highly dependent on the form of the underlying risk model with respect to time-related projection risk. The illustrative examples below incorporate several such features that are further discussed in subsequent chapters; specifically:

- Severity trend (and its associated uncertainty) is modeled as applying through the date of loss payment. All unpaid losses, therefore, continue to be exposed to this trend risk. Loss reserve risk models that incorporate calendar-year trend are discussed in Section 5.2.

- Severity trend risk is modeled according to the AR-1 (first order autocorrelated) process that is introduced in Section 3.2.

The example is intended to be typical of direct middle-market commercial liability insurance written in the United States, with a maximum policy limit of $2 million.

Before considering the effect of reinsurance, let us examine the impact of accumulated risk on the direct (i.e., BARE) results. Figure 2.5.14 compares probability density functions (PDFs) and cumulative distribution functions (CDFs) for the accident year alone versus the accident year plus as-if reserves.

**FIGURE 2.5.14: DISTRIBUTIONS OF UNDERWRITING LOSS —
CURRENT YEAR AND ACCUMULATED RESULTS**

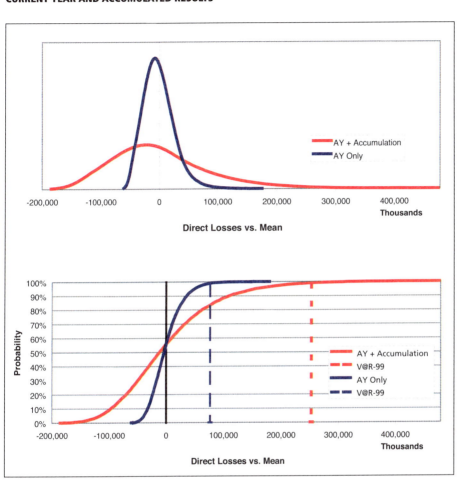

For a given outcome, we define capital consumed as the present value of losses and expenses minus the present value of underwriting funds available. For the accident year, funds available are premiums, and we have assumed breakeven underwriting. For the as-if reserves, funds available are the nominal value of the reserves. Present values are at 4 percent per annum. Figure 2.5.15 compares PDFs and CDFs for capital consumed.

FIGURE 2.5.15: DISTRIBUTIONS OF CAPITAL CONSUMED — CURRENT YEAR AND ACCUMULATED RESULTS

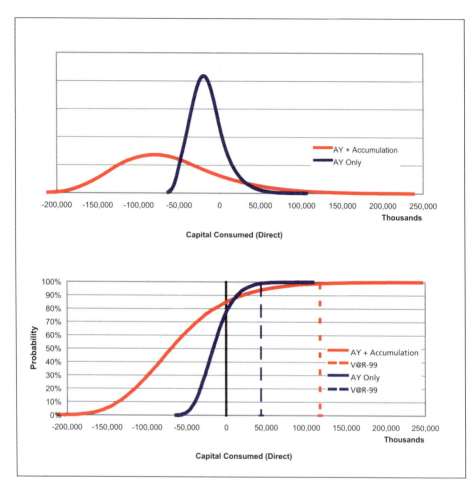

Clearly, the analysis of accumulated risk provides a dramatically different picture of the capital consumed by writing a long-tailed line of business.

Next, we add reinsurance to the picture. We illustrate a simple per-occurrence XOL program covering 1.5M x 0.5M. In order to properly reflect the impact of the trend-risk model, it is essential that the model of the ceded losses reflect not only the XOL process risk but also the XOL payment pattern and the leveraged effect of changes in severity trend on the XOL layer.

FIGURE 2.5.16: TAILS OF CAPITAL DISTRIBUTIONS

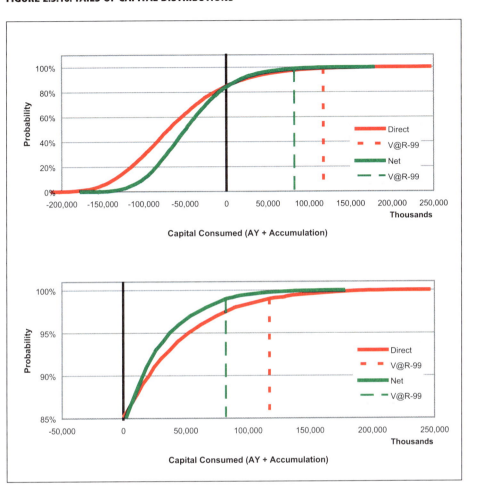

The reinsurance in the example is priced to a 5 percent underwriting loss, with no ceding commission and a 15 percent reinsurer expense ratio. Figure 2.5.16 displays the CDFs of the capital-consumed distributions, direct and net.

FIGURE 2.5.17: STRUCTURE COMPARISON WITH ROEs

		DIRECT	NET
Mean Profit (Discounted Basis)		14,555,893	10,865,516
Capital	V@R-99	117,190,899	82,032,910
	TV@R-99	139,381,010	97,578,009
Spread ROE	V@R-99	12.42%	13.25%
	TV@R-99	10.44%	11.14%

Figure 2.5.17 compares expected profit (cost) – direct, net and ceded – versus required capital according to several tail measures. This type of comparison can measure the value of reinsurance and compare competing reinsurance options, as has been described in the prior section.

Note that the required capital illustrated above is relative to the distribution for a stand-alone line of business, rather than to an allocation of company capital or capital cost. As such, the realistic capital levels are not as deep in the tail of the distribution as they would be for the company as a whole.

Reinsurance and Market Value

In an ideal world of business, every competitive action of a firm would be performed with the intent of increasing the value of the company. Where constraints force a decision between competing activities, the firm would presumably prefer those that increase value the most on a risk-adjusted basis. These statements are certainly true for publicly traded companies, where market value is a ready report card on the company's performance, but they likely hold for mutual companies as well.

The third paradigm for measuring value in reinsurance extends the notion in the previous section – that the stability garnered from reinsurance is a substitute for capital and can therefore be judged accordingly – to relate the concepts of capital consumption and stability to the ultimate value of the firm. The third paradigm is perhaps the holy grail of cost-benefit analysis.

We can all agree that the value of the firm is favorably impacted by the effective use of capital, stability of earnings and steady growth. Several academic studies [2] have chipped away at the relationships between capital, earnings, growth and value. Recent studies have found:

- Insureds demand price discounts of 10 to 20 times the expected cost of the chance of an insurer default (see Phillips, Cummins and Allen [3]).
- A 1 percent decrease in capital gives a 1 percent loss in pricing, and a 1 percent increase in the standard deviation in earnings leads to a 0.33 percent decrease in pricing (see Sommer [4]).
- A ratings upgrade is worth 3 percent in business growth, and a ratings downgrade can produce a 5 to 20 percent drop in business (see Epermanis and Harrington [1]).

The third paradigm is an area of ongoing research, but our research into this class of models is encouraging. Section 2.6 introduces FLAVORED models, which seek to measure the market value of risk management.

Conclusion

Cost-benefit analysis provides a useful methodology for insurers to quantify the value in their reinsurance transactions and to compare among alternative structures.

A good cost measure is the net decrease in the net present value of earnings expected from the program. Conversely, we find using combined ratios can give a distorted picture of the effects of reinsurance on earnings.

The simplest measure of benefit – our first paradigm – is the increased stability gained from the reinsurance transaction. Measures of stability, variance and standard deviation can give misleading results, as they can be lowered by eliminating the chance for favorable deviations. Looking at the distribution of differences in programs is also not as useful as looking at the differences in the distributions. Efficient frontier analysis is often a useful tool.

Benefit measures would ideally show the increased value of the firm (third paradigm) from the increased earnings from reduced financing costs, better claims paying ratings, etc. A reasonable substitute is to relate the increased stability that arises from the reinsurance program to capital requirements. Value in reinsurance can be measured versus a cost of capital or in terms of marginal ROEs. Several risk measures based on various financial accounts give similar comparisons.

2.6 Measuring the Market Value of Risk Management: An Introduction to FLAVORED Models

By John A. Major, ASA, MAAA

Introduction

This section is about quantifying the market value of risk management, forging a usable tool for practitioners by bringing together two distinct lines of research. On the one hand, there is a particular class of models we have taken the liberty of naming de Finetti-Lévy Asset Value of Optimized Risk, Equity and Dividends ("FLAVORED") models. The original forms date back to actuarial science circa 50 years ago, but the intervening years have seen tremendous extension and sophistication in their development by stochastic optimization and control theorists. On the other hand, there is the literature of corporate hedging within finance theory, also dating back about 50 years. In particular, Froot et al. ([29], [30]) developed a model to explain why risk management matters to financial firms, and Froot [28] refines this to apply more specifically to insurers.

Until very recently, each of these bodies of literature showed little or no acknowledgement that the other existed. Yet, as we shall see, they have converged to the point where a synthesis is imminent. This chapter will create one link in that synthesis, demonstrating how a version of the Froot, et al. model can be turned into a FLAVORED model. Moreover, the innovations in Froot [28] can be accommodated as well.

Why are these models important? Without a consensus on a value-based theoretical framework for risk management, analysts are left hypothesizing risk-reward preferences to guide corporate strategies. In practice, this means showing managers the risk-return tradeoffs of various items on the decision menu and letting them "make the call" (Venter [74]). The models discussed in this chapter are based on a market perspective of value and not on the idea of firms having risk preferences – just a preference for higher shareholder value. Whereas the usual approach considers a two-dimensional risk-versus-reward decision space, FLAVORED models put both risk and reward on the same dimension: market value.

This chapter presents a literary history of the models, the disconnect between the two streams and recent signs of convergence. Next, it shows how to take the Froot, et al. costly external capital model and turn it into a FLAVORED model. Finally, solutions and solution methods are discussed, and a new insurance-specific example is worked out by way of a general-purpose numerical solver.

A History of FLAVORED Models

The typical DFA model in insurance takes a form something like the following (Daykin, et al. [22]):

(Change in capital) = (profits) = (premiums) + (investment income) − (expenses) − (losses)

where some of the elements, such as premiums, are assumed known (deterministic); and some, such as losses, are unpredictable (stochastic). Details include the time period over which quantities and changes are measured, whether taxes are included in expenses or are ignored, whether investment income is considered deterministic or stochastic, etc.

Management strategies are reflected in parameter choices that may alter the characteristics of both deterministic (e.g., a reinsurance premium) and stochastic (e.g., how losses are altered by reinsurance) parts of the equation. Statistics of outcomes (risk measures, profit measures) are captured. One or more objectives are chosen, and the analyst's task is to figure out how the parameters could be set to achieve the objectives, or, failing a definitive solution, to offer a menu of alternatives that trade off various objectives.

Early Forms of the Model

In classical actuarial science, the objective was to minimize (or at least control) the probability of ruin. De Finetti [23] proposed changing the focus of actuarial science from ruin probability to the value of shareholder dividends. The equation for capital under de Finetti's optimal dividends model can be written as:

$$W_t = W_0 + \mu \cdot t - X_t - D_t \qquad [2.6.1]$$

where W represents the capital (alternatively, "equity," "surplus" or "risk reserve") of the firm at time t, μ is the constant rate of inflow of funds (e.g., net premiums), X is the cumulative uncertain outflow of funds (e.g., loss payments), and D represents the accumulated dividends distributed back to the firm's owners. With X being a random variable, equation 2.6.1 describes the firm's capital as a stochastic process. With X represented as a compound Poisson process (and no D), this is known as the Cramér-Lundberg model (Cramér [20]).

The objective here, however, involves not the minimization of ruin but the maximization of owner wealth:

$$M(w) = E\left[\sum_{t=0}^{\infty}(1+r)^{-t}\Delta D_t \,\Big|\, W_0 = w\right] \qquad [2.6.2]$$

where E signifies mathematical expectation and r is an appropriately chosen discount rate. This is familiar from finance as the discounted dividends model for the value of a firm.

The key mathematical object in this and all subsequent versions of the model is M(W), known as the M-curve. This is the relationship between the capital of the firm (W) and the market value of the firm (M).

Similar to the questions in ruin theory, questions here revolve around initial capital and risk management strategies; but the first question is: What is the optimal dividend strategy? De Finetti solved this in a simple case involving discrete time and discrete X values. It amounts to a "barrier" strategy, where all excess capital above a particular level β is paid back as dividends to the owners; but there are no dividends when capital is less than β.

Borch ([11], [12], [13], [14]) extended de Finetti's model in a number of directions, but retained its discrete-time perspective. Other researchers continued to extend optimal control theory, with applications often being to economics and finance. Variations on the "problem of optimal dividends," whether in a discrete or continuous setting, were solved again and again over the coming decades. Examples include Shubik and Thompson [69], Miyasawa [55], Takeuchi [70], Morill [58], Bather [5], Gerber [31], Porteus [63], Waldmann [75], Jeanblanc-Picqué and Shiryaev [45], Radner and Shepp [64], Milne and Robertson [54], Asmussen and Taksar [1], Paulsen and Gjessing [61], Højgaard [36], Taksar [71], Taksar and Zhou [73], Højgaard and Taksar ([38], [39], [40]), Taksar [72] and Asmussen et al. [2].

Typical 20th century models focused on a Brownian motion[17] risk process. See Gerber and Shiu [32] or Major [48] for more historical details. Many later papers broke away from Brownian motion, returning (with new levels of rigor and sophistication) to the classical actuarial risk models. Examples include Zajic [77], Højgaard [37], Mnif and Sulem [56], Azcue and Muler [4] and Gerber and Shiu [33].

Some papers introduced complications to the capital-generating process or constraints on firm behavior or made generalizations in other ways. Examples include Højgaard and Taksar ([41], [42]), Cadenillas et al. [15], Choulli et al. [18], Paulsen [60], Hipp [35], Chen et al. [17], Bäuerle [6], Guo et al. [34], Hubalek and Schachermayer [43], Dickson and Waters [25] and Decamps and Villeneuve [24].

We may characterize a general form of these models as the FLAVORED model:

$$dW_t = \mu(W_t, u_t) \cdot dt - dX(W_t, u_t) + dC(u_t) - dD(u_t) \qquad [2.6.3]$$

---

17 See the section, "Going-Concern Froot Model" for a definition.

where,
- W_t represents the capital (policyholder surplus, wealth) of the firm at time t;
- u_t represents a vector of management controls;
- μ represents the expected rate of change (drift) of wealth, which is a function of current wealth and the controls;
- X is a Lévy[18] stochastic process representing the cumulative risks to wealth, with its distributional properties being functions of wealth and control;
- C (respectively, D) is the nondecreasing cumulative external capital (respectively, dividends) supplied by (respectively, paid back to) shareholders, also under management control.

The equation 2.6.3 is a stochastic differential equation (SDE), the continuous-time counterpart to a discrete time series equation.[19]

The objective is again to maximize the market value of the firm given by the M-curve:

$$M(w) = E\left[\int_0^\infty e^{-rt}dD_t - (1+\kappa)\cdot \int_0^\infty e^{-rt}dC_t \mid W_0 = w\right] \quad [2.6.4]$$

where κ is a loading factor representing the cost of external capital.

The Disconnect with Finance Theory

Until the 21st century, the optimal dividends model retained a "provincial" flavor compared to mainstream finance theory. Its roots in actuarial science and operations research made it unfamiliar to many economists and finance theorists.[20] Its relationship to classical finance theory had not been explained, and its logic made it seem quaint compared to contingent claims analysis. This section describes the disconnect and discusses recent literature that addresses those issues in relation to full FLAVORED models.

The Modigliani and Miller ([53], [57]) theorem is the "Newton's Law" of finance theory. In the absence of "friction" and in a situation of fixed investment strategy, neither capital structure, dividend policy, nor risk management affect the firm's market value. To the extent that such frictions (such as bankruptcy costs, agency distortions, tax effects, cost of holding capital and costly access to external capital) exist, then capital structure, dividends and risk management can matter, but only to the extent that they serve to exacerbate or ameliorate the effects of the frictions. Modern texts on risk management (e.g., Culp [21], Doherty [27]) explain the application of risk management, capital structure and dividend policy in terms of the modes of violating the Modigliani and Miller assumptions.

---

18 A Lévy process generalizes Brownian motion and compound Poisson processes, including the two, and sums thereof, as special cases.
19 Basically, replace the differential d symbol with the discrete first-difference symbol Δ. See Itô [44] for a more formal treatment.
20 Google Scholar (http://scholar.google.com) shows at most 55 citations for a paper in the literature reviewed here, and only four others with more than 35 citations. In comparison, Froot et al. [30] shows 450 citations, Modigliani and Miller [57], 1,552, and Black and Scholes [9], 5,110.

In particular, Doherty [26], Froot, Scharfstein and Stein [30], Froot and Stein [29] and Froot [28] develop a one-period model to illustrate how one source of friction, costly external capital, affects market value and how risk management can serve to increase market value. We will return to this model in the next section.

A decade after Modigliani and Miller, Merton ([50], [52]) and Black and Scholes [9] sparked the revolution in mathematical finance that continues today. Actuaries became increasingly familiar and comfortable with "financial engineering" based on this work, but this did not help the disconnect between the optimal dividends literature and finance theory, because the optimal dividends problem *does not fit the financial engineering paradigm*.

Froot and Stein [29] write:

> [The] dominant paradigm... boils down to a contingent-claims model of the sort pioneered by Merton [52]. This type of model... assumes away exactly the sorts of imperfections that make [risk management] challenging and relevant. Indeed, it is only appropriate if either: i) the [firm] can frictionlessly hedge all risks... or ii) the Modigliani-Miller theorem applies, so that the [firm] has no reason to care about risk management in the first place.

Arbitrage-free pricing assumes there must be no positive NPV investment opportunities, but the existence of such forms the starting point of corporate finance theory. Froot and Stein continue, "[W]e want to have a model that is squarely rooted in the objective of maximizing shareholder value in an efficient market."

This would seem to be consistent with the objectives and approach of the optimal dividends literature. The pertinent question is this: Which Modigliani and Miller assumptions are being violated and how do those violations relate to the model? To some early authors, the obvious answer – no external finance[21] – might have been too obvious to deserve mention. To others, it is possible that the question did not even arise.

Later Models Start to Connect with Finance Theory

One of the more evident changes in the 21st century optimal dividends literature is that at least a passing mention of Modigliani and Miller has become *de rigueur*. Beyond a *pro forma* mention, some of these papers explicitly discuss the Modigliani and Miller assumptions and how the optimal dividends model violates them.

---

21 Peura [62] notes another source of friction embedded in the early models: "...indirect or opportunity cost of bankruptcy. This is the value lost due to irreversible discontinuation of operations which are fundamentally profitable on average. We can add direct bankruptcy costs to the model with little added difficulty." (The boundary condition becomes $M(0) = -K$ instead of $M(0) = 0$.)

More importantly, recent papers extend the optimal dividends model to allow for external financing, that is, capital flows from the investors back into the firm, making them full FLAVORED models. When this is allowed under Modigliani and Miller conditions (no cost, any amount), then the standard Modigliani and Miller result is obtained: The market value of the firm is the capitalized value of the expected profit flow plus the capital: $M = \mu/r + W$. Furthermore, risk management (i.e., costlessly reducing volatility of W) does not affect the market value and so is irrelevant. With an infinite cost of external capital, the model reverts to the dividends-only submodel. With finite nonzero cost, more interesting behavior is observed.

Sethi and Taksar [68] appears to be the first paper to extend the Brownian motion model to include external capital. However, they stipulate certain conditions on the functions $\mu(W)$ and $\sigma(W)$. Løkka and Zervos [47] appears to be the first paper to analyze the "standard" (constant drift and volatility) Brownian motion with costly external capital. More extensions of those results followed (e.g., Belhaj [7], Cai et al. [16] and Avram et al. [3]).

These papers, however, do not explain at length how their models relate to Modigliani and Miller; the ones discussed below do.

Peura [62] addresses the optimal dividends model with the possibility of recapitalization. It discusses the Modigliani and Miller irrelevance theorems and the literature on their violations, including an explicit discussion of the Froot et al. costly capital model.

Blazenko et al. [10] model insurance firms as being "regulated" in the sense that if $W < 0$, then shareholders must either add (frictionless) capital at a rate k, or abandon the business; hence, they distinguish economic ruin (abandonment) from technical ruin (financial distress).[22] They derive the optimal abandonment barrier and the value of the abandonment option. In the limit as $k \to \infty$, corresponding to a requirement of instantaneous makeup of the capital deficit, the usual Modigliani and Miller linear equation for $M(W)$ is obtained and the value of the abandonment option goes to zero. They conclude that in the presence of strong regulatory capital requirements, "the correct financial valuation methodology for management of an insurance business is discounted cash flow analysis rather than contingent claims analysis."

---

22 Without loss of generality, the capital constraint defining distress can be placed anywhere (e.g., at some barrier $\beta > 0$), which is more realistic in terms of how insurance regulation and ratings are conducted.

Rochet and Villeneuve [65] analyze distinct and simultaneous possibilities for "hedging" (against Brownian motion) and "insuring" (against a Poisson risk with constant severity), along with two forms of costly external financing. They write:

> [W]hen liquidity management and risk management decisions are endogenized simultaneously, the theoretical impact of profitability and leverage is non monotonic.... Moreover when insurance decisions are explicitly modeled, we find that the optimal patterns of hedging and insurance decisions by firms are exactly opposite: Cash poor firms should hedge but not insure, whereas the opposite is true for cash rich firms.... This may explain the mixed findings of empirical studies on corporate demand for hedging and insurance....

Froot et al. and FLAVORED Models

This section discusses the model of Froot et al. ([30], [29]) and shows how it can be adapted to become a FLAVORED model. An expanded discussion can be found in Major [49].

A Simplified Froot Model

At time $t = 0$, the firm chooses how much liquid capital, K, to hold. There is a cost of holding capital, however: Additional funds τK must be paid on the side. K is the firm's initial wealth, W_0. Between time 0 and time 1, business operations result in either an increase or decrease of W according to $\Delta W = \mu + \sigma Z$, where Z is a unit normal (Gaussian) random variable. At time $t = 1$, the firm may invest an amount I in an opportunity whose net present value is $M(I) - I$.

The quantity I may be less than or equal to $W_1 = W_0 + \Delta W$, or it may be greater than W_1, in which case the difference must be made up from external funds $e = I - W_1$ with associated funding cost $C(e)$. Assume that $M(0) = 0$. The net (of initial capital) market value of the firm is:

$$NMV = M(I) - e - C(e) - (1+\tau) \cdot K \qquad [2.6.5]$$

There are two questions:

1. What is the optimal value of K to maximize the expectation of the net market value of the firm?
2. Is there an advantage to replacing the stochastic ΔW with a constant $\Delta W = \mu$?

First, let us consider the frictionless situation, when the cost of holding capital τ and the cost of external funds $C(e)$ are both zero. The net market value of the firm is then $M(I) - e - K = M(I) - I + W_1 - K = M(I) - I + K + \Delta W - K = M(I) - I + \Delta W$. Therefore the answer to Question 1 is: Subject to constraints, the choice of initial capital K does not matter – only the choice of I. The expectation of the final market value is given by $M(I) - I + E[\Delta W] = M(I) - I + \mu$, so the answer to Question 2 is: Risk management does not matter, either.

This is a version of the Modigliani and Miller world, where neither capital structure nor risk management matters to the value of the firm. What is important is making the right investment decision to gain the maximum available NPV: $M(I) - I$.

In the case of costly capital, the analysis is not so simple. First, Froot et al. assume that the investment gross return $M(I)$ is concave, giving the NPV of $M(I) - I$ a single local and global maximum at some specific I. Furthermore, they assume $C(e)$ is convex. In assuming smoothness of $M(I)$ and $C(e)$, they are able to derive first-order conditions for optimality and analyze the comparative statics. Rather than repeat their analysis, we turn our attention to a very special case.

A Going-Concern Froot Model

Instead of the Froot model with an arbitrary terminal investment opportunity $M(I)$, consider that the time 1 investment is to *continue operations*. For concreteness, let us start by encapsulating the random ΔW "business operations" into a physical asset – a magic coin box. Consider the following version of the problem:

> You have a magic coin box that can hold up to W_{max} dollars in coins. Every fixed time interval, some coins randomly appear or disappear according to $\Delta W = \mu + \sigma Z$. If the box already holds W_{max} and more coins appear, the new coins are ejected and you keep them. (Call these dividends δ.) But once the box runs out of coins, it vanishes in a puff of smoke. Assume also that these random transitions are uncorrelated with any financial markets. Currently, the box has $W_0 = K \to \infty$ in it and will transition at the end of the next time interval. What is the fair market value,[23] M, of this device?

Our concern here is not to solve the problem but to elucidate its structure. We will, however, note some solution features.

---

23 Assume its sales value as a scientific or entertainment novelty is zero!

A basic pricing principle is that the expected return of an asset has to equal the appropriate risk-adjusted hurdle rate. Whether given by CAPM (Merton [51]), APT (Ross [66]) or another pricing model, the fact that the transitions are uncorrelated with financial markets means that the appropriate hurdle rate is the risk-free rate, which we will denote as r. The return is the sum of cash dispensed and capital gain (i.e., change in market value). So the requirement, which must be satisfied at any time t, is:

$$r = E[return] = E\left[\frac{Dividends + Capital\ Gains}{Value}\right] = E\left[\frac{\delta_{t+1} + M_{t+1} - M_t}{M_t}\right].$$

[2.6.6]

This can be rewritten as a recursive equation:

$$M_t = \frac{1}{1+r} E[\delta_{t+1} + M_{t+1}]$$

[2.6.7]

or expanded into extensive form:

$$M_t = E\left[\sum_{j=1}^{\infty} \frac{\delta_{t+j}}{(1+r)^j}\right]$$

[2.6.8]

but they all say the same thing (assuming the infinite series converges).

What if, instead of the random transitions, ΔW was exactly equal to the expected value μ (assuming μ ≥ 0) with certainty every time? Would it be worth more? It depends. That perpetuity is worth μ/r. If σ is large, μ is small and W is near W_{max}, it might be better to take the 50 percent chance of a large payoff instead of an ε-small certain stream.

So far, what we have described is a fixed, but not necessarily optimal, dividends policy. What if, in the brief moment after a transition occurs, we could open the box and remove some money? Would it ever be advantageous to do so? What is the best way? Such a possibility extends the problem to one of optimal dividends.

What if we had the option of adding money? Starting at W=W_{max}, the box will survive for another cycle with probability 1-q = Φ(W_{max}/σ). Consider the following strategy: If ΔW < 0, we replenish; if ΔW > 0, we pocket the proceeds. If the discount rate is correct and q is approximately zero,[24] we should be indifferent to this dividend stream, its certainty equivalent stream or selling the box for the capitalized value of those streams. The magic box now lives in the Modigliani and Miller world where risk management does not matter.

---

24 It should be noted that this model also incorporates a severe degree of "bankruptcy cost," another source of capital market friction and violation of Modigliani and Miller assumptions. In the typical corporate finance context, the assets of the firm consist of plant and equipment, as well as the good will arising from customer and supplier relationships. When a firm goes bankrupt, it typically does not see its factories disappear in a puff of smoke!

What if an extra cost of κ > 0 were incurred every time we added a coin to the box? That is, we expend 1+κ in order to increase W by 1. How would this change our strategy? Clearly, the odds have shifted and risk management matters now.

Notice how we have retained the essential structure of the Froot model. At time t = 0, we want to initialize the box with the optimal amount of funds K. Between time 0 and 1, a random process affects the wealth, W. At time t = 1, we have the option of adding funds (at a cost) to the box, and we want to do so in a way that maximizes the net value of the box (plus dividends, less our out-of-pocket) at that time.

What if we were not restricted to affecting the box at unit time intervals – after all, many small changes could be happening within each interval. We could consider the dynamics over arbitrary small intervals Δt. The possibility of overlapping (t, t+Δt) intervals makes the concept of the Z variables a bit difficult to formalize, so, instead, we use the random variable B_t to represent the cumulative sum of distinct random changes.[25] We can write the random transitions as:

$$\Delta W_t = W_{t+\Delta t} - W_t = \mu \cdot \Delta t + \sigma \cdot (B_{t+\Delta t} - B_t) = \mu \cdot \Delta t + \sigma \cdot \Delta B_t \quad [2.6.9]$$

We can use the same idea to track the accumulated amount of money that has been dispensed by or removed from the box up to time t, D_t, and the accumulated amount of money that has been added to the box, C_t. Then the stated equation for W can be written:

$$\Delta W_t = \mu \cdot \Delta t + \sigma \cdot \Delta B_t + \Delta C_t - \Delta D_t \quad [2.6.10]$$

The essential question is the same – given an initial amount of money in the box, W_0, what is the market value of the box? For any particular dividend (D) and capitalization (C) strategy, the answer is given by the extensive form valuation formula:

$$M_t = E\left[\sum_{j=1}^{\infty} e^{-r \cdot j \cdot \Delta t} \cdot \Delta D_{t+j \cdot \Delta t} - (1+\kappa) \cdot \sum_{j=1}^{\infty} e^{-r \cdot j \cdot \Delta t} \cdot \Delta C_{t+j \cdot \Delta t}\right] \quad [2.6.11]$$

where now we have used a continuous force of interest r instead of a finite-period interest rate. If external financing is too expensive to use at all, C_t will always be zero and the second term in brackets will be superfluous. The goal, then, is to craft the optimal dividends and recapitalization strategies so as to maximize this expected value; that, then, is the market value. Equation 2.6.10 is still analogous to the Froot model dynamics for W, and equation 2.6.11 is still representative of the market value of a going concern with costly external capital. Bankruptcy cost manifests itself in the restriction that ΔD and ΔC remain zero after W hits zero.

---

[25] That is, $B_{t+\Delta t} - B_t$ is distributed as a normal with mean zero and variance Δt. This is known as Brownian motion or a Weiner process.

By allowing the time step Δ→0, we finally arrive at a version of the full FLAVORED model as represented by equations 2.6.3 and 2.6.4.

Evaluating Risk Management with FLAVORED Models

Froot [28] augments the one-period model discussed above with several key elements specific to insurance firms: "The first feature is that customers – especially retail policyholders – face contractual performance risks.... Customers are thought to be more risk averse to these product performance issues than are bondholders." This insight can be incorporated into the general FLAVORED model by making the μ and X elements of the stochastic differential equation 2.6.3 be dependent on the current value of capital, W. This leads to versions of the problem that have not been solved analytically. They can, however, be solved numerically. In doing so, not only can optimal risk management strategies be determined, but their (market) value to the firm can be calculated as well.

This section reviews solutions for some simpler versions of the problem, as well as a more realistic state-dependent version.

The Vanilla Model

Gerber and Shiu [32] define the capital process as:

$$dW_t = \mu \cdot dt - \sigma \cdot dB_t - dD_t \qquad [2.6.12]$$

where μ and σ are constants, B is a standard Brownian motion, and dividend distribution D itself is the only control. They show that the optimal strategy is to distribute immediately all capital above a "barrier" point β. When W is less than β, no dividends are distributed. The barrier point can be interpreted as the optimal level of capital for the firm: If capital is above that, excess amounts are returned to the shareholder immediately; below that, all profits are retained until such time as it is reached.

Figure 2.6.1 shows the M-curve resulting from $\mu = 0.5$, $\sigma = 1$ and $r = 6$ percent. The resulting barrier is $\beta = 3.8$. Note that for $W > \beta$, the M-curve is linear with slope 1. One might expect the slope to be less than one, as a consequence of "frictional cost" of holding capital above β; but there is none in this model, because if the firm ever finds itself in that situation, it immediately dividends all excess back to the shareholders. As W→0, the M-curve also approaches zero. At the barrier, the value of M is the present value of a perpetuity at the rate of drift, $M = \mu/r = 8.33$. The barrier amount $W = \beta$ can be interpreted as the amount of risk capital necessary to support that perpetuity. Note that the *excess* of M over W is *not* the perpetuity value. For $W \geq \beta$, the excess of market value over cash, M-W, is equal to $\mu/r - \beta$, the perpetuity value less the required capital.

FIGURE 2.6.1: M-CURVE (FIRM VALUE) FROM BROWNIAN MOTION AND DIVIDENDS ONLY

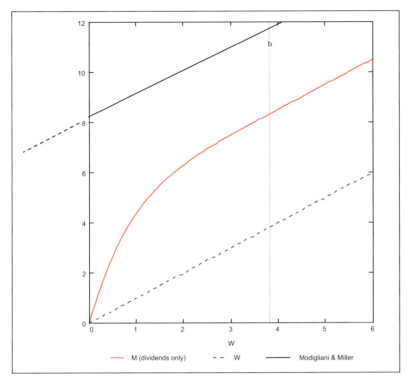

In Figure 2.6.1, an additional straight line is drawn above the M-curve. This represents the value of the firm under Modigliani and Miller conditions. With W = 0, the value is the perpetuity; and for greater W, the value increases dollar for dollar. The dotted extension to the left represents a situation discussed in Blazenko et al. [10]. If the firm were allowed to exist in a state of technical insolvency long enough for investors to add funds to bring W back into the positive range, investors would be willing to do so as long as the current W were not less than $-\mu/r$. Thus, the Modigliani and Miller straight line extends all the way to the horizontal axis.

Proportional Reinsurance

Bather [5] took the step of introducing no-load proportional (quota-share) reinsurance in the control vector. Equation 2.6.3 becomes:

$$dW_t = U(W_t) \cdot \mu \cdot dt - U(W_t) \cdot \sigma \cdot dB_t - dD_t \qquad [2.6.13]$$

where $0 \leq U(w) \leq 1$ is the fraction of the risk to retain.

The optimal dividend strategy is essentially the same as for equation 2.6.12 (with a slight downward shift in the location of the barrier β to 3.3). The optimal reinsurance strategy involves a second barrier, $\rho = 1.4$, above which all risk is retained (U = 1). For $W < \rho$, U(W) is linear in W down to U(0) = 0. Figure 2.6.2 compares the M-curve for this problem to the dividends-only version. It is interesting to note that the availability of reinsurance raises the value of the firm, even when $W > \rho$ and it is not being used.

FIGURE 2.6.2: M-CURVE FROM BROWNIAN MOTION, DIVIDENDS AND PROPORTIONAL REINSURANCE

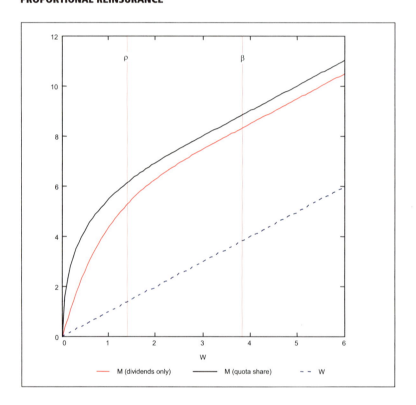

A Ratings-Cliff Problem

So far, the drift term μ has not depended explicitly on wealth W. A key feature of Froot's [28] model is that it does. This section presents the numerical solution of a FLAVORED model where it does as well, and also illustrates how to handle constant background growth by changing to an inflation-adjusted numéraire. Consider the following example:

The economy is currently undergoing 4 percent inflation with a 5 percent risk-free interest rate. The firm has book value (capital) of 10 billion and expected one-year inflation-adjusted growth in book value of 1 billion, if it maintains its rating. The standard deviation of this real profit is also 1 billion and it is assumed to follow a normal distribution (Brownian motion). The firm can cede a proportion of its business to a reinsurer at no net cost; but even if it ceded all of it, it would still have 100 million in operating expenses. Management estimates that if book value were to go below 7 billion, it would experience a ratings downgrade that would force it to experience real per annum losses of 500 million.[26] External financing is out of the question.

Some questions that might be raised include:

1. What is the optimal level of capital; does the firm need more, or is it overcapitalized?
2. Should it cede some business to the reinsurer, and if so, how much?
3. How does the market value of the firm respond to changes in its capital?
4. Does the availability of risk transfer bring value to the firm, and if so, how much?

The corresponding FLAVORED model is governed by an equation similar to 2.6.14 but with an extra $-bdt$ term, with $\sigma = 1$ (billion), $W_0 = 10$, $b = 0.1$, and $\mu(W)$ function defined by:

$$\mu = \begin{cases} 1.1, & W > 7 \\ -0.4, & W \leq 7 \end{cases}$$

[2.6.14]

The valuation rate is the real interest rate, $r = 0.01$. Note that the net profit of 1 billion (resp, –500 million) is the algebraic sum of $\mu = 1.1$ (resp –0.4) and $-b = -0.1$.

This results in qualitatively different behavior of the solution from what was seen above, even without risk transfer. Figure 2.6.3 shows the optimal dividends. This indicates two zones where dividends should be paid. The "typical" zone, where $W > 7$ corresponds to the strategy we saw in both previous examples: There is a threshold, in this case 12 or 12.5, beyond which all excess capital should be immediately distributed back to the shareholder. However, there is a second zone: Below capital of about 2.3, all capital should also be immediately distributed back to the shareholder, leaving the firm with zero, and therefore, going out of business.

---

26 In nominal terms, this is only a 100 million loss. The assumption here is that if the firm did not lower prices, it would lose business and enter a death spiral; so it is better to fight to retain market share and hope for improved underwriting results to enable it to regain its rating.

The answer to Question 1 is that the firm, currently at $10 billion, is undercapitalized. The optimal level is just more than $12 billion (with risk transfer; closer to $12.5 without) in real terms. Next year, the target would be 4 percent higher in nominal dollars. Capital above this level should be dividended back; but for now, profits should be retained.

FIGURE 2.6.3: OPTIMAL DIVIDENDS

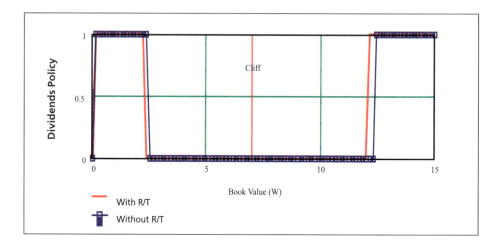

Figure 2.6.4 shows the optimal risk retention strategy. This, too, shows more zones than did previous graphs. For W > 7, the optimal control U behaves analogously to the previous constant-μ example. There is a high-W zone in which risk transfer is not conducted. As W gets lower and approaches the value 7, less of the risk is retained, as before.

New behavior emerges for W < 7. For W between the lower dividend barrier and 7, full risk is again retained. This behavior we may interpret as "hoping for the best" or "betting the farm." In zones where dividending takes place, the value of U is technically undefined.

The answer to Question 2 is that the firm should not transfer risk at this time. If capital goes below $8.8 billion, cessions should start, maxing out at 61 percent (39 percent retained) at the $7 billion cliff. Below the cliff, the mathematically optimal solution is to retain all business and hope for improving fortunes to enable a ratings upgrade. If capital decreases to $2.3 billion, as noted before, the firm should go out of business. [27]

---

[27] Conclusions regarding W below the ratings barrier should not be taken too seriously; there are likely to be other ratings boundaries and effects (e.g., rating agencies care about risk management), and the model does not adequately represent the value of the firm in runoff or as a candidate to be sold. Also, possible recapitalization has been assumed away.

FIGURE 2.6.4: OPTIMAL RISK RETENTION

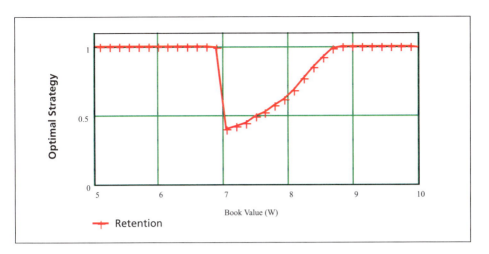

Figure 2.6.5 shows the M-curves. For W > 7, familiar features are seen. The curves rise steeply, then level off to 1-for-1 straight lines above the high dividend barrier of W=12 or 12.5. For W < 7, the value in the "hope for the best" zone curves downward to meet the 1-for-1 value line in the "go out of business" zone.

The answer to Question 3 is that around the current $10 billion in capital, every new dollar in capital increases firm value by about 1.20 (with risk transfer; 1.30 without). For lower levels of capital, the rate of market value change accelerates until it reaches a ratio of over 55:1 at the ratings cliff.

The difference in M-curves is shown in Figure 2.6.6. This answers Question 4: Availability of risk transfer adds $243 million (0.3 percent of firm value or 2.4 percent of capital) to the firm currently, but would be worth as much as $5 billion (6.8 percent, 71.4 percent, respectively) if the firm were at the ratings cliff.

FIGURE 2.6.5: M-CURVES FOR RATINGS DOWNGRADE PROBLEM

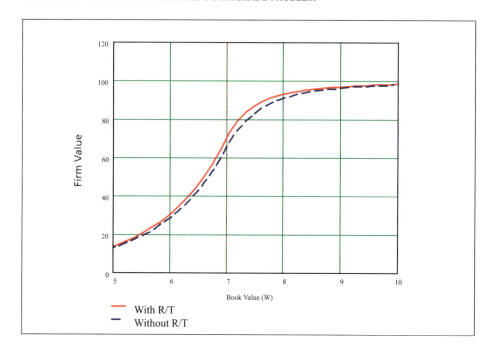

FIGURE 2.6.6: VALUE OF RISK TRANSFER

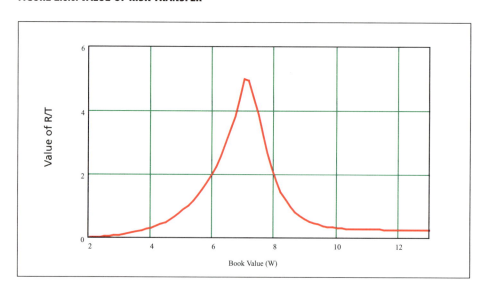

These examples had in common a Brownian motion risk variable X. More realistic modeling of insurance operations, especially where catastrophe insurance is concerned, requires jump diffusions or Lévy processes. These include Brownian motion and compound Poisson processes as special cases. With jumps, the model can represent the effect of excess of loss (XOL) reinsurance. For more about Lévy processes, see Schoutens [67] and Cont and Tankov [19].

Solution Methodology

This section discusses various approaches to solving FLAVORED models. To solve the model analytically, one typically refers to the Hamilton-Jacobi-Bellman (HJB) equation (Yong and Zhou [76], Øksendal and Sulem [59]). As is typical with partial differential equations, the solution method involves careful scrutiny of the boundary behavior of M and optimal U, divining their essential properties, correctly guessing their analytical forms and then teasing out specific values for all the parameters and coefficients.

It is instructive to consider how one might approach the problem via Monte Carlo simulation.

Given particular risk transfer and dividend/capitalization strategies, one may estimate the resulting firm value by simulating sample paths of W, starting with a particular initial W_0. Each sample path would be taken out to its first insolvency or to a length of time sufficiently long so that the discounted perpetuity of profits past that point is negligible in present value. Given enough sample paths, the expected value of the present value of dividends can be estimated by averaging.

Then another strategy would need to be tried, and another, until an apparently optimal strategy is found. Numerous techniques for improving the efficiency of simulation (e.g., importance sampling) and optimization (e.g., parameter search methods operating on a fixed set of sample paths) could be applied. The limitation posed by the fact that the simulations started with only one specific W_0 might be mitigated by taking some early time points, with different W values, as effective starting points, rather than rerunning the entire process for different W_0.

While this approach could work, its principal weakness is the fact that the control strategies being sought are functions and, therefore, require a high dimension to represent numerically. A reasonable number of basis functions (e.g., Tchebychev polynomials) might be considered for a parameterization of the function space, but the success of such an approach would depend on the nature of the (unknown) solutions to the particular model in question.

The proprietary numerical solver used is based on dynamic programming (Bellman [8]). The capabilities of the solver are quite general in that any relationship $\mu(W,u)$ and any conditional distribution of X on W and u, that can be represented in tabular or Algorithmic form, may be used (subject to finiteness restrictions).

By considering the nature of an optimal solution as it relates to the objective function, one is led to a version of the so-called optimality equation, also known as Bellman's equation:

$$M(W_t) = \max_{U}\left\{-(1+\kappa)\cdot dC + dD + e^{-r\,dt}\cdot E[M(W_{t+dt})|W_t]\right\} \quad [2.6.15]$$

This equation must hold if M is the solution to the optimal control problem. Intuitively, it says that the value of the firm at time t is equal to the net of capital to be raised or dividends about to be given back to the shareholder in the next infinitesimal period of time, plus the discounted expected value of the firm at the end of that time, given that optimal control is always exercised. Note the similarity between this equation and the recursive valuation Equation 2.6.7.

Regarding the right-hand side of the equation as an operator on a proposed M, it is evident that the solution for the optimal M is a fixed point of this operator. Relaxation methods can find that fixed point, solving for the optimal controls (U, C, D) and the value (M). See Kushner and Dupuis [46] for details.

The solver was implemented in C++. For the problem above, functions M, U and C were rendered on a 100-element grid, and time was discretized at dt = 0.01. Typical run times were around 10 minutes on a 1GHz Pentium® desktop.

Conclusions

This section first reviewed the history of the "optimal dividends" problem and FLAVORED models introduced by de Finetti and developed by many others working in the fields of actuarial science and stochastic optimization. These models were seen to represent the market value of a firm as the expected value of discounted dividends (which is consistent with Modigliani and Miller), when dividend policy and risk management strategy are optimized to maximize that expectation (which is consistent with violating Modigliani and Miller assumptions). Recent literature explaining the relation to Modigliani and Miller, in particular the role of external capital and bankruptcy cost, was reviewed.

Most of the FLAVORED models appearing in the literature do not include the addition of outside capital; this absence corresponds to prohibitively costly external capital in the Froot model. Versions of the model that do include external capital exhibit economically sensible behavior, and, in the limit where outside capital is frictionless, reproduce the Modigliani and Miller irrelevancy of risk management and dividend policy. We saw how the Froot et al. model of the value of risk management can be reconfigured to represent the market value of a going concern, and how a continuous-time version of that is a FLAVORED model.

The section also presented the FLAVORED model in its general form. While advances continue in the search for analytical solutions to particular versions of this model, it is unlikely that a closed form solution to the generic model will be found. For this reason, numerical solution techniques will be essential for the practitioner. Previously solved FLAVORED models were discussed, and a more realistic (less tractable) version was solved via a numerical dynamic programming solver.

In solving the models, not only were optimal risk management strategies determined, but their effect on market value was calculated as well.

General Modeling Considerations

3.1 Considerations on Implementing Internal Risk Models

By Donald F. Mango, FCAS, MAAA

Introduction
Successfully implementing an internal risk model (IRM; aka DFA model) in an organization requires much more than data collection and model running. There are planning, organizational change, leadership and communication implications that many companies need to factor into their timelines. Most firms underestimate the resource commitment, timelines and organizational impact. To put the magnitude of the impact on the firm in perspective, consider implementing a brand new general ledger or reserve review. Done right, an IRM will be the hub of risk decision making, impacting planning, pricing, reinsurance buying, capacity allocation and rating agency interaction.

This section draws on the experiences (good and bad) of several companies and outlines key decision points to help in planning and implementation. It is meant to highlight the broad spectrum of decision points and, in some instances, make specific recommendations.

Startup: Staffing and Scope
Low-tech organizational details like the ones listed in Figure 3.1.1 are often overlooked in IRM implementation planning. Insufficient clarity in these key areas can lead to organizational friction and avoidable energy loss in debate, rehash, conflict and overlap. It is also critical that scope and purpose be agreed upon by all key stakeholders at the start. An IRM has the potential to appear to be all things to all people. Expectation management is crucial to a successful implementation.

FIGURE 3.1.1: IRM START-UP — STAFFING AND SCOPE

Organization Chart	• Modeling team reporting line
	• Solid line versus dotted line (matrix) reporting
	• Multifunction oversight committee
Functions Represented	• Actuarial (reserving and pricing), finance, planning, underwriting, risk
Resource Commitment	• Mix of skill set – actuarial, underwriting, data management, documentation, communication
	• Full or part time – i.e., in addition to existing duties or full commitment
	• Temporary or permanent – i.e., loan or transfer
Critical Roles and Responsibilities	• Control of input parameters
	• Control of output data
	• Analyses and uses of output – i.e., templates, metrics
Purpose	• Quantify variation around plan, or provide objective view of distribution of results?
Scope	• Prospective underwriting year only, or including reserves, assets or operational risks?
	• Low detail on the whole company or high detail on one pilot segment?

Recommendations

- Reporting relationship – The functional reporting line for the IRM team is less important than having them report to a leader with a reputation for fairness and balance.
- Resource commitment – It is best to think of IRM implementation as the establishment of a new competency, which suggests transfer or outside hire of full-time employees.
- Inputs and outputs – These are controlled in a manner similar to that used with general ledger or reserving systems.
- Initial scope – Prospective underwriting period, variation around plan.

IRM Parameter Development

IRM development efforts (like many large-scale IT initiatives), which are charted in Figure 3.1.2, almost always extend past expected timelines. Variations in data quality, unique characteristics of product lines and differing risk attitudes all mean that many functional areas will want (and need) to be involved in the parameter development process. The more people that need to be involved, the longer the process will take – with the timeline extending more than linearly, unfortunately.

Expert opinion also plays a surprisingly significant role. Many hope that an IRM exercise will be primarily objective and scientific. However, just as in reserving, parameter estimation methods rarely perform so well as to allow seamless implementation of their output without the need for informed judgment. The lower the product data quality or availability, the higher the degree of judgment required.

Correlation assessment is particularly problematic. Not only does it have poor data support and high political sensitivity, it also spans business units. It will have a major impact on the aggregate portfolio risk profile as well as on capital allocation and pricing. Fundamentally, correlations cause risk sharing among business units, which drives home one implication of internal risk modeling: It allows a portfolio-based management approach, which means portfolio effects become part of the decision process.

Validation and testing of an IRM are very difficult, unlike typical large-scale model and system testing. There is usually no "current" IRM for comparison. Rather than detailed validation using control totals, users must review a series of tests involving many complementary decision variables. The goal is to gain comfort by a preponderance of circumstantial evidence of overall model quality and reasonableness.

FIGURE 3.1.2: IRM PARAMETER DEVELOPMENT

Modeling Software	• Capabilities
	• Scalability
	• Learning curve
	• Integration with other systems
	• Output management
Developing Input Parameters	• Process is heavily data driven
	• Requires fair amount of expert opinion
	• Involves many functional areas in the process
	• Requires clear assignment of final ownership
Correlations	• Line of business representatives cannot set cross-line parameters in isolation
	• Corporate-level ownership of these parameters required
Validation and Testing	• No existing IRM with which to compare
	• Multidimensional, multi-metric testing is required
	• Iterative testing with increasing scope and detail

Recommendations

- Modeling software – Be sure to assess how much is pre-built from the many capable model offerings versus user built and make sure that aligns with the capabilities of the IRM team.
- Parameter development – Include product expertise from underwriting, claims, planning and actuarial. Develop a systematic way to capture expert risk opinion.
- Correlation – Have the IRM team recommend correlation assumptions, which are ultimately owned by the CRO/CEO/CUO.
- Validation – Validate and test over an extended period. Align with educational offerings to bring all interested parties to the same basic understanding of probability and statistics.

Implementation

Many companies believe an "internal sell" rollout is best. This approach, illustrated in Figure 3.1.3, relies upon a cascading adoption, convincing key opinion leaders of the value and validity, who then become advocates convincing others. This approach sounds like the most inclusive and respectful to all the experts in the organization. However, in today's hectic corporate environment, the scarcest (hence most valuable) commodity is *priority*. With many competing initiatives, managers must choose which get priority and effort now and which must wait. In the internal sell model, priority setting is distributed to all key opinion leaders. Effective veto or stall power is also distributed: Any opinion leader, through overt or covert action, can slow the adoption process. The net result of these two effects is inefficiency in rollout.

Firms want to keep the opinion leaders engaged, while not allowing deliberate or inadvertent priority decisions to derail the implementation. One solution is to have senior management set the priority for IRM analysis and signoff. This way, opinion leaders are given reasonable timeframes within which to have their concerns voiced and addressed. However, the firm benefits from closely sticking to a pre-agreed implementation schedule. This discipline helps immensely with integration of an IRM into critical corporate calendar items like planning.

An IRM will attract interested (and impacted) parties from all parts of the organization. It is imperative that the IRM implementation team be prepared to communicate across the entire organization in a predictable, consistent manner. Don't underestimate the appetite for information.

The impact of an IRM on an organization can be profound. One good way to ease the transition is by pilot testing. Assign a multidisciplinary team to use real data – either a high-level representation of the whole firm or detailed representation of one segment – and produce additional decision support material in parallel to the existing company processes. Simultaneously, offer educational opportunities to the leadership to ensure consistent understanding of key concepts in probability, statistics and risk model evaluation and usage.

FIGURE 3.1.3: IRM ROLLOUT

Priority Setting	• Importance of priority – company may not spontaneously make the necessary investments to support implementation • Approach and style: Ask (sell) versus tell (mandate) • Priority and timeline must be driven from the top
Interest and Impact	• Visibility and interest • Communication plans • Education plans
Pilot Test	• Simultaneous release of decision support material • Real data, real analysis, real business units • Multidisciplinary team: Actuarial, Underwriting, Finance, Planning, Risk • Piloting means model indications initially receive no weight – a learning and familiarization exercise • Subsequent rounds give increasing importance in decision process
Education Process	• In parallel with pilot test • Bring leadership to same point of understanding

Recommendations

- Priority setting – Have top management set the priority for implementation.
- Communications – Plan for regular communication to broad audiences.
- Pilot testing – Allows effective preparation of the company for the magnitude of change.
- Education – Target training to bring leadership to similar base level of understanding.

Integration and Maintenance

The best way to integrate the IRM into the organization is by aligning its input and output stages with key points on the corporate calendar. In keeping with the analogy to the reserve review, it is preferable not to do major updates more than twice a year. Minor changes can be handled by modifying the scale of impacted segments.

Centralized control and storage of input and output sets (similar to reserving data) is also important. Taking it a step further, consider controlling the analytical templates used to manipulate the IRM outputs for various application purposes. Misuse and abuse of the outputs can undermine the credibility of the IRM.

The IRM integration and maintenance process is illustrated in Figure 3.1.4.

FIGURE 3.1.4: INTEGRATION AND MAINTENANCE

Cycle	• Integrate into major corporate calendar: planning, reinsurance purchasing, portfolio reviews or capacity allocation • Mandatory inclusion of IRM output as part of decision support
Updating	• Frequency and magnitude of updates • Simple scale adjustments for minor changes
Controls	• Centralized storage and control of input sets and output sets (date stamped) • Endorsed set of analytical templates – avoids misuse and abuse of information

Recommendations

- Cycle – Integrate into planning calendar at a minimum.
- Updating – Perform a major input review no more frequently than semi-annually. Minor updates can be handled by modifying the scale of the impacted portfolio segments.
- Controls – Maintain centralized control of inputs, outputs and possibly even application templates.

3.2 Modeling Parameter Uncertainty

By Gary G. Venter, FCAS, MAAA, and Spencer M. Gluck, FCAS, MAAA

Introduction

Modeling insurance losses typically involves postulating frequency and severity distributions for each line of business. But the uncertainty about which distributions actually apply turns out to be a significant risk for insurance companies. In fact, for the larger companies, which achieve stability through spread of business, the risk of assuming the wrong distributions or the wrong parameters for the right distributions often overshadows the other risk issues.

Some aspects of this risk are estimation risk, projection risk and model risk. Estimation risk arises from having only a sample of the universe of possible claims to use for estimating the parameters of distributions. Projection risk is the possible error in projecting past trends into the future. Model risk is the uncertainty that arises from having the wrong models to start with.

Impact of Parameter Risk

To illustrate the impact, an example of projection risk will be used. If the frequency and severity distributions are known, there is a standard formula for the CV (or coefficient of variation – the ratio of standard deviation to mean) of total losses. It is the frequency variance-to-mean ratio plus the square of the severity CV, all divided by the frequency mean. This ends up showing a lot of risk for small insurance companies, but increasing stability for larger companies.

To model projection risk, consider the losses as the sum of the individual claims times a random factor for future cost levels. Whatever variance that factor has does not decrease with increased business; the same factor applies to all the claims. It is similar to pricing risk – if the prices are too low, you cannot make up for that with volume.

As an example, consider a Poisson frequency distribution and a severity distribution with CV = 7, which is fairly high. Thus, a small company will be fairly volatile with these parameters, while a large company will be stable. Then multiply losses by a random factor 1+J, which is constant for all claims for a year, and has mean 1. As the CV of 1+J increases, so does the risk for the large company.[28] However, the effect on the smaller company is less dramatic, as it is already volatile.

Figure 3.2.1 illustrates the impact of the CV of J on the CV of aggregate losses for small, medium and large companies, as measured by expected number of claims N.

---

28   CV^2 increases by a factor of $1+CV_J^2$ plus an additional CV_J^2.

FIGURE 3.2.1: CV OF TOTAL LOSS

CV(J) E(N)	2,000	20,000	200,000
0.05	16.6%	7.1%	5.2%
0.03	16.1%	5.8%	3.4%
0.01	15.8%	5.1%	1.9%
0.00	15.8%	5.0%	1.6%

This result is translated into its impact on loss ratio distributions in Figure 3.2.2. Here the expected loss ratio is 65 percent. With just frequency and severity risk, the 99th percentile loss ratio for the large company is 67.4 percent, which is unrealistically stable. Giving J a CV of 5 percent increases this to 73.3 percent, which is more realistic, but perhaps still more stable than usually seen.

FIGURE 3.2.2: LOSS RATIO RISK

CV(J)=0.05	E(N)=2,000	20,000	200,000
90th	79.2	71.0	69.4
95th	84.1	72.8	70.8
99th	94.1	76.4	73.3
CV(J)=0			
90th	78.5	69.2	66.3
95th	83.1	70.5	66.7
99th	92.5	72.9	67.4

For the large company, projection risk has materially increased overall uncertainty, but this is less true for the smaller companies.

Projection Risk
A Simple Trend Model
A trend line fit to the loss cost history can project future loss levels, and there is a standard statistical procedure for putting prediction intervals around the projection. This provides quantification of the projection risk. It is based in part on how well the trend line fits the historical pattern.

A problem with this approach, however, is that often the history is itself based on estimates of past claims which have not yet settled. This increases the projection uncertainty beyond that quantified by traditional methods. This problem can arise with projections of average claim cost, because of open claim estimates, and claim frequency rates, due to incurred but not reported claims and losses (IBNR).

FIGURE 3.2.3: RISK IN TREND

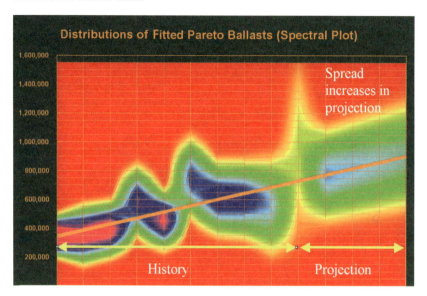

Figure 3.2.3 illustrates this issue with a trend of the mean of Pareto distributions fit to claim sizes in each historical period. The fitting procedure has its own associated uncertainty, which is represented by the concentration plotted around each historical point. The projection uncertainty shown results from the combination of the uncertainty in each historical point and the uncertainty in the fitted trend line.

More advanced regression procedures correct the prediction intervals for the effect of uncertainty in the historical points.

Severity Trend and Inflation

Claim severity trend observed in insurance data often differs from measurements of general inflation, or even more specifically targeted inflation indices. Severity trend has often been greater, with the excess over inflation sometimes described as social inflation or superimposed inflation (we will continue with the latter terminology). In U.S. practice, claim severity trend is most often modeled directly from insurance data, with no specific reflection of general inflation, and superimposed inflation is observed rather than modeled directly. For some lines of business (typically property and auto collision), specific inflation indices may be used in preference to trends from insurance data.

Another approach is to correct the payment data using general inflation indices, and to then model the residual superimposed inflation. The subsequent projection then requires a projection of general inflation. This approach has the advantage of reflecting a dependency between claim severity trend and general inflation. Conceivably, other functional forms relating claim severity trend to general inflation could be explored.

An enterprise risk model will necessarily include a macroeconomic model, including future inflation rates. Unless the modeler believes that claim severity trend is completely independent of general inflation (an unlikely proposition), it will be essential that the claim severity trend model reflect appropriate dependency between trend and inflation, thereby incorporating inflation uncertainty as an element of projection risk, and creating appropriate dependencies with other elements of the enterprise risk model.

Trend As a Time Series
The previous simple trend model also represents the most common approach to trend. As in all models, the model structure contains implicit assumptions. In the case of the simple trend model, the implicit assumption is that there is a single underlying trend rate that has been constant throughout the period of the historical data and will remain constant in the future, throughout the projection period. The only potential error is misestimation of the rate.

Whether the trend model is of all trend or superimposed inflation, history rarely bears out this simplifying assumption, except over limited time periods. It is unlikely that any useful macroeconomic model would model future inflation in this manner.

As an alternative, consider a model of the future trend rate as a first order autocorrelated time series, or AR-1. This is the simplest form of a mean-reverting time series.[29] The true underlying mean is unknown; it is estimated from the data, analogous to the single trend rate in the simple trend example. The additional assumptions for the AR-1 model are the autocorrelation coefficient and the annual disturbance distribution, which are postulated to be 80 percent and Normal (mean zero, standard deviation 2.5 percent), respectively.[30]

Figure 3.2.4 displays an example of projection risk under the constant trend model. The trend is fitted to 10 historical parameter values, each of which is itself subject to estimation error with 10 percent CV.

---

29 Inflation and interest rates, for example, are most commonly modeled as mean-reverting.
30 A fit of the AR-1 model to annual U.S. Consumer Price Index inflation from 1968 through 2005 yields autocorrelation of 80 percent and annual volatility of 1.6 percent. The volatility was judgmentally rounded up to reflect the greater volatility of insurance trends.

FIGURE 3.2.4: PROJECTION INTERVALS WITH FIXED TREND RATE MODEL

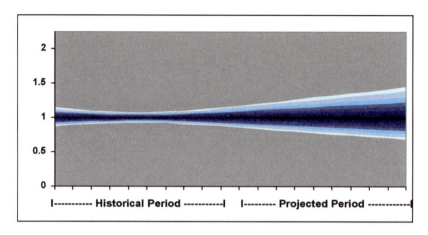

The projection intervals widen with time due to the uncertainty in the estimated (fixed) trend rate. With a 10-year-forward projection period, the 1-in-100 result is a +45 percent error.

In Figure 3.2.5 below, the additional uncertainty of the AR-1 process is added to the model.

FIGURE 3.2.5: PROJECTION INTERVALS WITH AR-1 TREND MODEL

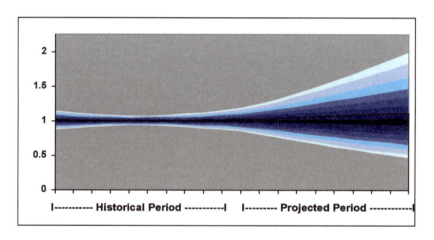

Under this model, the relationship of projection risk and time is substantially more pronounced. The effect is modest for near-term projections and significant for long-term projections. The 10-year-forward projection now has a 1-in-100 error of +100 percent. The choice of model form is particularly important for long tail lines of business, where the standard simple trend model will likely understate the projection risk.

Parameterizing time series models has its own pitfalls. A substantial number of data points is advisable. If the time period of the data is too limited to exhibit a range of behaviors, the resulting model will be similarly limited and will understate risk potential. For these reasons, it may be advisable to focus on large data sets and long time periods, with less emphasis on more limited insurer-specific data.

Estimation Risk

The preferred method for estimating parameters of frequency and severity distributions from historical data is maximum likelihood estimation (MLE). Its appeal is based on the fact that, for large samples, MLE has the smallest estimation error among unbiased estimators. For small samples, this may not hold, but better alternatives, if any, are not widely known.

The likelihood of a distribution for a set of data is essentially the probability of observing that data from a sample of that size from the distribution. MLE tries to find the parameters that maximize the likelihood for each distribution. These can be compared across distributions, with a penalty for distributions with more parameters.

For any particular distribution, the uncertainty about the best-fitting parameters depends on the shape of the likelihood surface. If this is very flat near the maximum, then a wide variety of parameter sets have almost the same likelihood. This increases the uncertainty about the parameters. But if the surface is very sharply peaked at the maximum, that maximum value has much less uncertainty about it.

This notion is formalized by the 2nd derivatives of the likelihood with respect to the parameters. These basically measure steepness of the decline in likelihood as the parameters deviate from the maximum. It is actually the matrix of all 2nd partial derivatives of the negative of the log of the likelihood (called the information matrix) that is used for this. The inverse of that matrix is the covariance matrix for the parameters of the distribution. Details can be found in the *Loss Models* [1] textbook read by actuarial students.

Figure 3.2.6 illustrates this as a bivariate normal distribution for the parameters of a ballasted Pareto. The diagonal ridge in the surface indicates some ambiguity between high-mean light-tail and low-mean heavy-tail distributions as explanations for the data at hand. Thus, there is correlation between the parameters. This shows up as a distribution that is not completely symmetric. The probabilities of parameter sets near the MLE estimator are all fairly high, but this falls off when moving further away from the estimated parameters.

FIGURE 3.2.6: JOINT NORMAL DISTRIBUTION

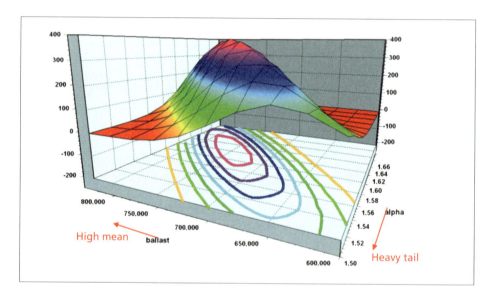

For large data sets, the parameters are close to being multivariate normal distributed with the covariance matrix from the information matrix. But for smaller data sets, there are problems with the normal assumption. First, the standard deviations of the parameters can be high enough to give significant probability to negative values of the parameters, which is not always meaningful. Second, for heavy-tailed distributions like the Pareto, the distribution of the parameters can itself be heavy-tailed.

This is known exactly in the case of the simple Pareto distribution $S(x) = (\theta/x)^\alpha$ for $x > \theta$. If θ is given, the MLE for α is the reciprocal of the average of the log of the observations. The log of a simple Pareto variate is exponentially distributed, and the sum of exponentials is gamma distributed, so the estimated α is inverse gamma distributed. This is a distribution shaped something like the lognormal, but more heavy-tailed.

Simulation tests of fits of other distributions to small samples have found lognormal distributions to provide a reasonably good fit to the parameter distributions. Thus, a pragmatic approach to quantification of estimation uncertainty is to use the standard covariance matrix from MLE, but assume the parameters follow a joint lognormal distribution with that covariance matrix.

FIGURE 3.2.7: CONTOURS

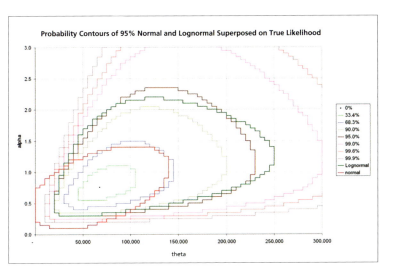

An example of this is illustrated in Figure 3.2.7, which shows the true probability contours for a fitting exercise and the 95th percentile contours for the normal (red) and lognormal (green) approximations. The true 95th percentile contour is the brown one that is very close to the lognormal green one. The normal distribution contour is pretty far away by comparison.

Model Risk
Fitted Distributions
There are some rules for selection of the best distribution for a data set that use the likelihood function and penalties for number of parameters. Instrat® tends to favor the Hannan-Quinn Information Criterion, or HQIC, which adds a per parameter penalty to the negative of the loglikelihood set to the log of the log of the number of observations in the data set. This is a compromise between other information criteria which add larger or smaller penalties.

But the selected distribution might not be the right one. A possible response is to assign probabilities of being right to all the better-fitting distributions. This could be based on the exponentiation of the HQ metric, for instance, or a Bayesian posterior distribution. Then a simulation model could first select a distribution from those distributions, which would be used throughout a single scenario, then select the parameters from the joint lognormal distribution of parameters for that particular distribution. The resulting distribution would be fixed for all losses in that scenario. The next scenario simulated would start this over with another selection of the distribution to use.

Projection Models

The prior discussion demonstrated the sensitivity of results to the form of the projection models. Alternative models should be tested for validity against available data, but it is also likely that these tests will be less than conclusive in indicating a preferred model form. Common sense judgment is essential to ensure that the model is structurally consistent with the underlying process that it represents. Reference to other databases is advised.

The goal of many modeling exercises is a best projection, and parsimony improves the stability of that projection. The goal of a risk modeling exercise is a realistic spread of potential outcomes; parsimony remains a virtue, but excessive emphasis on parsimony can lead to unrealistically stable projections. A parsimonious model has imbedded assumptions, and the potential inaccuracy of those assumptions is not, in general, reflected. Adding flexibility (i.e., complexity, additional parameters) transfers assumptions from the structure to the parameters, thus allowing the risk model to reflect the uncertainty in the assumptions.

Conclusion

Parameter risk is a key source of variability, especially for larger companies. Its components – projection risk, estimation risk and model risk – can all be quantified and applied in a simulation model.

3.3 Modeling Dependency: Correlations and Copulas

By Gary G. Venter, FCAS, MAAA

Introduction

Each line of insurance is typically modeled with its own parameters; but in the end, the distribution of the sum of the lines is needed. To get the distribution of the sum, the dependencies among the lines must be taken into account. If there are catastrophe events, for example, all of the property damage lines could be hit at the same time. Other changes could hit all of the liability lines. Sometimes, liability is hit in a major catastrophe as well. When there is the possibility of correlated large losses across lines, the distribution of the sum of the lines gets more probability in the right tail.

Unfortunately, even though the univariate distribution of the sum is the core requirement, with dependent losses, the multivariate distribution of the individual lines is necessary to get the distribution of the sum. That quickly leads to the realm of copulas, which provide a convenient way to combine individual distributions into a single multivariate distribution.

Modeling Dependent Losses

Instrat® has done a fair amount of research in approaches for quantifying not only the overall correlation but also where in the distribution the correlation takes place. Rodney Kreps [2] has pioneered a methodology to combine independent and perfectly correlated scenarios to model how much of the correlation occurs in the right tail. Essentially, he uses different functions on the unit interval to control how much weight goes to the independent versus the perfectly correlated cases, with more weight going to correlated cases the closer it gets to 1.

Figure 3.3.1 shows a sample generated from one of the joint distributions based on this methodology. Here, the correlated and independent pieces clearly stand out (line versus scatter), with less independence with larger losses (fewer scattered points in upper right).

FIGURE 3.3.1: PARTIAL PERFECT CORRELATION

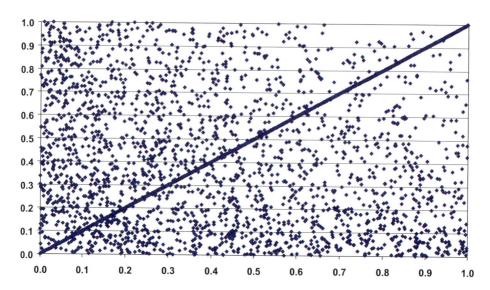

Copulas

As mentioned above, copulas provide a convenient mechanism to combine individual distributions into a multivariate distribution. A copula $C(u,v)$ is a function that expresses a joint distribution function $F(x,y)$ in terms of $F_X(x)$ and $F_Y(y)$, the individual (so-called marginal) distribution functions for X and Y. The combination is $F(x,y) = C(F_X(x), F_Y(y))$. It is clear from this expression that C is a distribution function on the unit square. Actually, C is a joint distribution of uniform distributions on [0,1]. Expressing distributions this way can be generalized to combining many distributions, not just two. It turns out that any multivariate distribution is a copula applied to the individual marginal distributions.

By selecting among the many available copulas, a good deal of control can be exercised over where the correlation takes place. Several bivariate copulas are discussed below. For instance, a copula with a great deal of concentration in the right tail is the heavy right tail (HRT) copula, whose density function on the unit square is graphed in Figure 3.3.2. The strong weight in the joint right tail is indicated by the higher probability there.

FIGURE 3.3.2: HRT COPULA DENSITY

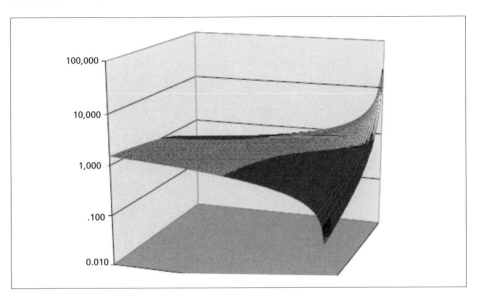

Some Particular Copulas

Some well-known copulas and a few designed particularly for loss severity distributions are reviewed here. The density and copula functions and Kendall's τ correlation coefficient are given, as well as simulation procedures.

The Frank Copula

Define $g_z = e^{-az} - 1$, then the Frank copula with parameter $a \neq 0$ can be expressed as:

$$C(u,v) = -a^{-1}\ln[1 + g_u g_v/g_1], \text{ with conditional distribution}$$
$$C_1(u,v) = [g_u g_v + g_v]/[g_u g_v + g_1],$$
$$c(u,v) = -a g_1(1+g_{u+v})/(g_u g_v + g_1)^2, \text{ and Kendall's } \tau \text{ of} \quad [3.3.1]$$
$$\tau(a) = 1 - 4/a + 4/a^2 \int_0^a t/(e^t-1)\, dt.$$

For $a \neq 0$, this will give negative values of τ.

C_1 can be inverted, so correlated pairs u,v can be simulated using the conditional distribution. First, simulate u and p by random draws on [0,1]. Here, p is considered a draw from the conditional distribution of $V|u$. Since this has distribution function C_1, v can then be found as $v = C_1^{-1}(p|u)$. The formula for this, which can be found from the formula for C_1, is $v = -a^{-1}\ln\{1+pg_1/[1+g_u(1-p)]\}$.

Once u and v have been simulated, the variables of interest X and Y can be simulated by inverting the marginal distributions, i.e., $x = F_X^{-1}(u)$ and $y = F_Y^{-1}(v)$.

Gumbel Copula
This copula has more probability concentrated in the tails than does the Frank copula. It is also asymmetric, with more weight in the right tail. It is expressed as:

$$C(u,v) = \exp\{-[(-\ln u)^a + (-\ln v)^a]^{1/a}\}, \ a \geq 1.$$
$$C_1(u,v) = C(u,v)[(-\ln u)^a + (-\ln v)^a]^{-1+1/a}(-\ln u)^{a-1}/u.$$
$$c(u,v) = C(u,v)u^{-1}v^{-1}[(-\ln u)^a + (-\ln v)^a]^{-2+2/a}[(\ln u)(\ln v)]^{a-1}\{1+(a-1)[(-\ln u)^a+(-\ln v)^a]^{-1/a}\}.$$
$$\tau(a) = 1 - 1/a.$$

[3.3.2]

Unfortunately, C_1 is not invertible, so another method is needed to simulate variates. This procedure starts by simulating two independent uniform deviates, u and v, and then solving numerically for $1 > s > 0$ with $\ln(s)s = a(s-u)$. Then, the pair $[\exp(\ln(s)v^{1/a}), \exp(\ln(s)(1-v)^{1/a})]$ will have the Gumbel copula distribution.

Heavy Right Tail (HRT) Copula and Joint Burr
For some applications, actuaries need a copula with less correlation in the left tail but high correlation in the right tail (i.e., for the large losses). An example follows:

$$C(u,v) = u + v - 1 + [(1-u)^{-1/a} + (1-v)^{-1/a} - 1]^{-a}, \ a > 0.$$
$$C_1(u,v) = 1 - [(1-u)^{-1/a} + (1-v)^{-1/a} - 1]^{-a-1}(1-u)^{-1-1/a}.$$
$$c(u,v) = (1+1/a)[(1-u)^{-1/a} + (1-v)^{-1/a} - 1]^{-a-2}[(1-u)(1-v)]^{-1-1/a}$$
$$\tau(a) = 1/(2a + 1).$$

[3.3.3]

The conditional distribution given by the derivative $C_1(u,v)$ can be solved in closed form for v, so simulation can be done by conditional distributions as in the Frank copula.

A joint Burr distribution is produced when the a parameter of both Burrs is the same as that of the HRT.

Given two Burr distributions, $F(x) = 1 - (1 + (x/b)^p)^{-a}$ and $G(y) = 1 - (1 + (y/d)^q)^{-a}$, the joint Burr distribution from the HRT is:

$$F(x,y) = 1 - (1 + (x/b)^p)^{-a} - (1 + (y/d)^q)^{-a} + [1 + (x/b)^p + (y/d)^q]^{-a}. \quad [3.3.4]$$

The conditional distribution of $y|X=x$ is also Burr:

$$F_{Y|X}(y|x) = 1 - [1 + (y/d_x)^q]^{-(a+1)}, \text{ where } d_x = d[1 + (x/b)^{p/q}]. \quad [3.3.5]$$

By analogy to the joint normal, this can be called the joint Burr — the marginal and conditional distributions are all Burr. In practice, the overall correlation can be set with the a parameter, leaving the p and q parameters to fit the tails and b and d to set the scales of the two distributions.

The Normal Copula

Useful for its easy simulation method and generalized to multidimensions, the normal copula is lighter in the right tail than is the Gumbel or HRT, but heavier than the Frank copula. The left tail is similar to the Gumbel.

To define the copula functions, let $N(x;m,v)$ denote the normal distribution function with mean m and variance v, $N(x)$ abbreviate $N(x;0,1)$ and $B(x,y;a)$ denote the bivariate standard normal distribution function with correlation = a. Also let $p(u)$ be the percentile function for the standard normal, so $N(p(u)) = u$. Then with parameter a, which is the normal correlation coefficient:

$$C(u,v) = B(p(u),p(v);a).$$
$$C_1(u,v) = N(p(v);ap(u),1-a^2).$$
$$c(u,v) = 1/\{(1-a^2)^{0.5} \exp([a^2 p(u)^2 - 2ap(u)p(v) + a^2 p(v)^2]/[2(1-a^2)])\}.$$
$$\tau(a) = 2\arcsin(a)/\pi. \qquad [3.3.6]$$

The Kendall τ is somewhat less than a. Figure 3.3.3 illustrates a few of the values.

FIGURE 3.3.3: VALUES OF τ AND α

α	0.15643	0.38268	0.70711	0.92388	0.98769
τ	0.10000	0.25000	0.50000	0.75000	0.90000

Simulation uses the conditional distribution C_1. Simulate $p(u)$ from a standard normal and then $p(v)$ from the conditional normal C_1. The standard normal distribution function can then be applied to these percentiles to get u and v.

Describing Copulas

Venter [3] describes methods for identifying characteristics of copulas by calculating functions of the copula. Looking at these functions for the data and comparing them to those for several copulas, the copula that is most applicable to the data can be determined.

The upper and lower tail dependence coefficients of a copula provide quantification of tail strength. These can be defined using the right and left tail concentration functions R and L on (0,1):

$$R(z) = Pr(U>z|V>z)$$
$$L(z) = Pr(U<z|V<z)$$
[3.3.7]

The upper tail dependence coefficient is the limit of R as $z \to 1$, and the lower tail dependence coefficient is the limit of L as $z \to 0$. For many copulas, these coefficients are zero. This means that for extreme values, the distributions are uncorrelated, so the large-large or small-small combinations are not likely. However, this is somewhat misleading, as the slopes of the R and L functions for some copulas can be very steep near the limits. Thus, there can be a significant degree of dependence near the limits, even when it is zero in the limit. Thus, R(z) for z a bit less than 1 may best show large loss relationships.

The left tail function approaches unity for z near 1, so does not distinguish much between copulas there, and similarly for the R function near 0. Thus, they can be combined into an *LR* function, which is L below 1/2 and R above 1/2. This LR function is graphed in Figure 3.3.4 for the copulas discussed above and for the Clayton copula, a heavy left tailed copula.

FIGURE 3.3.4: LR FUNCTIONS

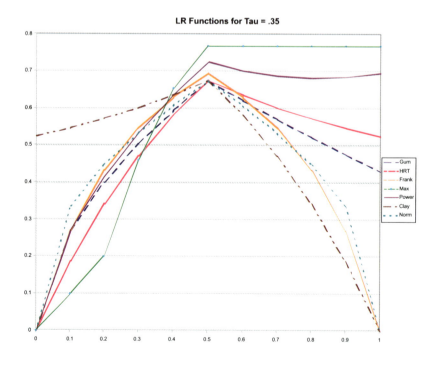

Another way to compare the tail behavior of copulas is to look at the resulting joint distributions for a pair of variates with that copula. Figures 3.3.5 and 3.3.6 are contour plots of the joint density functions of a pair of lognormal (0,1) distributions for the Frank and Gumbel copulas. The greatest concentration of probability is near the modes, which are close to the means at <1,1>. The graphs go out in the tail to values of 10 times the mean. For the Gumbel copula, the joint distribution has higher probability of both variates being large, even though the overall correlation (rank and τ) is the same as for the Frank copula.

FIGURE 3.3.5: FRANK LOGNORMAL PAIRS

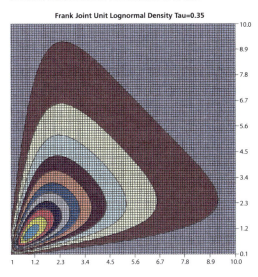

FIGURE 3.3.6: GUMBEL LOGNORMAL PAIRS

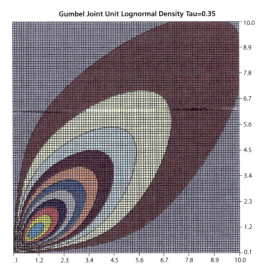

Illustration of Catastrophe Loss by Line

As an application of copula theory, several copulas were fit to the bivariate distribution of auto and property claims in French windstorms by Belguise and Levi [1]. The log of auto and property losses for each event is shown in Figure 3.3.7.

FIGURE 3.3.7: AUTO VS. PROPERTY LOSSES

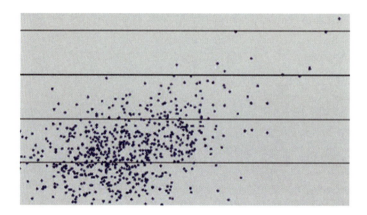

There is a somewhat amorphous blob of data for small events, but the largest events were large in both lines. Thus, we have an example of correlation being mainly in the tail. The L and R functions for the data and a few distributions are shown in Figure 3.3.8. It is clear that the HRT copula provides the best fit.

FIGURE 3.3.8: AUTO VS. PROPERTY L&R FUNCTIONS

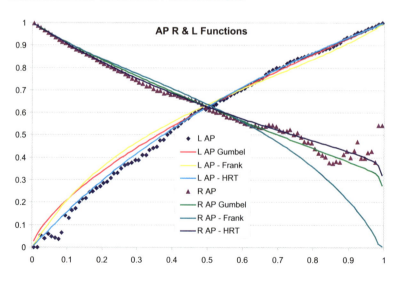

Multivariate Copulas

While there are quite a few copulas available for bivariate distributions, only the t-copula and the normal copula are commonly known for more variables. Both of them take a correlation matrix as input, so they have complete flexibility about the possible correlation structure.

The t-copula has an additional parameter n for heaviness of tail. The normal copula is uncorrelated for very large and for very small losses, while the t can be very strongly correlated in the tails, if desired. The t also has a bit more possibility of inversely related observations. The density of the bivariate t with n=5 is shown in Figure 3.3.9.

FIGURE 3.3.9: T-COPULA

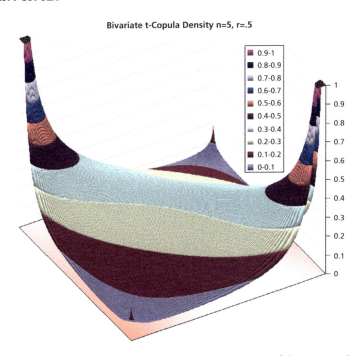

With only one parameter to control tail strength, the more highly correlated pairs tend to have more tail correlation as well. Some other multivariate copulas have more parameters, so they can be more flexible here, but they do not necessarily allow as wide a variety of correlation matrices to begin with.

The tail correlation increases as n decreases. For large n, the t-copula approaches the normal copula. Figure 3.3.10 shows the ratio of the density of the t-copula above with n=5 to that with n=50.

FIGURE 3.3.10: T-COPULA DENSITY RATIO

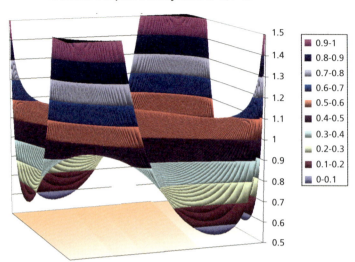

Bivariate t-Copula Density Ratio n=5, r=.5

While the higher ratios at the left and right (which are at the points <0,0> and <1,1>) are to be expected from the higher tail correlation, the even higher ratios near the off-diagonal corners are a bit surprising. To maintain the overall correlation as the normal copula, the t has more probability in all four corners. Since the normal copula goes to zero in the off-diagonal corners, the ratios get very high there.

Fitting Copula to Data

As in the two-line catastrophe loss example, copulas are generally fit by maximum likelihood; but in complicated cases, the sum of squared errors (SSE) between empirical and fitted copulas might be useful. Also, the product of bivariate likelihood functions can be maximized, if this is easier. In judging goodness of fit, more descriptive functions are available as well. Figure 3.3.11 shows a fit of three trivariate copulas to changes in currency exchange rates for three currencies against the U.S. dollar. One is the t-copula. The other two, called MM1 and MM2, are not described here, as the point is about methodology.

The product of the bivariate MLE estimates for MM1 was quite close to the full trivariate MLE. It should be noted, however, that there are many local maxima for both likelihood functions; so we cannot be absolutely sure that these are the global maxima. Only the bivariate estimates were done for MM2. The SSE parameters, which are shown in Figure 3.3.11, were quite a bit different from the MLE's.

FIGURE 3.3.11: PARAMETER ESTIMATES FOR THREE COPULAS

	MM2		MM1			t	
	SSE	MLE bi	SSE	MLE bi	MLE tri	MLE bi	MLE tri
δ12	2.62588	1.50608	3.69513	2.14275	2.1094	0.491	0.490
δ13	0.80055	0.43963	1.52005	1.19832	1.1152	0.262	0.266
δ23	3.2E-07	0.0103	1	1	1	0.097	0.097
p1	0.49881	0.37649	0.49963	0.40533	0.37175		
p2	0.5	0.5	0.5	0.5	0.5		
p3	0.26236	0.49625	0.29097	0.5	0.5		
θ	0.19599	0.2209	1.08308	1.0939	1.1234	20.53	20.95

The t parameters were done trivariate and product of bivariates for comparison. We use a beta distribution version of the t that allows fractional degrees of freedom. Comparisons of fits were performed using graphs of the empirical and fitted J and χ functions in Figures 3.3.12 through 3.3.17. These functions are defined as:

$$J(z) = -z^2 + 4\int_0^z \int_0^z C(u,v)c(u,v)dvdu/C(z,z) \text{ and } \chi(z) = 2 - \ln[C(z,z)]/\ln z.$$

[3.3.8]

As z→1, these approach Kendall's τ and the upper tail dependence R, respectively.

In two of the three J graphs, the t-copula is clearly the best fit; but MM2 is close for Sweden-Canada. In the third J graph, MM2 is the best. MM1 is always worse for this data. The t is also best in two of the three χ graphs, but not much better than MM2 for Sweden-Canada. In the third graph, each of the three is best in some range; but MM1 is probably the best choice. Overall, MM2 seems to provide almost as good a fit as t, but not quite.

FIGURE 3.3.12: SWEDEN – JAPAN J FUNCTION

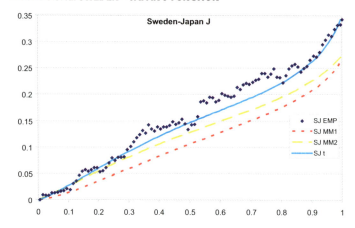

FIGURE 3.3.13: SWEDEN – CANADA J FUNCTION

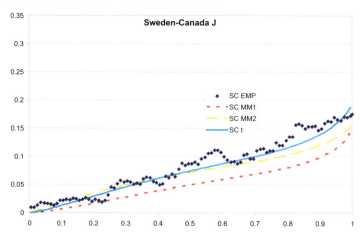

FIGURE 3.3.14: JAPAN – CANADA J FUNCTION

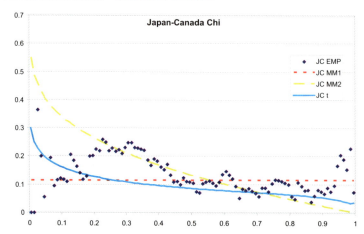

FIGURE 3.3.15: SWEDEN – JAPAN χ FUNCTION

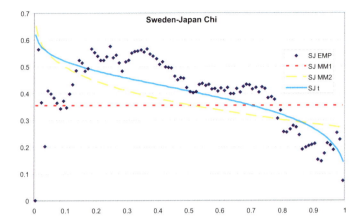

FIGURE 3.3.16: SWEDEN – CANADA χ FUNCTION

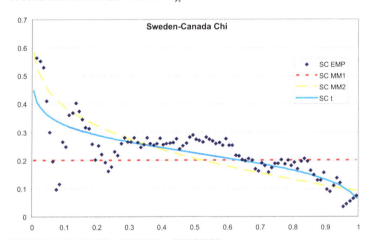

FIGURE 3.3.17: JAPAN – CANADA χ FUNCTION

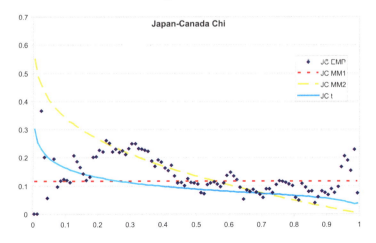

3.4 Timeline Simulation

By Rodney E. Kreps, FCAS

The Essence

In the usual collective risk model, actuaries ask the question: "How many events are there in a time period?" This question is followed by: "How big is each event?" In a timeline formulation, we ask: "How long is it to the next event?" followed by "How big is this event?" This change of focus is the subject of this chapter.

With a timeline formulation, the emphasis is on the instantaneous frequency – the propensity to generate a claim of some type at any point in time. The number in a time period emerges as a counting exercise. This point of view is a mathematically equivalent formulation for all of the commonly used distributions. Furthermore, the notion of frequency, rather than count, is what claims people and actuaries are really thinking about. A statement like "the frequency of fender-benders goes up in the winter" is intuitively clear and goes to the heart of the matter; whereas, "the number of fender-benders over a specified time period smaller than a season goes up in the winter" just sounds awkward.

Why have actuaries used collective risk models? Some contributing factors have been: because the data we see is arranged by period, such as accident year or quarter; because we can calculate interesting properties, such as the moments of the aggregate distribution; because the implicit assumption of the independence of frequency and severity is empirically often good; and because the available computing power limited the calculation.

Properties of a Timeline Formulation

Timeline simulation is obviously more realistic than collective risk modeling because events in the real world do occur on a timeline. Further, since events can be and often are influenced by prior events, causal relationships can and should be modeled explicitly. Since we are working one claim at a time, we can ask at any point for all of the influences on the claim's instantaneous frequency and severity. The whole history is available, although there might be some interesting modeling around questions of incomplete information. Exposure, itself a random variable, can simultaneously drive the frequency of large losses in a line, the aggregate distribution of bulk[31] losses and the written premium. A change in inflation will affect auto parts prices; a change in the unemployment rate will affect workers compensation claims, and so on. The benefit of a timeline formulation is that the interpretation becomes intuitive. The challenge becomes how to actually model the effects.

---

[31] In principle, we could individually simulate all losses. In practice, losses are divided up into small losses, large losses and catastrophe losses. The latter two are individually simulated, and the aggregate amount of the former is modeled. The losses calculated in bulk are sometimes known as "attritional" losses. The collective risk model (supplemented by considerable parameter risk to match real data) allows us to parameterize the aggregate distribution.

We do not need to assume that frequency and severity are independent, provided we have some sensible model that connects them, such as a quantification of "successful large claims engender more of the same." The success of a new theory of liability (think toxic mold) spawns many more suits.

Seasonality, trend and calendar-year influences have a natural implementation. The generation of events is separated from the reporting on events. Going from annual to quarterly reporting enables the same events to be viewed on a time-line, with just the relevant time intervals changed. Discounting, even with multiple discount rates, can be done on an individual payment basis. Accident-year, report-year, policy-year and calendar-year reports are just summaries of different subsets on the same events on a timeline, so consistency is automatic. Management decision rules based on periodic or even instantaneous reports can be implemented.

Whereas a timeline formulation allows any collective risk model to be implemented, it also allows many kinds of calculations to be performed exactly rather than by hopeful approximation. One example is the European index clause in its various forms, which requires indexation by a possibly random index at the times of occurrence and payment(s). In a collective risk model, the times are forced to be at the middle or end of intervals. In a timeline formulation, they can be at arbitrary times. Another example is in the area of multiple payments. Currently, these can be difficult to work with if there is a variable number of them, or where their number or amount is not determined at the time of occurrence, or where there is an exotic pattern, such as a number of small ALAE payments followed by a big loss or not, on a probabilistic basis. Another example is the effect of changing exposures on a causal basis, such as reducing writings in response to a large catastrophe or series of them.

Practice

In this section, we will discuss the implementation of timeline simulation. In the next, we will refer to a few examples and their implementation in an available companion spreadsheet. The examples will illustrate the principles given here, as well as lead the reader through one particular implementation of the timeline formulation.

Basics of Timeline Simulation

The fundamental paradigm is that events appear on a timeline, changing the state of the world. Events can be randomly generated or scheduled, or they can arise in response to other events. The latter property leads to event cascades. Time runs to a prespecified horizon and then reports (possibly including known future events) are made on the events on the timeline. Reports can also be made on a periodic or even instantaneous basis.

An event is essentially anything of interest at a particular time. For most DFA analyses, prototypical events would be cash flow amounts at particular times, with tags indicating the type of accounting entry, the line of business, perhaps the location and anything else of relevance. Exogenous variables, such as the CPI values, can also be events of interest.

Fundamentally, what defines "of interest" is the kind of reports that are desired, which in turn are determined by the kinds of questions the analysis is trying to answer. Most frequently, these questions are couched in financial terms and often in terms of impact on an insurance company's financial statement. Income statements are sums of dollars and counts of events during specified time intervals, identified by accounting entry type and line of business. Sometimes, in order to generate an event of interest – for example, a reinsurance cession – other informative events will be required, such as exterior index values, which then become of interest.

Some examples of possible event generators are losses (catastrophe, non-catastrophe and bulk), contracts such as reinsurance treaties and cat bonds, reserve changes, dividends paid or received, asset value changes, surplus evaluations, results of management decisions, etc. Events that come from an event generator carry appropriate tags, defined in terms of the reports of interest and the requirements of other generators. Even the reports themselves can trigger events if other event generators need their data.

At the time an event is generated, the entire prior history is available to it. So, for example, a direct premium event generator in a line of business may respond to the latest exposure measure event, as may a loss event generator for that line in setting its frequency of large losses and the severity of aggregated losses. If an event generator needs some kind of information to operate, then that kind of information must be available on the timeline. Almost all information is in events on the timeline, including internal states of event generators themselves if the states are of interest to other event generators. Although this requirement can lead to many events on a timeline, it means that each simulation has perfect transparency. One can walk the timeline and see exactly the state of the world that led up to any event.

The other information is the state of the world at time zero. It may include such things as initial asset and liability values and other items on the balance sheet, initial frequencies and exposures, etc. In order to include parameter uncertainty, it will also include the randomly chosen parameter values for the current timeline realization.

Event generators will at any one time generally operate in one of three modes: random, scheduled and responsive. However, a generator may use several modes. For example, a reinsurance contract has (at least) a scheduled mode for deposit ceded premium paid and a responsive mode for the ceded loss generated by a direct loss.

In random mode, at any point in time the generator has an instantaneous frequency. It is taken to be constant until the next event of any sort (which may be a time signal). The time for an event then arises from a random draw on waiting time. Another way of saying this is that the simulation is piecewise Poisson. More complex modeling is certainly possible, but not apparently needed yet.

In scheduled mode, a generator will generate an event at a known time. The characteristics of the event, for example, the size of loss, can depend on anything that has happened up until that time, such as inflation. An example could be a loss event with several payments. The generator may set the time for each payment either on a fixed or random basis, and the loss amount may be known before the event time or may need to be calculated at the time of payment. As another example, reserve changes are usually done at periodic scheduled intervals.

In responsive mode, a generator simply responds to another event. It may generate an immediate response event, or schedule it for a later time. It may generate more than one event in response to a single event. For example, a reinsurance contract, in response to a direct loss, may generate a ceded loss and a reinstatement premium. Those events in turn may be responded to by other generators.

Operation of Timeline Simulation

We start from zero with a state of the world, some parts of which will be randomly chosen because of parameter uncertainty and possibly frequency mixing. The simulation process is as follows:

1. Start at zero and poll all the sources for their current instantaneous frequencies.
2. Ask if there is a random event before the next scheduled event.
3. If there is, use it; and if not, use the scheduled event.

The event, random or scheduled, may generate immediate and/or subsequent events, leading to an event cascade. For example, an incurred loss may put payments on the schedule whose delay times from occurrence may be fixed or themselves random. A loss payment may create a ceded loss by one or more reinsurance treaties, and these in turn may generate other events, such as reinstatement premium.

When the sequence of immediate events is finished, we poll all the sources for their (possibly new) instantaneous frequencies, and repeat. We continue until the next random event is beyond the chosen time horizon. As mentioned earlier, this simulation can be characterized as piecewise Poisson. If a frequency has an explicit dependence on time, then it is necessary to schedule time signal events so that the change in frequency can be noted. When the time signals need to occur depends on how fast the frequency is changing.[32] In the case of hurricane seasonality, monthly time signals are satisfactory for current data.

For connection to the current usage in frequency distributions, a Poisson is simply a constant instantaneous frequency; and a negative binomial is an initial draw from a gamma distribution to get an instantaneous frequency for each timeline. An arbitrary annual frequency distribution can be used by initially drawing a number of events for each year and then assigning random times within years, ignoring values past the time horizon.

For the severities, the current practice is to randomly generate the incurred value and then have one or more payments that sum to the incurred. Generally, a payout pattern is matched either by breaking up the incurred value into a fixed number of payments at exact periodic (annual, quarterly, etc.) intervals or by having a single payment at a random exact number of periods later. While neither of these options is particularly realistic, they can be done on the timeline.

It is also possible to have more exotic possibilities, some of which will be discussed in the "Examples" section below. For instance, we can model a random time to the first payment, a random amount dependent on random inflation and then a decision as to whether there is a subsequent payment or not, resulting in a change in the incurred value; and then repeat the whole process at the next payment time.

It turns out to be helpful to not only allow events to carry arbitrary codes, such as Part A Loss and Part B Loss for a contract, but also to allow them to publish details about the event that may be of interest to other generators. For example, if there is a surplus share contract, the generated loss also publishes the policy limit from which it came. The essential principle for transparency is that everything necessary to understand a result should be on the timeline. It should be possible to pick any event at a given time, say a reinstatement premium, and unambiguously walk the timeline backward to see the ceded loss, why the ceded loss was the amount that it was and so on back to the original event of the cascade.

---

[32] The interval between time signals should be small compared to the inverse of the time derivative of the frequency.

Examples

In this section, we will discuss a few examples and their implementation in the companion spreadsheet.[33] The spreadsheet is a complete timeline simulation tool, with all code available to the reader. Once understood, the big problem is that it is slow, rather than that it is hard to construct a model.

For any given simulation, it is possible to look at the timeline and see exactly what happened and why. For example, Figure 3.4.1 illustrates one timeline from a formulation that has a random source and a reinsurance contract on that source. The source is named "Large Auto Losses" and is a pure Poisson with frequency 6 and a single payment that is a Pareto with mean $390,724. The contract has an occurrence limit of $100,000 with a retention of $400,000, and an annual limit of $300,000 and a deductible of $50,000, with an 80 percent participation. In the timeline, the source for every event is either "Large Auto Losses" or another event. For example, the direct paid loss (code DPL) at time 0.0378477 is the source for the "contract touched" event at 0.0378478; and that is the source of the ceded paid loss (code CPL) at 0.0378479. The amount of ceded loss is 80 percent of $100,000, less the $50,000 annual deductible.

FIGURE 3.4.1: SAMPLE TIMELINE SIMULATION

TIMELINE	AMOUNT	SOURCE	CODE
0.0000000			
0.0378477	$629,062.66	Large Auto Losses	DPL
0.0378478		0.0378477	100 XS 400
0.0378479	$40,000.00	0.0378478	CPL
0.1680589	$164,658.94	Large Auto Losses	DPL
0.1808943	$106,692.78	Large Auto Losses	DPL
0.3750555	$96,299.17	Large Auto Losses	DPL
0.4024014	$73,943.39	Large Auto Losses	DPL
0.4526555	$171,295.84	Large Auto Losses	DPL
0.4895300	$2,422,921.23	Large Auto Losses	DPL
0,4895301		0.4895300	100 XS 400
0.4895302	$80,000.00	0,4895301	CPL
0.7256551	3,324,210.24	Large Auto Losses	DPL
0.7256552		0.7256551	100 XS 400
0.7256553	$80,000.00	0.7256552	CPL
0.7918963	$1,243,311.46	Large Auto Losses	DPL
0.7918964		0.7918963	100 XS 400
0.7918965	$40,000.00	0.7918964	CPL

---

33 The companion spreadsheet is available at http://ERMBook.guycarp.com.

It can be seen that there are three more large losses, which respectively cede 80,000, 80,000 and 40,000. The last is less than 80,000 because the aggregate limit for the contract has been reached. Further losses would cede nothing.

On the reports page, we see the totals of various amounts of interest for this realization. The total DPL is 8,232,395.71; the total DPL discounted at 4 percent is 8,046,674.69. The discounting uses the actual times, of course. Figure 3.4.2 is an excerpt of the companion spreadsheet.

FIGURE 3.4.2: SPREADSHEET OUTPUT

INCLUSIVE SUMMATION	
Time Interval Covered	
from time	0.00
to time	1.00
Coverage Included	
type	DPL
Result:	**8,232,395.71**

FIRST YEAR CEDED PREMIUM	
Time Interval Covered	
from time	0.00
to time	1.00
Coverage Included	
type	CCP
Result:	—

INCLUSIVE DISCOUNTED SUMMATION	
Time Interval Covered	
from time	0.00
to time	1.00
Coverage Included	
type	DPL
discount rate	4%
Result:	**8,046,674.69**

REINSTATEMENT PREMIUM	
Time Interval Covered	
from time	0.00
to time	1.00
Coverage Included	
type	RPP
Result:	—

INCLUSIVE COUNT	
Time Interval Covered	
from time	0.00
to time	1.00
Coverage Included	
type	DPL
Result:	**9%**

FIRST YEAR CEDED LOSS	
Time Interval Covered	
from time	0.00
to time	1.00
Coverage Included	
type	CPL
Result:	**240,000.00**

We can also see that we have no ceded premium, which means either that we received a very good deal from the reinsurer or that we probably need to extend the model.

The example shown in Figure 3.4.3 has a negative binomial frequency and Pareto severity. Perhaps of more interest is the payout pattern. There is an initial payment, followed by a random number of randomly timed payments. To simplify, the amounts are all made the same. The number of subsequent payments is Poisson,[34] with mean number of payments of 5.4, and the interval times between payments are exponential with mean 0.25. The source name is "Casualty 2," and the payment behavior is meant to have more of the randomness that might characterize a casualty line.

When the generator is invoked, the subsequent payments go to the schedule. On one particular timeline, after the first invocation, the first claim, which occurred and had a payment at time = 0.0012108, has three additional payments at random times, as shown in the following schedule:

FIGURE 3.4.3: RANDOM CLAIM PAYMENTS – ONE CLAIM

TIME	AMOUNT	SOURCE	CODE	ORIGINAL WORKSHEET NAME	SOURCE NAME
0.4955255	$39,852.12	0.0012108	DPL	gamma mix	Casualty 2
0.9198603	$39,852.12	0.4955255	DPL	gamma mix	Casualty 2
0.9858654	$39,852.12	0.9198603	DPL	gamma mix	Casualty 2

After the next step, a new claim has occurred and had a payment at time = 0.01457231 (after the first claim). This new claim has a second payment that occurs before the first claim's second payment. The subsequent payments on both claims are shown in Figure 3.4.4.

---

[34] This compounding, which is negative binomial with Poisson, could clearly be done with other distributions or in several stages of compounding just as easily.

FIGURE 3.4.4: RANDOM CLAIM PAYMENTS – TWO CLAIMS

TIME	AMOUNT	SOURCE	CODE	ORIGINAL WORKSHEET NAME	SOURCE NAME
0.3930491	$151,835.83	0.1457231	DPL	gamma mix	Casualty 2
0.4955255	$39,852.12	0.0012108	DPL	gamma mix	Casualty 2
0.9198603	$39,852.12	0.4955255	DPL	gamma mix	Casualty 2
0.9858654	$39,852.12	0.9198603	DPL	gamma mix	Casualty 2
1.4835023	$151,835.83	0.3930491	DPL	gamma mix	Casualty 2
1.8480726	$151,835.83	1.4835023	DPL	gamma mix	Casualty 2
1.9190961	$151,835.83	1.8480726	DPL	gamma mix	Casualty 2
2.0185829	$151,835.83	1.9190961	DPL	gamma mix	Casualty 2

The first part of the resulting timeline is shown in Figure 3.4.5.

FIGURE 3.4.5: SAMPLE TIMELINE SIMULATION

TIMELINE	AMOUNT	SOURCE	CODE
0.0000000			
0.0012108	$39,852.12	Casualty 2	DPL
0.1457231	$151,835.83	Casualty 2	DPL
0.3930491	$151,835.83	0.1457231	DPL
0.4955255	$39,852.12	0.0012108	DPL
0.5017110	$34,325.14	Casualty 2	DPL
0.5249812	$34,325.14	0.5017110	DPL
0.5963269	$40,529.29	Casualty 2	DPL
0.6088104	$34,325.14	0.5249812	DPL
0.6114640	$34,325.14	0.6088104	DPL
0.7423930	$123,014.70	Casualty 2	DPL
0.7621211	$84,410.25	Casualty 2	DPL
0.7634110	$23,858.52	Casualty 2	DPL
0.7869403	$23,858.52	0.7634110	DPL
0.8062894	$26,161.09	Casualty 2	DPL
0.8300506	$26,161.09	0.8062894	DPL
0.8462430	$84,410.25	0.7621211	DPL
0.8595786	$84,410.25	0.8462430	DPL
0.8953636	$23,858.52	0.7869403	DPL
0.9126039	$26,161.09	0.8300506	DPL
0.9198603	$39,852.12	0.4955255	DPL
0.9723323	$23,858.52	0.8953636	DPL
0.9858654	$39,852.12	0.9198603	DPL
1.0540800	$26,161.09	0.9126039	DPL

Here, as on all timelines, you can pick up any one event, say the $23,858.52 loss at 0.9723323, and track back through the preceding events at 0.8953636 and 0.7869403 to the original event of this cascade at 0.70634110. What you do not see at time 0.9723323 is that the last payment of this series is actually at 3.0050366. In the spreadsheet, of course, you can filter on the original source event and see the whole cascade, as in Figure 3.4.6.

FIGURE 3.4.6: FILTERED CLAIM CASCADE

TIMELINE	AMOUNT	SOURCE	CODE
0.7634110	$23,858.52	Casualty 2	DPL
0.7869403	$23,858.52	0.7634110	DPL
0.8953636	$23,858.52	0.7869403	DPL
0.9723323	$23,858.52	0.8953636	DPL
1.9169860	$23,858.52	0.9723323	DPL
1.9333161	$23,858.52	1.9169860	DPL
3.0050366	$23,858.52	1.9333161	DPL

As a more complex example, consider this suggestion toward a model of loss and legal fees. It pays legal fees and then either wins or loses in court. There is an initial direct incurred loss (DIL), and then typically a stream of relatively small loss adjustment expense (LAE) payments followed by a large direct paid loss (DPL) with no change in the incurred value. Sometimes there are no payments, and there is a takedown of the incurred. There are a variable number of payments (the mean number increases with the claim size) at random times, with a mean delay between them of 0.5, and the legal payment totals are about 30 percent of the original incurred. The larger claims, having more payments on average, will tend to take longer to settle since the mean delay time is fixed. At the end, there is a "good lawyer" parameter. If the final outstanding is less than this parameter, the (high) legal fees are presumed successful and the final payment is zero, with a takedown in the incurred occurring half a day after the final payment.

Figure 3.4.7 is a sample timeline showing a typical claim and a closed-without-payment claim. The published details are the current outstanding value for the combined loss and LAE claim.

FIGURE 3.4.7: SAMPLE VALID CLAIM AND CLOSED-WITHOUT-PAYMENT CLAIM

TIMELINE	AMOUNT	SOURCE	CODE	PUBLISHED DETAILS OF THE STATE OF THE WORLD
0.0000000				
0.2448359	$419,219.31	general liability	DIL	419,219
0.3678098	$342,062.14	general liability	DIL	342,062
0.3693098	-$342,062.14	0.3678098	DIL	
0.7704962	$65,262.54	0.2448359	LAE	353,957
1.2563849	$25,844.79	0.7704962	LAE	328,112
1.5310431	$23,325.41	1.2563849	LAE	304,787
3.1242009	$14,474.64	1.5310431	LAE	290,312
3.4553438	$290,311.95	3.1242009	DPL	—
3.4568438	$0.00	3.4552338	DIL	

Figure 3.4.8 is a sample timeline showing a claim where the lawyer prevailed. This timeline is filtered on the original event.

FIGURE 3.4.8: FILTERED CLAIM HISTORY WITH PAID LOSS

TIMELINE	AMOUNT	SOURCE	CODE	PUBLISHED DETAILS OF THE STATE OF THE WORLD
0.6616716	$160,938.71	general liability	DIL	160,939
1.4325739	$18,785.62	0.6616716	LAE	142,153
1.5764449	$9,514.91	1.4325739	LAE	132,638
4.8165814	$28,994.72	1.5764449	LAE	103,643
5.6598165	$0.00	4.8165814	DPL	103,643
5.6613165	-$103,643.45	5.6598165	DIL	

Other examples include the European index clause in some of its incarnations, an excess of loss contract that has a backup and the backup contract. There is also a contagion example, where the presence of a claim increases the frequency for more claims.

Epilogue

The suggestion is "Try it, you'll like it." There is much more control over interacting events in a timeline formulation, and it is easier to express intuitions. Perhaps most importantly, a timeline formulation encourages a different way of thinking that leads to new kinds of simple models.

As an example, it is folk wisdom that larger claims close later. One model is to take the time to payment to be distributed, say exponentially, with the mean time proportional to the size of loss. While this assumption is most likely not how claims actually are distributed, it shows the ease of creating a model with few parameters that can generate count and dollar triangles and be compared to data. As another example, cancellation on treaties with seasonal effects can and should be done pro rata on exposure (via the frequency changes) rather than on time; although modeling will need to be on a pro rata basis until such time as these nuances are included in reinsurance contracts.

However, there are very few actuarial models that work on this level. The big challenge is going to be to create and then parameterize such models, starting with doing maximum likelihood on actual time delays. A case in point is accident-year paid development data. In timeline simulation, we model accidents as happening uniformly in a year and then a single payment that has a distribution of the time delay from occurrence. The accident-year data is the time from zero to payment, which is the sum of the time to occurrence plus the payment delay and, thus, the convolution of two random variables. Since our data comes in this form, we need to be able to produce a payment time delay distribution by fitting to it.

Clearly, one solution (which corresponds to the collective risk model) is to say that, for accident-year data, payments happen either when the accident occurs, exactly one year afterward, exactly two years after and so on with no payments at other intermediate times. However, it is hard to believe that claims departments actually work in this manner. Another solution has been found, using a piecewise linear continuous payment distribution. It usually is possible to fit a payment pattern exactly, but this results in an unreal density. Compromising between the quality of the fit and a more believable payment density results in consistently graduated payout patterns.

Operational and Strategic Risk

4.1 Operational Risk

By Donald F. Mango, FCAS, MAAA and Gary G. Venter, FCAS, MAAA

Definition

The use of the term "operational risk" in banking first came to prominence in the mid-1990s and, along with the major banking scandals around that time, in many ways contributed to the evolution of the role of the Chief Risk Officer. This is a role that is spreading from the banking industry to the insurance industry.

Operational risk is defined by the Basel Committee on Banking Supervision as "the risk of loss resulting from inadequate or failed internal processes, people and systems or from external events. This definition includes legal risk, but excludes strategic and reputational risk." [1]

This definition is deceptively short for such a broad area. To elaborate, the Basel Committee issued a July 2002 consultative paper, "Sound Practices for the Management and Supervision of Operational Risk," where they defined the following seven types of operational risk loss events at category level 1 [2]:

- **Internal fraud.** Acts of a type intended to defraud, misappropriate property or circumvent regulations, the law or company policy, excluding diversity/discrimination events, which involve at least one internal party. Examples include intentional misreporting of positions, employee theft and insider trading on an employee's own account.

- **External fraud.** Acts by a third party, of a type intended to defraud, misappropriate property or circumvent the law. Examples include robbery, forgery, check kiting and damage from computer hacking.

- **Employment practices and workplace safety.** Acts inconsistent with employment, health or safety laws or agreements, or which result in payment of personal injury claims, or claims relating to diversity/discrimination issues. Examples include workers compensation claims, violation of employee health and safety rules, organized labor activities, discrimination claims and general liability (for example, a customer slipping and falling at a branch office).

- **Clients, products and business practices.** Unintentional or negligent failure to meet a professional obligation to specific clients (including fiduciary and suitability requirements), or from the nature or design of a product. Examples include fiduciary breaches, misuse of confidential customer information, improper trading activities on the bank's account, money laundering and sale of unauthorized products.

- **Damage to physical assets.** Loss or damage to physical assets from natural disaster or other events. Examples include terrorism, vandalism, earthquakes, fires and floods.

- **Business disruption and system failures.** Disruption of business or system failures. Examples include hardware and software failures, telecommunication problems and utility outages.

- **Execution, delivery and process management.** Failed transaction processing or process management, and relations with trade counterparties and vendors. Examples include data entry errors, collateral management failures, incomplete legal documentation, unapproved access given to client accounts, non-client counterparty misperformance and vendor disputes.

The committee defined subcategories of these loss events at category level 2 and further suggested example activities at level 3. However, the committee has left it to the banks to define appropriate heterogeneous groupings.

While inevitably banking focused, the Basel Committee definition has gained substantial visibility and acceptance as the field of ERM has developed over the last ten years. However, there is not yet consensus on this categorization. But as many financial conglomerates have both banking and insurance operations, and are regulated by the same authority with converging regulatory ideas (e.g., Financial Services Authority (FSA) in the UK and Australian Prudential Regulation Authority (APRA) in Australia), one can easily imagine that greater use will lead to wider acceptance.

Many firms include reputational and strategic risks under the operational risk banner. One example for insurers comes from the ERM framework of the UK. FSA breaks down the universe of insurer risk as illustrated in Figure 4.1.1 (note the placement of strategic risk).

FIGURE 4.1.1: UK FSA RISK MAPPING

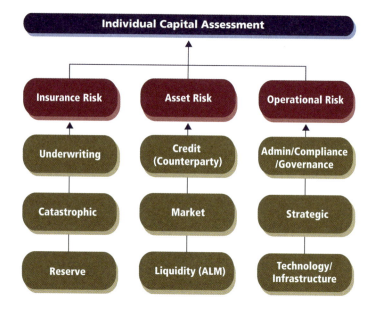

This figure is very similar to Figure 1.2.1, with some different words used to describe the components of operational risk.

In some ways, except for regulatory requirements, one could argue that it does not matter whether strategic or reputational risk is included in operational risk, as long as it is considered in isolation and not overlooked altogether.

Figure 4.1.2 shows some examples of insurer exposures to each subcategory of the Basel II definition:

FIGURE 4.1.2: INSURER EXPOSURES TO BASEL II SUBCATEGORY

SUBCATEGORY	EXAMPLES OF INSURER EXPOSURE
Internal Fraud	Employee theft, claim falsification
External Fraud	Claims fraud, falsifying application information
Employment Practices and Workplace Safety	Repetitive stress, discrimination
Clients, Products and Business Processes	Client privacy, bad faith, red-lining
Damage to Physical Assets	Physical damage to own office, own automobile fleets
Business Disruption and System Failures	Processing center downtime, system interruptions
Execution, Delivery and Process Management	Policy processing, claim payment errors

Inevitably, the definitions by regulators are compromises. However, useful practical refinements and insights have been added by ORX[36] and ORIC[37], which have developed operational risk loss data consortiums for the global banking industry and the UK insurance industry, respectively.

Operational Risk in Insurers

A.M. Best periodically issues studies of the causes of impairments or insolvencies in the U.S. insurance industry. Figure 4.1.3 summarizes the breakdown of the causes for insolvencies between 1969 and 2002, as reported in its 2004 study.

FIGURE 4.1.3: PRIMARY CAUSES OF P&C COMPANY IMPAIRMENTS (SOURCE: A.M. BEST)

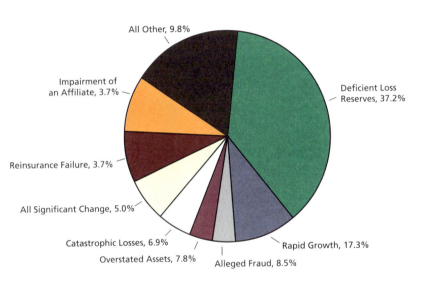

The A.M. Best findings are consistent with those in "Failed Promises: Insurance Company Insolvencies," a 1990 U.S. Congressional Report by the Committee on Energy and Commerce Subcommittee on Oversight and Investigations. That report attributed insurer failures to underreserving, underpricing, insufficiently supervised delegation of underwriting authority, rapid expansion, reckless management and abuse of reinsurance. Australia's HIH Royal Commission, looking into the collapse of one of Australia's largest insurers, arrived at similar conclusions[38].

---

36 ORX is the Operational Riskdata eXchange Association (www.ORX.org).
37 ORIC is the Association of British Insurers Operational Risk Insurance Consortium (www.abi.org.uk).
38 Available online at www.hihroyalcom.gov.au/finalreport/indext.htm.

Mark Verheyen [7] questioned whether the conclusions from A.M. Best, "Failed Promises" and HIH indicate that, in fact, operational risks are the primary causes of insurer failures. He further suggested that "the significant sources of operational risk are implicitly included in regulatory and rating agency capital models." Indeed, the capital charges for premium, reserves and growth are in some part proxies for operational risk. This is a compelling reason to unbundle them from underwriting risk and consider them explicitly rather than implicitly.

This is precisely the reason that in banking, operational risk has been added to market and credit risk (Basel I). Operational risks have brought down many banking institutions (e.g., Barings, Long-Term Capital Management) and undermined the confidence in the banking system. Now that it is clearer that operational risks have heavily contributed to insurance impairments and insolvencies, they require explicit consideration in order to more fully protect the insurance industry and the underlying policyholders.

The Risk Fulcrum: Plan Loss Ratios
Insufficient reserves are technically a condition of every impairment and insolvency. Identifying "reserve deficiencies" as the cause of impairment is akin to citing "heart stoppage" as cause of death. It is factually accurate, but not very informative or useful.

The root reason for insurer failure is the accumulation of too much obligation (exposure) for the supporting asset base. Insufficient carried reserves are the symptom of a series of company analyses and managerial decisions. They are lagging indicators of insufficient initial reserving – which is primarily driven by optimistic plan loss ratios – or premature reserve releases. In fact, if one wanted to begin exploring the operational risk dynamics of an insurer, the "fulcrum" of that risk may well be the plan loss ratio determination process. The planning process could be the "perfect storm" of potential failure of people, processes and systems.

Consider the following thought experiment: Lemur Insurance writes a substantial book of long-tailed business. We will assume "long-tailed" means that historically it takes five years from policy year (PY) inception for 50 percent of the ultimate losses to be reported and 10 years for 90 percent to be reported.

Lemur (like most insurers) always "makes plan," especially its premium goals, as often bonus schemes are driven off these targets. The premium targets are to a large extent driven by the assumed plan loss ratio – ostensibly an unbiased, realistic forecast of the loss ratio for the upcoming underwriting period. If a line of business is forecast to be at a lower loss ratio next year, it is almost certainly a line the company will want to grow in. If the firm has a reasonable model for forecasting plan loss ratios, then such growth decisions make sense.

Lemur sets its plan loss ratios using a "bridging model," where more mature prior-year ultimate loss ratios (taken from the reserve review) are bridged forward using estimates of year-over-year loss cost and price level changes. The plan loss ratio selection, is based on a set of these bridged loss ratios, based on mature prior years.

Reserve review ultimate losses for immature prior years (those five years and younger) are calculated using the Bornhuetter-Ferguson (B-F) method, with expected loss ratios (ELRs) equal to the initial plan loss ratio for each prior year. This means that in the most recent few years, a prior-year ultimate loss ratio is quite close to its plan loss ratio.

One operational problem with such a bridging process is the high degree of interdependence and autocorrelation it induces among prior-year ultimate loss ratios. Absent any other information, optimistic older prior-year loss ratios can propagate forward and lead to optimistic plan loss ratios. By simply following this process, underwriters can inadvertently string together a series of optimistically forecasted prior years. This is equivalent to betting a slate of long shots at the racetrack: The chance of hitting them all is quite small.

Eventually, Lemur's older prior years begin to deteriorate, and via the bridging, the B-F ELRs for the newer prior years also increase. This "reserve conflagration" actually represents unanticipated model risk – pure operational risk – associated with Lemur's loss ratio and reserving process. The conflagration of loss ratio increase creates a dilemma for Lemur's management: Either book the indicated deficiency and suffer a rating downgrade, or convince their auditors of the need to legitimately change their reserving process. Needless to say, they foresee no success with the latter tack, so they opt for the substantial reserve increase. The downgrade puts the firm at a claims-paying rating below levels acceptable to their core clientele. This leads to massive nonrenewing and no new business volume. Six months later, with the franchise in ruins, Lemur is put into runoff.

What are the proximate causes of Lemur's demise? The underwriters decry the poor performance of Lemur's actuarial staff: We followed directions and made plan, they say. The actuaries blame management, who in turn point the finger at the inherent, irreducible unpredictability of long-tailed business. This is the nature of insurance, they claim. This "pure insurance risk" argument is well-known in the industry. The fundamentally volatile loss-generating process, plus the confluence of economic and social forces, means even the most skillful forecasters can only get so close to the true answers. Forecasting errors such as happened to Lemur are inevitable and benign, indicating no wrongdoing.

While this argument makes the actuaries feel better about their own poor track record, the separation between underwriting (reserving) risk and operational risk is unclear. A forensic analysis of Lemur's plan loss ratio process reveals at least three explanations:

1. The plan loss ratio model could not accurately forecast the loss ratio.
2. The plan loss ratio model could have accurately forecasted the loss ratio, but was improperly used.
3. The plan loss ratio model did accurately forecast the loss ratio, but their indications were unpopular and therefore ignored.

A similar analysis of their reserving process reveals the same explanations:

1. The reserve review models could not accurately forecast reserves.
2. The reserve review models could have accurately forecasted reserves but were improperly used.
3. The reserve review models did accurately forecast reserves, but their indications were unpopular and therefore ignored.

Explanation #1 lines up well with the inherent uncertainty argument and helps many professionals save face. However, were #1 the truth, there is some operational risk – the plan loss ratio process failed to accurately forecast the loss ratios (process and system failure). If no competitor had any more success in this product line, then we could accept #1 in totality, without operational risk implications. But if there were competitors with better forecasting models, then Lemur's planning system failed to deliver its intended product, namely accurate loss ratios.

Explanation #2 is pure people failure (improper use), and #3 is process and governance failure, what former president of the Faculty and Institute of Actuaries Jeremy Goford calls "corner office risk."

Operational Risk and Cycle Management

Rather than list all the many possible operational risks insurers face, we will demonstrate the relevance of some of the critical risks in a setting that is familiar: cycle management. While meaning different things to different people, cycle management can be thought of as the prudent management of underwriting capacity as market pricing fluctuates in what is known as the underwriting cycle. The industry knows all too well that irresponsible, simplistic strategies ("maintain market share") during soft markets increase the likelihood of impairment, failure and destruction of franchise value. While there is much debate and speculation over the true causes of underwriting cycles, we can analyze a typical fictional insurer's response strategies from the perspective of people and process performance. We might ask:

1. Does the company have a proactive cycle management strategy? If not, does it believe it needs one?
2. Does the company know where in the cycle the market stands at any given time?
3. Are underwriters making decisions that are consistent with #1 and #2?

We will assess Foresight Insurance from a system performance perspective. That is, an insurer is a financial security system, a persistent pool of money. Policyholders can be thought of as members who purchase the right to access the system at a future time, should they need to. System performance assessments of, for example, utilities focus on stability, availability, reliability and affordability. Users depend on the system, and performance perturbations have undesirable ripple effects. So through this lens, we have to ask if Foresight is stable, available, reliable and affordable. Would an effective cycle management process improve its performance assessment?

Performance Assessment Under Naïve Cycle Management

As a starting point, consider Foresight's performance as it follows the "maintain market share" strategy. As price adequacy drops via either pure price decreases or expansion of coverage, Foresight maintains premium volume but takes on more exposure. For a period of time, Foresight appears to its constituents to be performing well. Policyholders see premium decreases, coverage expansion or both. Prior policyholders are still getting their claims paid. However, once the cycle hits bottom and Foresight can no longer avoid recognition of its mounting claim exposures from the recent past, the situation changes dramatically. Foresight may be downgraded below a level acceptable to some policyholders, forcing them to switch carriers – failures on both a stability and availability basis. Foresight's insolvency means many policyholders will receive only partial recoveries on claims – failures in reliability and affordability. One might question how default is an affordability issue, since in insurance usage, that term typically refers to premiums. However, a partial claim payment means the policyholder must bear a portion of the cost itself, which for large claims it may well be unable to afford.

Performance Improvement Via Cycle Management

Foresight knows a naïve strategy will likely lead to poor performance, so its managers wish to implement effective cycle management. Many similar firms fail to deliver on their initial commitment due to the overwhelming scope implied in cycle management. Essentially, an insurer must reengineer its underwriting decision processes. Given the continuous nature of the business (e.g., renewals, claims), for most insurers such an undertaking would be like rewiring the house with the lights still on. It is daunting because it impacts so many critical areas simultaneously: planning, underwriting, objective setting and incentive bonuses.

Respecting those realities, Foresight could still achieve meaningful process improvements by focusing on intellectual property, underwriter incentives, market overreaction and owner education.

Intellectual Property

The majority of an insurer's franchise value is in intangible assets, also referred to as intellectual property. Examples include the experts in underwriting, claims, finance and actuarial; the proprietary databases of policyholder information (purchased via underwriting losses); the forecasting systems (pricing and reserving); and market relationships and reputation. Like all assets, these require care and maintenance. They are time-consuming to build and easy to lose or destroy. Therefore, prudent managers must focus on maintaining the core assets throughout the cycle. This has several implications. First, they must retain their top talent throughout periods of capacity retraction and continue to grow and develop their skills. Second, they must maintain a presence in their core market channels. Finally, they must maintain a consistent pattern of investment in systems, models and databases.

Underwriter Incentives

Cycle management requires adaptability and responsiveness. Typical underwriter incentive plans are written once a year, with hard-coded bonus formulas tied to making "the plan," which is based on one assumed market situation. This structure is the antithesis of flexibility. In order to ensure underwriting decisions are in line with the corporate objectives and needs at the time the decisions are being made, the incentive plans need to be based on how well underwriters supported the portfolio goals throughout the year. Those goals will be fluid and changing based on inevitable market condition changes. If prices drop to an unacceptable level, underwriters may have to stop writing new business, with complete confidence that their bonus, and their long-term employment prospects at the firm, will be unaffected.

Market Overreaction

The industry has a proven track record of aggregate overreaction in both directions. Market prices and coverage soften far below sensible levels, until the pain becomes too great, at which point the prices and restrictions overcorrect to the other extreme. In anticipation of such overreaction, Foresight may find another reason to prudently manage capacity. The firms with the most available capacity during the price-improvement phase will reap windfall profits that can offset many years of small underwriting losses.

Owner Education

Foresight's owners must understand that under cycle management, certain financial figures may appear out of step with their peer companies. For example, premium volumes will drop. While those unfamiliar with insurance may see this as a decline in revenue (an undeniably bad signal for most types of firms), in an insurer practicing prudent cycle management, it is a sign of good stewardship of the franchise and the financial security system. Premium is an aggregate result of (i) amount (and nature) of exposure taken on, and (ii) price per unit of that exposure. It is imperative that owners understand what they are seeing and do not make ill-advised calls for top-line growth or increased market share at the worst possible point in the cycle.

Another example is the overhead expense ratio. Again, for most types of firms, the ratio of overhead expense to revenue is a critical indicator of operational efficiency. Based on the prior discussion of intellectual property, though, one can see that the portion of current-year overhead expense related to expert underwriter salaries, or IT costs for the claims and underwriting systems, could in fact be considered capital investments in these assets. One could make a compelling case that an underwriter's activity this year will produce benefits to the firm in subsequent years. That would argue for less emphasis on the overhead expense ratio.

A case in point can be found in the 2004 Berkshire Hathaway letter to shareholders. Figure 4.1.4 is taken from that letter[39].

---

[39] Available online at www.berkshirehathaway.com/letters/2004ltr.pdf.

FIGURE 4.1.4: BERKSHIRE HATHAWAY RESULTS

**PORTRAIT OF A DISCIPLINED UNDERWRITER
NATIONAL INDEMNITY COMPANY**

YEAR	WRITTEN PREMIUM (IN $ MILLIONS)	NO. OF EMPLOYEES AT YEAR-END	RATIO OF OPERATING EXPENSES TO WRITTEN PREMIUM	UNDERWRITING PROFIT (LOSS) AS A PERCENTAGE OF PREMIUMS (CALCULATED AS OF YEAR-END 2004)
1980	$79.6	372	32.3%	8.2%
1981	59.9	353	36.1%	(.8%)
1982	52.5	323	36.7%	(15.3%)
1983	58.2	308	35.6%	(18.7%)
1984	62.2	342	35.5%	(17.0%)
1985	160.7	380	28.0%	1.9%
1986	366.2	403	25.9%	30.7%
1987	232.3	368	29.5%	27.3%
1988	139.9	347	31.7%	24.8%
1989	98.4	3320	35.9%	14.8%
1990	87.8	289	37.4%	7.0%
1991	88.3	284	35.7%	13.0%
1992	82.7	277	37.9%	5.2%
1993	86.8	279	36.1%	11.3%
1994	85.9	263	34.6%	4.6%
1995	78.0	258	36.6%	9.2%
1996	74.0	243	36.5%	6.8%
1997	65.3	240	40.4%	6.2%
1998	56.8	231	40.4%	9.4%
1999	54.5	222	41.2%	4.5%
2000	68.1	230	38.4%	2.9%
2001	161.3	254	28.8%	(11.6%)
2002	343.5	313	24.0%	16.8%
2003	594.5	337	22.2%	18.1%
2004	605.6	340	22.5%	5.1%

Note that this "portrait of a disciplined underwriter" shows, over a 25-year stretch, significant fluctuations in premium volume but far fewer fluctuations in number of employees. The result, predictably, is fluctuation in the ratio of operating expense to written premium, often to levels unthinkable to many management teams (e.g., 40 percent). National Indemnity is fortunate to have an owner (Warren Buffett) who understands the franchise he has built, who gives his underwriters clear guidance and incentives and has demonstrated over time that their jobs will be preserved during soft markets.

Agency Theory Perspective

Agency theory looks at management as the agents of owners, but agents with potentially divergent interests ([4], [5], [6]). The private interests of management create a type of operational risk faced by most widely held companies. One goal of agency theory studies is how to align management and owner interests, and another is to understand the impacts of potential divergence.

Some of this is difficult to quantify and to fund for. It is hard to ask an employee or even a consultant to compute the probability that the CEO will be overpaid at the expense of the shareholders. Even if this were quantified, would you want to increase capital to fund for this risk?

More generally, what is the probability that the incentive compensation plan will lead to inappropriate managerial behavior and decision making? Rather than quantifying and funding for such risks, studying the plan and understanding its incentives and, if necessary, adjusting it would be more useful.

It is often difficult to align management and owner interests. For instance, a start-up company can agree to pay management a percentage of the increase in its market cap after five years. That might give investors and management the same perspective. But if the management has a certain attitude towards risk, it could decide to take very risky actions to try for a major increase in firm value, figuring they could end up either very wealthy or right where they are now. This is essentially incenting them to gamble with someone else's money.

Paying management in stock grants or stock options is often viewed as a way to harmonize management and shareholder incentives, but this too could backfire. It is quite possible that shareholders become much more diversified than management, which then becomes more risk averse. A widely held company could be run like a closely held family enterprise as a result.

In the insurance industry, it is not just senior management incentives that are an issue. Production incentives are not uncommon but can lead to sloppy underwriting or mispricing. Recognizing and controlling this risk is central, although it might be worthwhile to try to quantify its probability and potential impact and even hold some capital for it. Using MGAs to produce business has similar risks.

There are no simple answers to the problems of agency theory. Different people may react differently to any given incentive program, depending on their own risk preferences. Being aware of the potential problems and monitoring results are key. Perhaps there is a role for independent board members in this process.

Operational Risk Management in Banking and Manufacturing

Many operational risks are common to all businesses, but identifying them as risk sources and managing their impacts can avoid unexpected problems and lead to profit opportunities. This section will cover some general operational risks and explore the elements of good operational risk management used in banks and manufacturers.

General Operational Risks

- Pension funding issues combine financial and HR components. Sometimes, changes in funding adequacy are not highlighted in financial statements; so this is not given as much focus as other issues, but it can have significant economic impact. Models that incorporate financial risk with firm demographics would be needed for quantifying this risk.

- IT failure risk has been quantified to some degree. Besides traditional hardware and software failure, there are new issues of virus and other Internet attacks. Monitoring and control with contingency planning is critical, but quantification and funding of the residual risk is possible.

- Other HR risks include loss of important staff, perhaps due to misdesign of compensation and benefit programs, employee liability, fraud by employees, rogue trader risk, inadequate training, errors, rule breaking, incompetence, etc. Again, identification and control of these risks are more critical than their quantification and funding. They also have opportunity elements. These risks, as well as property damage, etc., have some insurance coverage available, so analyzing the company as a client can help quantify such risks.

- Reputational risk can arise from product tampering, bad press coverage, etc. Firms' reputations and images have even been severely damaged from off-hours behavior of key employees. It is not clear that adding extra capital would help in such cases. Thus, for much of operational risk, the primary role of ERM would seem to be identification and management of such risks rather than quantification and funding for them.

- Lawsuits can be brought for anything from making too much money to making too little. Sometimes, a company can feel it has proper business practices, but these can be misinterpreted or reinterpreted through changing standards of jurisprudence. Monitoring behaviors is important for this, but perhaps there is a role for funding as well. Corporate culture can also make a difference, but this may be difficult to determine in a risk analysis.

Control Self-Assessment (CSA)

The Institute of Internal Auditors (IIA, www.theiia.org) defines control self-assessment[40] as "a process through which internal control effectiveness is examined and assessed. The objective is to provide reasonable assurance that all business objectives will be met." The focus on internal controls is consistent with internal auditing professional standards. According to IIA standards, the primary objectives of internal control are to ensure:

1. The reliability and integrity of information.
2. Compliance with policies, plans, procedures, laws, regulations and contracts.
3. The safeguarding of assets.
4. The economical and efficient use of resources.
5. The accomplishment of established objectives and goals for operations or programs.

According to the IIA's Professional Practices Pamphlet 97-2, "Assessing and Reporting on Internal Control", the IIA supports the COSO[41] recommendation that organizations "should report on the effectiveness and efficiency of the system of internal control, which is defined as:

> …a process, effected by an entity's board of directors, management and other personnel, designed to provide reasonable assurance regarding the achievement of objectives in the following categories:

1. Effectiveness and efficiency of operations.
2. Reliability of financial reporting.
3. Compliance with applicable laws and regulations."

---

40 Institute of Internal Auditors, "A Perspective on Control Self-Assessment." Available online at www.theiia.org/iia/download.cfm?file=345.
41 COSO is the Committee of Sponsoring Organizations of the Treadway Commission, which sponsored development of the U.S. research report titled "Internal Control – Integrated Framework."

Key Risk Indicators (KRIs)

Davies and Haubenstock [3] provide the following definition of risk indicators:

> Risk indicators are a broad category of measures used to monitor the activities and status of the control environment of a particular business area for a given operational risk category. While typical control assessment processes occur only periodically, risk indicators can be measured as often as daily. Risk indicators help keep the operational risk management process dynamic and risk profiles current. As the use of risk indicators becomes integrated into a risk management process, indicator levels/measures must have a frame of reference, commonly referred to as escalation criteria or trigger levels. These levels represent thresholds of an indicator or a tolerance that, when passed, require management to step up its actions.

KRIs are forward-looking, leading indicators of risk, whereas historical losses are inevitably backward looking.

Mark Verheyen [7] suggested the following insurer KRIs:

- Production — hit ratios, retention ratios, item count, pricing levels (renewal business and new business), rate per unit of exposure;
- Internal controls — audit results, audit frequency;
- Staffing — employee turnover, training budget, premium per employee, policies per employee;
- Claims — frequency, severity, new classes of loss.

Six Sigma

Six Sigma is a management framework born out of the manufacturing world, which was originally invented by Motorola in 1985. It has connections to Total Quality Management (TQM) and Statistical Process Control (SPC). The name means that customer-specified tolerances for output quality (defects) are plus/minus three standard deviations ("sigma") from the mean (hence, Six Sigma). Major corporations that use Six Sigma include Motorola, General Electric, Honeywell (Allied Signal) and Ford.

Six Sigma provides a framework encompassing process redesign, project management, customer feedback gathering, internal communication, design trade-offs, documentation and control plans. This framework is typically applied in two different settings: existing process improvement and predictive design. While developed in manufacturing, Six Sigma has value in financial services, where there is a predominance of high volume processing, and has been used as a means of operational risk mitigation. Specifically, Six Sigma can help firms identify and eliminate chronic process issues: inefficiencies, errors, overlaps and gaps in communication and coordination. The end result will be reduced operational loss potential, from potentially both a frequency and severity perspective.

Some examples of insurer processes that might benefit from process improvement are:

- Underwriting — exposure data verification, exposure data capture, price component monitoring, classification and hazard selection.
- Claims — coverage verification, ALAE, use of outside counsel and initial case reserve setting.
- Reinsurance — treaty claim reporting, coverage verification, reinsurance recoverables, disputes, letters of credit and collateralization.

Operational Risk Modeling

A comprehensive operational risk management system is akin to a captive insurance company. This suggests that a centralized operational risk management group is a *de facto* insurance captive manager. The portfolio consists of *all* the operational risk exposures that are either transferred (insured or transferred to the capital markets) or retained, regardless of whether retention is by virtue of decision or by necessity (because some risks are either not insurable or no insurance exists). Drawing on the key elements of insurance portfolio risk management, the necessary steps for operational risk portfolio management might therefore include:

1. Identify exposure bases for each key operational risk source. Examples include payroll, head count, policy count, endorsement count, claim count and premium volume. Typically, these are KRIs whose levels are regularly recorded by each business unit (BU) and monitored by the centralized operational risk group.
2. Measure the exposure level for each BU for each operational risk source. This might be based on exposure modeling, experience modeling and industry data, supplemented by (large) loss scenarios and adjusted for the future business environment, or a combination of any of these. The goal is the best assessment of exposure using the best and most appropriate techniques available.
3. Estimate the loss potential (frequency and severity) per unit of exposure for each operational risk, reflecting the existing level of internal controls and process effectiveness.
4. Combine #2 and #3 to produce modeled BU loss frequency and severity distributions.
5. Estimate the impact (reduction) of mitigation, process improvements or risk transfer on the BU loss frequency and/or severity distributions.

Structurally, this exercise is no different than standard property-casualty (general insurance) actuarial analysis. The difference is that many of these exposures have never been covered under any insurance program, so (ironically) there is no loss history on some of these insurer operational risks. It is worth noting that some of this loss information may be in existence, although it may not have been recorded for managing operational risk per se. For example, the general ledger accounts might well record some "operational risk" losses. Consequently, it is well worth investigating internal systems to discover what operational risk loss information might be recorded, perhaps in an uncoordinated manner, and systematize and institutionalize its future collection.

Also, Step #5 will likely be an area where significant expert opinion is required. It is unlikely that organizations will have significant amounts of operational loss data both before and after every possible mitigation effort. Banks use Control Self-Assessments (CSAs) as a source of information to help gauge the degree of process and control improvement.

This is similar to the determination of the mandated premium discounts for tort reform. Actuaries do not have the luxury of "rerunning the experiment" before and after tort reform – that is, what would the claim experience have been had these reformed tort laws been in effect over the past several years? Significant detailed analysis of claim and policyholder information is required, along with informed estimation and judgment.

Conclusions

Our understanding of operational risk is in its infancy, especially as regards quantitative modeling. Each step we make in our progress merely increases its importance. It is essential that ERM practitioners do not lose sight of operational risk simply because it is soft, difficult, poorly understood or lacking historical track record. It is just these characteristics that make operational risk fertile ground for historically relevant research, with undeniable benefits to flow to our industry and economy.

4.2 Strategic Risk

By Donald F. Mango, FCAS, MAAA

Strategic Risk – History and Definition

The concept of strategic risk (SR) is not well defined and therefore not well understood. The problem may start because the word *strategy* itself is neither well defined nor well understood. The Merriam-Webster Online Dictionary provides three definitions:

1. (a) the science and art of employing the political, economic, psychological and military forces of a nation or group of nations to afford the maximum support to adopted policies in peace or war, (b1) the science and art of military command exercised to meet the enemy in combat under advantageous conditions, (b2) a variety of or instance of the use of strategy

2. (a) a careful plan or method: a clever stratagem, (b) the art of devising or employing plans or stratagems toward a goal

3. an adaptation or complex of adaptations (as of behavior, metabolism or structure) that serves or appears to serve an important function in achieving evolutionary success <foraging strategies of insects>

Taking liberties, and with willingness to expand the military context to general organizations and corporations, the proposed unified definition of *strategy* is:

- A science and art of planning,
- Using political, economic, psychological and organizational resources,
- To achieve major organizational goals.

This unified definition corresponds well with the definition in the report of the General Insurance Research Organization (GIRO)[42] Working Party on "The Application of Strategic Models to Non-Life Insurance Markets" (www.actuaries.org.uk/files/pdf/proceedings/giro2005/Massey.pdf).

> A strategy is a long term series of actions designed to take a company from its current state to its desired future state, and aims to provide a sustainable competitive advantage over other companies in the same market.

---

[42] GIRO is the non-life insurance research group of the Faculty and Institute of Actuaries, the actuarial body of the United Kingdom. See www.actuaries.org.uk.

The GIRO Working Party goes on to clarify what strategy is not:

1. Strategy goes beyond pure business planning and, in particular, considers a wider breadth of issues. Formulating a company's strategy requires an understanding of the market it is competing in, where it sits relative to its competitors and how it will compete and outperform its rivals.

2. Strategy is also not tactics; the two are often confused. Tactics tend to be short-term measures and are described in significant detail. Strategy is broader themes/features/styles that a company may want to exploit.

Another possible source of confusion regarding *strategic risk* may be that two loaded terms – "strategic" and "risk" – are combined in one phrase, without clear grammatical demarcation. Reasonable people could interpret the phrase quite differently. Some of the definitions focus on strategic risk-taking – intentional risk-taking as an essential part of the company's strategic execution; others are aimed at strategic risk – unintentional risks as by-products of strategy planning or execution.

As an example, consider this definition offered by the Office of the Comptroller of Currency (OCC) in its 1998 document *Emerging Market Country Products and Trading Activities*:

> Strategic risk is the risk to earnings or capital arising from adverse business decisions or improper implementation of those decisions. This risk is a function of the compatibility between an organization's strategic goals, the business strategies developed to achieve those goals the resources deployed against these goals and the quality of implementation. The resources needed to carry out business strategies are both tangible and intangible. They include communication channels, operating systems, delivery networks and managerial capacities and capabilities. The definition of strategic risk focuses on more than an analysis of the written strategic plan. Its focus is on how plans, systems and implementation affect the franchise value. It also incorporates how management analyzes external factors that impact the strategic direction of the company[43].

The OCC's definition is strategic risk of the second kind – unintentional risks as by-products of strategy planning or execution. Its inclusion of systems is interesting and is symptomatic of the confusion. Compare this definition with the definition of operational risk from the Basel Committee on Banking Supervision (the Committee)[2]:

---

43 Available at www.occ.treas.gov/handbook/emkt.pdf.

> The risk of loss resulting from inadequate or failed internal processes, people and systems, or from external events. This definition includes legal risk, but excludes strategic and reputational risk.

Note the Committee's specific exclusion of strategic risk, but its inclusion of systems failure, which the OCC included in strategic risk. This instance of overlap is far from unique. In fact, many operational, reputational, financial and hazard risks could also potentially be of strategic origin or significance.

Strategic Risk Management Research to Date

The first instance of the term "strategic risk management" (SRM) in scientific literature appears to be in Miller [5], "A framework for integrated risk management in international business." Miller highlights the confusion regarding inconsistent definitions of the term "risk." It can refer to unanticipated, negative variation in business outcome variables (i.e., effects) or to factors (external or internal) that impact on the risk experienced by the firm (i.e., actual sources of risk). Miller adopts the following usage convention:

- Risk refers to unpredictability in corporate outcomes (effects); and
- Uncertainty refers to the unpredictability of environmental or organizational variables that impact corporate performance (sources).

Miller's "strategic risk" actually refers to "strategic moves that can potentially mitigate the risks associated with the uncertainties" outlined in the previous section of his paper. Thus, what we have so far defined as strategic risks, Miller would consider strategic uncertainties – unpredictable impacts of strategies. It is a little ironic that the person credited with coining the term actually uses it in a manner quite different from that used in much of the risk management literature.

Another of the seminal papers on strategic risk is: "Toward a Contingency Model of Strategic Risk Taking," by Baird and Thomas [1]. Like Miller, Baird and Thomas return to the origins of what science there is and find clarity and precision to be somewhat lacking. They reference a 1921 work by Knight [4] as the source for defining risk as "a condition in which the consequences of a decision and the probabilities associated with the consequences are known entities." They differentiate this from uncertainty, in which neither consequences nor probabilities are known. They define strategic risk-taking as:

"Corporate strategic moves that cause returns to vary, that involve venturing into the unknown, and that may result in corporate ruin – moves for which the outcomes and probabilities may be only partially known and where hard-to-define goals may not be met."

Baird and Thomas outline the following important elements of strategic risk:

- Voluntariness of exposure
- Controllability of consequences
- Discounting in time
- Discounting in space
- Knowledge of risky situation
- Magnitude of impact
- Group/individual factors

Concerns with risk have been factored into strategic decision making using several simplistic approaches:
- Obtaining more accurate forecasts
- Adjusting factors empirically
- Raising thresholds for required returns
- Estimating best, probable and worst case outcomes—i.e., rudimentary scenario analysis and
- Considering selected probabilities on key factors

Slywotzky and Drzik [7] describe SRM as a means to devise and deploy a systematic approach for managing strategic risk, categorized as follows:

1. Industry – capital intensiveness, overcapacity, commoditization, deregulation, cycle volatility
2. Technology – shift, patents, obsolescence
3. Brand – erosion or collapse
4. Competitor – global rivals, gainers, unique competitors
5. Customer – priority shift, power, concentration
6. Project – failure of R&D, IT, business development or M&A
7. Stagnation – flat or declining volume, price decline, weak pipeline

Ironically, Slywotzky and Drzik list as risks what Miller would consider uncertainties or sources. Still, their contribution is valuable as a cataloguing of the major components of a strategic risk analysis.

Hertz and Thomas [3] develop the concept of SRM further to strategic risk analysis, whereby risk analysis:

"is an input for the strategy development process, aiding strategy formulation, evaluation, choice and implementation. No distinction is drawn between strategic risk analysis and strategy formulation. Instead, both are viewed as parts of an iterative, adaptive and flexible policy dialogue process."

This definition focuses on how to make better strategy decisions and therefore would correspond closely to the strategic error concept. Hertz and Thomas' work is also valuable in providing a detailed, practical example of integration of risk analysis into a corporate strategic decision making process.

Examples of Strategic Risks for an Insurer
It is instructive to see how many of the strategic risks from Slywotzky and Drzik might impact an insurer:

- Industry – capital intensiveness, overcapacity, commoditization, deregulation, cycle volatility
  Magnitude of risk: very high
  Insurance markets suffer from all of these conditions.

- Technology – shift, patents, obsolescence
  Magnitude of risk: low
  Except for possible innovations in distribution for personal lines via the Internet. One area of potential technological innovation is data management.

- Brand – erosion or collapse
  Magnitude of risk: moderate
  Essentially, insurance "products" are claim checks. Therefore, it is difficult for insurers to differentiate based on product content. Either the check is good, or it isn't. Therefore, insurers often differentiate on price or services. If one interprets the insurer's "brand promise" as including a reputation for fair claims handling, then loss of this reputation through adverse press or class action suits could definitely destroy franchise value.

- Competitor – global rivals, gainers, unique competitors
  Magnitude of risk: moderate
  Predatory pricing is a significant risk, since market share can be grabbed fairly easily by carriers willing to write the coverage at a discount to incumbent carriers.

- Customer – priority shift, power, concentration
  Magnitude of risk: moderate
  This risk is probably a bigger issue for large commercial insurance business.

- Project – failure of R&D, IT, business development or M&A
  Magnitude of risk: high
  Companies have a long track record of value-destroying mergers and acquisitions. They are also notoriously small investors in R&D and IT, which is ironic given the nature of the intellectual capital franchise.

- Stagnation – flat or declining volume, price decline, weak pipeline
  Magnitude of risk: high
  This risk is highly correlated to cycle volatility management. Insurers have a difficult time redeploying their assets, since they are essentially intellectual assets with a large degree of task specificity and stickiness. Insurers also suffer from extensive reporting lags and potentially mismatched revenue and expense. It could be argued that part of the impetus driving insurers to continue to write business at inadequate prices is the need to fund current-year fixed costs ("plant" expenses).

Some other examples of strategic risks using the Slywotzky and Drzik framework are:

- (Competitor) Entrance into new (or significant growth in existing) lines or territories with inadequate underwriting expertise, pricing systems, price monitoring capabilities, policy servicing capabilities, understanding of regulatory requirements, claims handling staff, etc.

- (Project) Mergers or acquisitions entered into without contemplating integration costs or timelines, cultural incompatibilities, reserve deficiencies, etc.

- (Competitor) Destructive competition from multiple competitors simultaneously targeting the same market segment (unilateral planning, failure to anticipate strategic changes of competitors).

- (Stagnation) Flawed organizational response plans to market price cycles, including maintaining premium volume and market share during price declines, and improper performance incentives for underwriters.

- Planning (particularly plan loss ratio setting) process not fully integrated to internal financial indicators, external benchmarks, which fails to update, susceptible to systematic optimism.

Strategic Risk Management and Scenario Planning

Effective strategic risk management begins with scenario planning. Schoemaker [6] wrote a seminal paper on scenario planning, "Scenario Planning: A Tool for Strategic Thinking." He describes several key characteristics of scenario planning:

- The range of future outcomes is simplified into a limited number of possible states called scenarios, each of which tells a story of how various elements might interact under certain conditions.
- Scenarios are tested for internal consistency and plausibility.
- The scenarios are used to explore the joint impact of various uncertainties.
- Scenarios change several variables at one time, trying to capture the new states that will develop after major shocks or deviations in key variables.
- Scenarios are more than just simulation output. They include subjective interpretations of factors that often cannot be explicitly modeled.

Schoemaker summarizes as follows: "In short, scenario planning attempts to capture the richness and range of possibilities, stimulating decision makers to consider changes they would otherwise ignore."

Schoemaker outlines the key steps in the scenario planning process:

1. Define the scope – time frame and scope of analysis (geographic, product segments).
2. Identify the major stakeholders – customers, suppliers, competitors, employees, shareowners and regulators.
3. Identify basic trends – include their influence on the organization.
4. Identify key uncertainties – unknown leverage points of impact.
5. Construct initial scenario themes – combine key elements.
6. Check for consistency and plausibility – are trends compatible within the chosen timeframe? Do the outcomes fit together? Are major stakeholders placed in realistic positions?
7. Develop learning scenarios – the goal is to identify themes that are strategically relevant. Naming the scenarios is also important.
8. Identify research needs – flesh out the understanding of trends and uncertainties.
9. Develop quantitative models – assess whether certain interactions should be formalized via a quantitative model.
10. Evolve toward decision scenarios – iterative process to converge to scenarios used to test strategies and generate new ideas.

Scenario Planning – Insurance Example

Clearly, scenario planning represents a significant departure from typical industry planning practice. However, an insurer could implement a rudimentary form of scenario planning. The prerequisite leap would involve moving from one detailed but almost certainly wrong plan to a set of less detailed plans based on key scenarios. Scenario planning is a first-order approximation of the range of possible states of the world.

The best place to try scenario planning at an insurer would be in the process used to determine the plan portfolio mix, defined as the planned combinations of written premium and corresponding written loss ratios by line of business. Loss ratio will be a function of price level. We will assume the company can accurately monitor price *changes* on renewal business.

Traditional Unilateral Planning Approach

A traditional insurer planning exercise begins by defining key plan components (by line of business):

- Base loss ratio
- Cost trend
- Price change
- Target premium volume
- Loss ratio

This plan is built upon "plan estimates," which arguably should be unbiased, realistic expectations but may be more optimistic due to the pressing need to meet overall corporate profit or premium volume targets. Once developed and presented to senior management, "the plan" can often take on a life of its own. Managers are reluctant to deviate from plan, despite market conditions. Underwriting units want to "make their plan numbers," by any means necessary, which creates pressure to book plan targets despite market realities. What may have initially been intended as a summary of bottom-up, reality-based figures can become an institutionalized fiction that requires enormous energy to maintain against the inevitable tide of financial reality.

To demonstrate the risk to the organization of the traditional planning approach, we will isolate our focus on one line of business (LOB):

- Base loss ratio   80%
- Cost trend   6%
- Price change   0%
- Target premium volume $100M
- Plan loss ratio   84.8% = 80% * (1.06)

With the best of intentions, it is likely that regardless of how the underwriting year plays out, the message to ownership and the initial financials will be very close to these figures. For example, if *actual* price change is -10 percent, the following may still occur:

- Recorded price change   0%
- Written premium volume $100M
- Recorded loss ratio   84.8% (based on 0% price change)
- Actual loss ratio   94.2% = 84.8% / (1.0 – 10%)

Not only will the company now have an unforeseen reserve deficit, it may have an overall portfolio mix that is not what it intended. In other words, had the leadership known at planning time that this LOB would be priced at a 94.2 percent loss ratio, it may have wanted far less volume – perhaps $50 million rather than $100 million. It may even have issued an edict to hold price and let premium volume fall where it may. However, without having thought through the possibilities, whatever responses they ended up with were an aggregate result of various bottom-up decisions. The commitment to one (and only one) plan leads to organizational inertia, inflexibility that is unrealistic and potentially detrimental to the firm.

Basic Scenario Planning (SP) Example

Consider the planning for our LOB under SP. The single point estimate for price change would be expanded as follows:

Scenario	Price Change	Likelihood
Optimistic	+5%	10%
Realistic	0%	50%
Pessimistic	-10%	40%

SP requires the firm to decide in advance:

- The possible range of outcomes or scenarios, with relative likelihood; and
- Its responses should each scenario come to pass.

The (controllable) decision variables are price change and premium volume. They are interlinked, of course, by the demand curve. For example, the firm could produce something like this:

Price Change	Likelihood	Response Plans
+5%	10%	$150M @ +5% (ride the wave)
0%	50%	$100M @ 0% (as expected)
-10%	40%	$50M @ -10% (bail out)

The three response plans would need to be laid out in enough detail to give them sufficient operational weight to drive decision making and behavior. That is, the firm would produce a "set of optional plans," one of which would be activated based on how market conditions play out. In concert with this, the firm would need market monitors to assess which scenario appears to be playing out.

Several advantages are gained from this small change:

- The company thinks through responses beforehand. They can prescreen and agree on the best response. They can also save time during crises by having strategic action plans laid out and ready for use.

- Organizational inertia is reduced, because a degree of flexibility is now built into the system. The unrealistic urge to "make the numbers" at all costs is reduced.

The resulting portfolio mix is tailored to the market realities that emerge.

Model Expansion

Expanding the example, the firm would develop a combined scenario set including all lines of business. A great deal of coordination would be required by the corporate planning team to craft the LOB perspectives into credible, internally consistent corporate scenario sets. Of particular interest is the inclusion of co-movement potential (e.g., market shocks, multiline price deterioration). The response plans will also be more politically charged, as limited underwriting capacity must be allotted across the organization. While this capacity allotment will be difficult, it is better for the organization to go through this during a scenario planning process than in the heat of a market crisis.

Advanced Scenario Planning and Enterprise Risk Modeling

Scenarios are really manually constructed equivalents to generated simulations from an ERM model. Over time, as firms grow more comfortable and skilled in their modeling efforts, their ERM models should produce rich, credible sets of scenarios. The scenarios, in turn, open up the possibility of dynamic strategy testing. That is, the firm can use its ERM model to determine the most effective decision making approach, where effectiveness can be tested across a broad spectrum of simulated scenarios. This use of ERM modeling represents proactive strategic risk mitigation, even strategic reward maximization.

There are examples of such strategy testing in asset risk management. Asset strategies are tested by simulating the returns of portfolios selected by different strategies. Each strategy is represented as a set of asset selection rules. These rules are repeatedly applied to "rebalance" the portfolio in response to the environment changes as the simulated scenario progresses. Examples of rebalancing activities might include selling bonds that have matured, reducing allocation to an asset class that has appreciated in value relative to other classes or buying more taxable or tax-exempt investments in response to portfolio tax position. This process is repeated for each strategy, for each scenario. The "best" portfolio is the one whose distribution of total returns is valued most highly. The evaluation can be based on both reward goals and risk constraints.

The first step in strategy testing is the capture and encoding of essential environmental variables necessary to determine the "state of the world" and, therefore, ultimately used to select the course of action.

Users must also define performance quality in terms of desirable goals (e.g., net income, economic value) and undesirable downside constraints (e.g., maximum tail-value-at-risk).

Finally, the user must specify action rules that describe portfolio responses to market environment changes. As an example, a strategy to "hold price" would respond to market price decreases by holding firm to price and losing substantial premium volume and market share. Another strategy example might be the allocation of underwriting capacity based on anticipated price adequacy levels. The key is to express these responses as a set of mathematical rules that the simulation model can convert into portfolio changes.

Agent-Based Modeling and Strategic Interaction Effects

The process just described represents unilateral strategy testing – testing of one market participant's strategic actions in a static market environment. There is another dimension of strategic risk that cannot be captured in such an approach – the risk of negative impacts due to the interaction effects of many market participants executing their strategies simultaneously.

Capturing the dynamics of simultaneous action requires agent-based modeling (ABM). ABM is a method for studying systems composed of interacting "agents" – independent entities capable of assessing the environment, selecting courses of action and effecting change on the environment based on those selected courses. Complex systems also have what are called "emergent properties" – qualities or characteristics that arise from the interactions of the agents. Typically, one cannot predict these properties simply by aggregating the properties of the individual member agents.

The real quantum leap in strategic risk assessment comes from modeling strategic interaction effects in a simulated insurance market populated with "insurer agents" following various strategies. Some could be disciplined technical pricers, while others could chase market share. The user could then test the likely impact on the market, and on its own results, of following various strategies. This exercise goes farther than previous strategic risk assessments by including the interaction effects of multiple agents competing.

As an example, a user might plan (in isolation) to target a market segment identified (using public information) as profitable. It could develop detailed plans of how much premium it will write at what profitable loss ratio. Such a plan sounds viable in principle and looks good on paper. However, it may fail to factor in the possibility that many competitors have come to the same conclusion regarding this market segment (as the information is public). If all these competitors commit to growth in that segment, the competition will lead to price decreases that (ironically) undermine the profitability that made the segment attractive in the first place.

Summary

What we have outlined here is the beginning of strategic risk management for insurers. Clearly, there is significant organizational learning and change required, as well as education of key stakeholders regarding the new landscape. However, it is our contention that this effort will be rewarded with superior operating performance.

Insurance Hazard Modeling

5.1 Severity and Frequency Distributions

By Steven B. White, FCAS, MAAA and Gary G. Venter, FCAS, MAAA

The textbook "Loss Distributions" [3] provides a thorough introduction to frequency and severity distributions used in insurance. We assume that text as background but may repeat some of it for perspective.

Severity Distributions

All of the severity distributions considered have closed form[44] densities and continuous distribution functions defined on all or part of the positive real numbers, although mass points can be added by policy limits, etc. All but one[45] distribution derives in some way from the incomplete beta function. Most of the distributions in the literature are related to the distributions listed here, all of which were introduced to the insurance literature in Venter [8] and independently to the economics literature in McDonald[46] [6]. Klugman in [3] and its predecessors used Venter's terminology "transformed beta" for the parent distribution instead of the more compact GB2 that McDonald used in his textbook, so that name has somewhat stuck in the insurance discussions. But since White was a student of McDonald, we tend to use both terms.

Math Background

Background is included here for the two functions that go beyond simple arithmetic: the beta and gamma functions. The gamma function is the continuous interpolation of the factorial function b!. For some reason relating to mathematical elegance, this is shifted by 1 so $\Gamma(b+1) = b!$ for integer b. Also for integer b, $b! = b(b-1)!$, which is extended to $\Gamma(b+1) = b\Gamma(b)$ for any real[47] b other than non-positive integers. The formal definition is:

$$\Gamma(b) = \int_0^\infty y^{b-1} e^{-y} dy \qquad [5.1.1]$$

The incomplete gamma function at b and x is defined by taking the integral just up to x. Since the integrand is positive, this is an increasing function of x; so dividing the incomplete gamma by the gamma produces a probability distribution.

---

[44] Here the gamma function is considered to be closed form, but the incomplete gamma and beta are not.
[45] The inverse Gaussian, which also can be related but it is more of a stretch.
[46] McDonald has been the more devoted father, writing numerous papers featuring these distributions.
[47] The gamma function is infinite at negative integers, so this formula requires some construing there.

The beta function is the ratio $\beta(P,Q) = \Gamma(P)\Gamma(Q)/\Gamma(P+Q)$, which comes up often in combinatorics. It has two equivalent definitions as integrals, called beta type 1 and beta type 2. These are the integral from 0 to 1 of $y^{P-1}(1-y)^{Q-1}$, and the integral from 0 to ∞ of $y^{P-1}/(1+y)^{P+Q}$, respectively. The second one (B2) is more commonly used in insurance, since its support is the whole positive line. Again, taking the integral to x instead of ∞ gives an increasing function of x, which can be normalized to be a probability distribution. For P = 1, the beta integrals are just of powers of 1 – y or 1 + y, so they can be calculated in closed form. This leads to a number of closed form special cases.

The gamma function integral converges more quickly than the beta due to the negative exponential versus the inverse power function. This makes the distributions from the beta more heavily tailed in some sense.

The distributions are finally spelled out by taking a scale and power transform of x. That is, $(x/\theta)^\tau$ is taken to follow the beta or gamma distribution. This is where the terms transformed gamma, transformed beta and generalized B2, or GB2, arise.

Typical notation is to call the Q parameter α and the P parameter β. This leads to beta distributions whose moments exist in the interval $(-\beta\tau, \alpha\tau)$. This is not the convention Instrat® usually follows, however; so when we use that parameterization, we will replace τ by γ and call it the γ-parameterization. Our usual practice is to take P as β/τ and Q as α/τ. This gives moments in the range $(-\beta, \alpha)$. Doing this consistently allows immediate interpretation of the α and β parameters of any distribution shown. As will be discussed shortly, this holds for the gamma-based distributions as well, as they are limiting cases of the beta. The shortcoming is that arriving at P=1 requires setting $\tau = \beta$, which is not always as easy to interpret. Since τ is the power parameter, it is sometimes clearer to see it in the formula instead of replacing it with β.

Limiting and Special Cases of the Transformed Beta

The limiting cases are quite clear in the τ-parameterization, however. When $\alpha \to \infty$, the transformed beta becomes a power transformed gamma distribution, for which all positive moments exist. The reciprocal of a beta variate is a beta with switched parameters, which leads to the fact that when $\beta \to \infty$, the transformed beta becomes a distribution of a variable whose reciprocal follows the transformed gamma. This is called the inverse transformed gamma. For it, all negative moments exist, but the positive moments stop at α. This much was known in the original papers, and McDonald even showed that when both α and $\beta \to \infty$, the lognormal results. All positive and negative moments exist for the lognormal. The F with 2α and 2β degrees of freedom is the generalized Pareto (transformed beta with $\tau=1$), with $\theta=\alpha/\beta$.

What the τ-notation makes clear is what happens when $\tau \to \infty$. The transformed beta density in this notation is a normalizing constant times $x^{\beta-1}[1+(x/\theta)^{\tau}]^{(\alpha+\beta)/\tau}$. The term in brackets goes to 1 if $x<\theta$, while the 1 can be ignored in the limit if $x>\theta$. This shows the limit is the split simple Pareto, which is a power curve below θ and the simple Pareto above θ. Figure 5.1.1 plots out the limiting cases. The special cases are a little easier with the γ-parameters, and these are shown in Figure 5.1.2. The transformed gamma also has special cases, which are the gamma, Weibull and exponential; and all of these have inverses that are special cases of the inverse transformed gamma. The chi-square distribution is just a form of the gamma.

The transformed beta with both τ and $\beta \to \infty$ is the simple Pareto, which has support only on $x>\theta$. This is a limiting case of both the split simple Pareto and the inverse transformed gamma. Figure 5.1.3 illustrates this. The power including the uniform is its inverse.

FIGURE 5.1.1: LIMITING CASES OF TRANSFORMED BETA DISTRIBUTION
(Inverse- Transformed Gamma, Split Simple Pareto, Transformed Gamma, Simple Pareto = Inverse Power, Power Distribution, Lognormal)

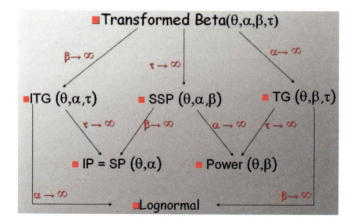

FIGURE 5.1.2: SPECIAL CASES OF TRANSFORMED BETA DISTRIBUTION
(Burr, Generalized F = Generalized Pareto, Inverse Burr, Paralogistic, Pareto, Inverse Pareto, Inverse Paralogistic, Loglogistic)

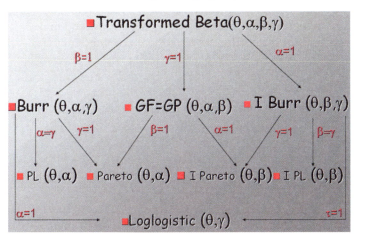

FIGURE 5.1.3: INVERSE TRANSFORMED GAMMA AND SPLIT SIMPLE PARETO

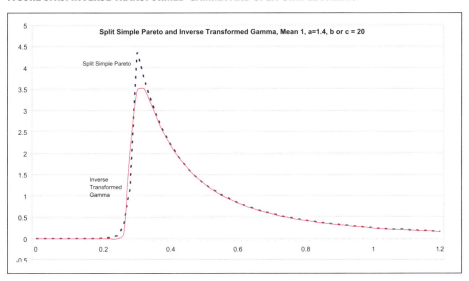

The generalized beta distribution, which is called the GB1 by McDonald, is based on the beta type 1 function previously mentioned $y^{P-1}(1-y)^{Q-1}$; while applying the same transformation $(x/\theta)^\tau$ as used in the transformed beta and transformed gamma distributions. That is, $(x/\theta)^\tau$ is taken to follow the beta type 1. The generalized beta parameters τ, η and θ correspond directly with the A, Q and B parameters of the GB1. The generalized beta β parameter has the same transformation as the β parameter in the transformed beta where β/τ is equal to the P parameter in the GB1.

The GB1 is different from the transformed beta and transformed gamma in that it is not defined over all positive values. It is defined in the range $0 \leq x \leq \theta$. Since there is an upper bound to the possible losses, the distribution is defined to have all positive moments and gives moments in the range $(-\beta, \infty)$. Also, since there is a theoretical upper bound to the losses, the GB1-based distributions tend to be short tailed. This can be useful for distributions where there is an upper bound to the possible losses and is commonly used to define the damage ratios used by some of the catastrophe model vendors.

Limiting cases of the GB1 include the transformed gamma as $\eta \to \infty$, which will also include the lognormal as a limiting case since it is a limiting case of the transformed gamma. Special cases of the GB1 include the power distribution when $\tau=1$ and $\eta=1$ and the uniform distribution, shown in Figure 5.1.4, which is the power distribution when $\beta=1$.

The inverse of the GB1 can be used when there is a logical lower bound to a loss distribution that is greater than zero. Limiting cases of the inverse GB1 include the inverse transformed gamma as $\alpha \to \infty$. The simple Pareto is a special case when $\tau=1$ and $\beta=1$. So this provides for a nice generalization of the simple Pareto.

FIGURE 5.1.4: UNIFORM AS A LIMIT OF τ AND $\alpha \to \infty$

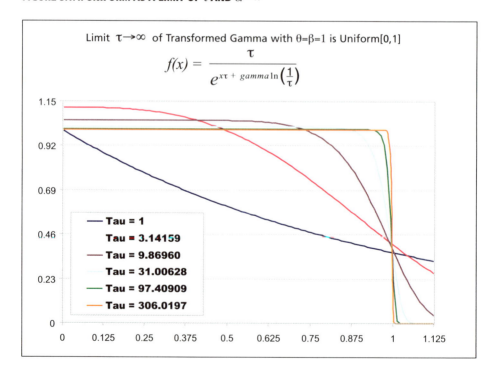

Other special cases are the folded versions of popular distributions on the whole real line. A symmetric distribution with mode 0 can be folded to be on the positive line only. That is, the density function is started at zero and is doubled on the positive line. Unfolding is accomplished by adding or subtracting half of the folded CDF from 1/2, depending on whether or not x is positive. For instance, by using the Excel function BETADIST for the GB1, the student's t distribution function with v degrees of freedom is:

$$F_{tv}(X) = \tfrac{1}{2} + \tfrac{1}{2} \, sign \, (X) BETADIST[1/(1+v/x^2), \tfrac{1}{2}, v/2]. \quad [5.1.2]$$

Unfolding the folded normal, which is a transformed gamma special case, gives the normal distribution:

$$\Phi^{\Delta}(x) = \tfrac{1}{2} + \tfrac{1}{2} \, sign \, (X) GAMMADIST[x^2/2, \tfrac{1}{2}, 1, 1], \quad [5.1.3]$$

again using Excel's function.

Interpreting the Parameters

Omitting normalizing constants, the transformed beta in the τ-parameters can be written:

$$F(X) \propto (x/\theta)^{\beta-1} \div \left[1 + (x/\theta)^{\tau}\right]^{\tfrac{\alpha+\beta}{\tau}} \quad [5.1.4]$$

What do these parameters do? We already know that moments exist in $(-\beta, \alpha)$. That means in effect that α determines the heaviness of the tail, and β determines the shape of the distribution and the behavior near zero. It turns out that τ can move around the middle, while θ is just a scaling parameter.

Alpha (α)

Positive moments $E(X^k)$ exist only for $k < \alpha$. Thus, α determines the tail heaviness, with smaller α giving a heavier tail. The ballasted Pareto

$$F(x) = 1 - \left(1 + x/\theta\right)^{-\alpha} \quad [5.1.5]$$

will be used to illustrate tail heaviness, as it is easy to deal with and has the same tail heaviness as the general case.

One way to measure tail heaviness is to look at the ratio of a high percentile to the median. For a large company, say with 50,000 expected claims, a fairly large claim would be one of the five largest – say the 1/10,000 probability claim. The Pareto 1 - 1/Bth percentile is $\theta (B^{1/\alpha} - 1)$. At B =10,000; this is $\theta (10^{4/\alpha} - 1)$. The ratio of this percentile to the median (B=2) is $(10^{4/\alpha} - 1)/(2^{1/\alpha} - 1)$. This is very sensitive to α, especially for α between 1 and 2, where it often is. The ratio of the fairly large claim to the median is 9254 when $\alpha=1.01$, while it is a considerably lower 788 when $\alpha=1.5$. Thus, the estimate of α could have a big impact on excess loss probabilities.

FIGURE 5.1.5: DENSITY BEHAVIOR NEAR ZERO

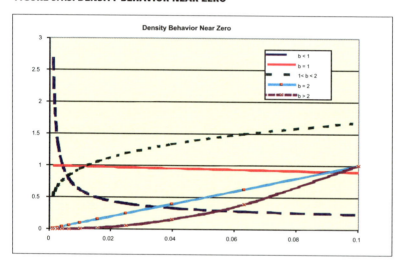

Beta (β)

Negative moments $E[(1/X)^k]$ exist just for $k<\beta$. The beta parameter governs the behavior of the distribution near 0. In that region, the density is close to a constant times $(x/\theta)^{\beta-1}$, so the derivative of the density is proportional to $(\beta-1)x^{\beta-2}$. This can be used to ascertain the shape of the density for smaller claims, which really determines the overall shape of the distribution. If $\beta<1$, the slope of the density at zero is negative infinity; so the density is asymptotic to the vertical axis. For $\beta=1$, the slope is a negative number, due to the constant of proportionality (not shown). The mode of the distribution is at zero in both of these cases. For $1<\beta<2$, the slope at zero is positive infinity; so the density is rising and tangent to the vertical axis. For $\beta=2$, the slope is a positive number, and for $\beta>2$, the slope is zero; so the density is tangent to the horizontal axis. For $\beta>1$, then, there is a positive mode.

Figure 5.1.5 shows the behavior near zero and how that depends on β. In this and other graphs, α, β ,τ are labeled a, b, c. Since the right tail is an inverse power curve, the behavior near zero determines the overall look of the distribution. The case β>2 gives the usual shape of a density function people think of, which rises gradually then more steeply before falling off with the inverse power relationship.

The transformed beta, in this case, looks like a heavy-tailed lognormal. The case β=1 is also seen a lot, for instance, in the exponential and ballasted Pareto distributions.

Tau (τ)

The τ parameter introduces a power transform x→x^τ into the transformed beta. This transformation tends to move the middle of the distribution around. A useful measure of where the middle is is the mode, as related to the mean. The ratio of mode to mean, when the mean exists (α>1) and the mode is positive (β>1), is for the most part an increasing function of τ for fixed α and β. Figure 5.1.6 shows the mode-to-mean function when α=1.4 and β=2; and Figure 5.1.7 shows the same function for the same α for the inverse transformed gamma, which is the limit of the transformed beta as β goes to infinity.

FIGURE 5.1.6: INVERSE TRANSFORMED GAMMA MODE-TO-MEAN FUNCTION

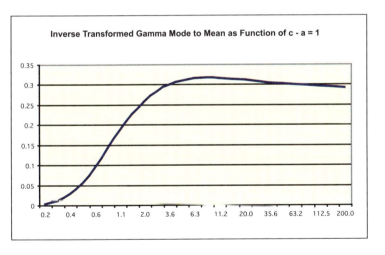

FIGURE 5.1.7: TRANSFORMED BETA MODE-TO-MEAN FUNCTION

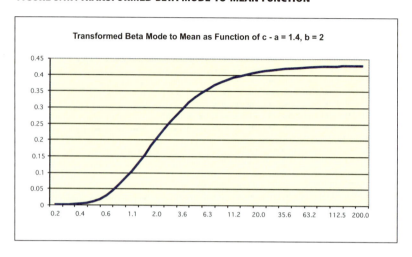

The value of α in Figures 5.1.6 and 5.1.7 is large enough to have some cases with a reasonably high mode – for example, 40 percent of the mean – but α is still small enough to be of potential use in U.S. liability insurance. For $\beta=2$, the ratio is a strictly increasing function of τ. For the limiting case of $\beta=\infty$, the ratio reaches a peak and then declines slightly. This is also the behavior for large values of β.

Since it is mostly an increasing function of τ, something near the highest value of the mode-to-mean ratio for a given α and β is provided by the limit of the transformed beta as τ goes to infinity. This is the split simple Pareto distribution. Its density f(x) is proportional to $(x/\theta)^{\beta-1}$ for x<θ and to $(x/\theta)^{-\alpha-1}$ for x>θ. The density is continuous but not differentiable at θ, which is the mode when $\beta > 1$. The mean is $\theta\alpha\beta/[(\beta+1)(\alpha-1)]$. Thus, the ratio of mode-to-mean is $(\alpha-1)(\beta+1)/\alpha\beta = (1-1/\beta)(1+1/\alpha)$. This is increasing in α and decreasing in β.

For low values of α, the mode-to-mean ratio cannot get very high; as the mean is increased by the heavy tail. The ratio for the split Pareto distribution is close to the upper limit for the transformed beta with a given α and β; so for low values of α, the τ parameter is not going to be able to have much effect on the mode for any transformed beta distribution.

The ratio declines for increasing β, but rather slowly. It is paradoxical that for this limiting distribution, the maximum mode-to-mean ratio is as β approaches 1; while for the transformed beta, the mode is zero at $\beta=1$. The split simple Pareto at $\beta=1$ is the uniform Pareto, which is uniform up to θ and Pareto after that. Thus, its mode is undefined, or it could be considered to be the whole interval [0, θ].

To illustrate the effect of the τ parameter, and thus the mode, on the density function, several cases are illustrated in Figure 5.1.8. All the distributions have α=2, β=3 and mean=1. Thus, it is τ that is moving the mode around. The mode is seen to increase with τ.

FIGURE 5.1.8: EFFECT OF THE TAU PARAMETER

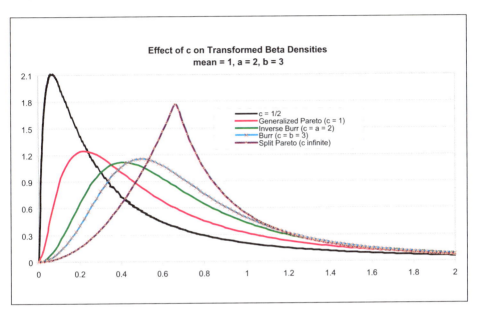

Another effect of low values of τ can be to increase the tails, even though this might not show up in moments. An interesting example is the Weibull distribution, for which α is infinite; so all positive moments exist, and β=τ. Taking β=τ=0.2 gives a fairly heavy-tailed distribution for which all positive moments exist. This has been traditionally used in the U.S. workers compensation line. As an example, take θ=100, with a mean of 12,000. In this case, the pretty large loss ñ 1-in-10,000 claim ñ is 6.6 million, or 550 times the mean. This is heavier-tailed by this measure than most Pareto distributions. For instance, with α=1.4, this ratio is 287. The cv^2 for this Weibull distribution is 251, so the cv itself is almost 16. For contrast, a lognormal with the same mean and cv would have the 1-in-10,000 loss about 4,750,000. The Weibull has another strange feature, however. As β is so small, negative moments do not exist except for powers closer to zero than -0.2. This means that a lot of the distribution is packed in towards zero. In fact, about 33 percent of the claims are less than 1, and the median claim is 16. The comparable lognormal, which can be given in the limit of α and β both going to infinity, has only 0.2 percent of its claims at less than 1, even though the mode is 3. The median claim is 756 for this distribution.

A small τ can pump up the tail of the transformed beta as well. For instance, taking α=1.4 and β=τ=0.2 gives a Burr distribution where the 1-in-10,000 claim is 910 times the mean, and more than 50 percent of the claims are below 1/12,000th of the mean. Keeping this value of τ, but letting β get larger, can allow the fairly large claim to be a high multiple of the mean without so many small claims. For instance, taking β=1, the fairly large loss is 795 times the mean, and only 7 percent of claims are below $1 when the mean is $12,000. Taking β up to 5, keeping α=1.4 and τ=0.2, these numbers come down to 673 times and 0.1 percent, which is still very heavy tailed without pushing so many claims to unrealistically small sizes. Although this distribution has a positive mode, it is at 0.065 percent of the mean, or 7.8 for a mean of 12,000, so it is close to zero.

Theta (θ)

The parameter θ is a scaling factor. Its effect is just like rescaling the x-axis. For instance, to convert a distribution expressed in British pounds to Canadian dollars, just multiply the scale parameter by 3 (for example). Then a probability for an amount expressed in Canadian dollars would be the same as for the equivalent amount expressed in British pounds.

In the GB1 distribution, interpretation of the τ and β is similar to the transformed beta. The θ parameter is a linear scaling of the distribution, with the added meaning of providing an upper bound to the curve. The η parameter is similar to the α in the transformed beta in that it defined the right-tail behavior of the curve; but where α defines the behavior around ∞, η defines the behavior about the upper bound θ.

Where Did β and τ Go?

Several two-parameter cases of the transformed beta have just the α and θ parameters. To understand what they are doing, it is helpful to know how β and τ were disposed of. Some examples:

- Ballasted Pareto: β=τ=1, so moments in (-1, α), mode zero. Closed form and invertible.

- Loglogistic: α=β=τ, so moments in (-α,α), and thus the mode is positive if the mean exists, but is probably fairly small with a low steepness. Closed form and invertible.

- Inverse Weibull: β infinite, τ=α, also closed form and invertible for simulation. Mode is always positive.

- Inverse Gamma: β infinite, τ=1, so mode is positive but usually less than for inverse Weibull. Not closed form.

- Simple Pareto: β=τ=infinity, so positive mode, infinite steepness, F(mode) = 0. The opposite extreme from the ballasted Pareto for β and τ. Invertible.

- Uniform Pareto: τ infinite, β=1. Mode ambiguous – whole range from 0 to θ is uniform. Intermediate between ballasted and simple Pareto and mirror image of inverse gamma in parameters. Invertible.

Frequency Distributions

The most commonly used frequency distributions in claim modeling are the Poisson and negative binomial distributions.

The Poisson distribution has a variance equal to the mean. The probability (P) of k claims under a Poisson distribution is given by the density formula:

$$P_k = \frac{\lambda^k e^{-\lambda}}{k!} \qquad k=0, 1, 2, \ldots \qquad [5.1.6]$$

In the usual parameterization of the negative binomial, the variance is a fixed multiple of, but greater than, the mean. Negative binomial distributions are in the (a,b,0) class, which means that for k>0, there are values a and b so that probabilities follow the recursive relationship $p_k = (a+b/k)p_{k-1}$. It has two positive parameters, r and β, with mean = rβ and variance = rβ(1+β). Probabilities are given by $p_0 = (1+β)^{-r}$ and in the recursion a = β/(1+β) and b =(r-1)a.

This parameterization of the negative binomial can be derived as a Poisson distribution with an uncertain λ distribution, where the distribution of λ follows a gamma distribution. A different means of looking at the negative binomial is viewing it as a Poisson distribution with contagion, which is explained by Heckman/Meyers [2]. One improvement of this method over the standard view is that it has the negative binomial variance to mean ratio defined as an increasing function of the expected number of claims rather than a fixed static value. A fixed or static variance-to-mean ratio typically understates the true volatility of claims as the number of claims increases.

This parameterization of the negative binomial relates the parameters to a change in exposure units. If you assume that β is fixed and r = qn for some fixed q when there are n exposure units, then the expected number of claims is βqn, and the variance is βqn(1+β), with a variance-to-mean ratio of 1+β. If, on the other hand, you assume that r is fixed and β = qn, then the mean is rqn and the variance is rqn(1+qn), with variance/mean = 1+qn, which increases with n.

There is a quite useful three-parameter frequency distribution that has a great deal of flexibility in matching the first three moments. This is called the Poisson extended truncated negative binomial (PETNB), which takes a bit of explaining. Zero-truncated frequency distributions are formed from regular frequency distributions by replacing the probability of no claims by zero and spreading the original probability at zero proportionally to all the other probabilities. When this is done for the negative binomial, the range of possible parameters is somewhat expanded, giving the extended truncated negative binomial (ETNB). If there is a Poisson distribution of number of events, and an extended truncated negative binomial distribution of number of claims per event, the compound distribution is the Poisson extended truncated negative binomial.

To be more specific, the ETNB distribution has two parameters, r and β. For the NB, these have to be positive but r can be positive or in (-1, 0). That is the extended part. Probabilities for the distribution are defined by $p_0 = 0$, $p_1 = \beta r/[(1+\beta)^{r+1}-1-\beta]$ and for k>1, $p_k = p_{k-1}[1+(r-1)/k]\beta/(1+\beta)$.

For the PETNB with Poisson λ, the first three moments are given by:

$$mean = \mu = \lambda r\beta/[1-(1+\beta)^{-r}]$$
$$variance = \sigma^2 = \mu\{1+\beta+r\beta\}$$
$$E([N-EN]^3) = \mu_3 = \mu + \beta(1+3\mu)(1+r)+\beta \quad [5.1.7]$$

From the empirical moments, the parameters can be solved as:

$$r = 1/[(\mu_3 - 3\sigma^2 + 2\mu)\mu/(\sigma^2 - \mu)^2 - 1] - 1$$
$$\beta = (\sigma^2/\mu - 1)/(1+r) \quad [5.1.8]$$
$$\lambda = [1-(1+\beta)^{-r}]\mu/r\beta.$$

The probabilities are calculated by a recursive scheme, which is the Panjer [4] recursion for the Poisson, namely: for ETNB probabilities as p_k

$$p_0 = 0, p_1 = \beta r/[(1+\beta)^{r+1}-1-\beta]$$
$$p_k = p_{k-1}\beta(r+k-1)/[k(1+\beta)], \; k = 2,3,... \quad [5.1.9]$$

PETNB probabilities are denoted as g_k

$$g_0 = e^{-\lambda}$$
$$g_k = (\lambda/k)\sum_{j=1}^{k} jp_j g_{k-j} \quad [5.1.10]$$

Estimation of Loss Distributions

Elementary methods of parameter estimation for distributions involve matching some features of the distribution, such as moments or percentiles. Moment matching actually does not seem too bad for frequency distributions, but it is inefficient for severity. For instance, Brazauskas and Serfling [1] calculated for a Pareto distribution with reasonably large samples; a sample size 80 percent larger is needed for moment matching to give the same degree of accuracy as maximum likelihood estimation (MLE) would give for the original sample. Thus MLE has become the standard estimation method for severity distributions.

The likelihood function L for a sample and a distribution, evaluated at a set of parameters, is the conditional probability of a sample of that size being the exact sample drawn, given those parameters. This is usually a small number, in the underflow range, so typically the log-likelihood function l is used. For individual exact observations, the contribution is the density at that value. If all that is known is that the value is in a range, the probability of being in that range is the contribution. This includes the case where the range is infinite, as where the claim has been censored by a policy limit. If the claims are subject to a deductible, then claims below the deductible are not observed; so the individual and range probabilities are all conditional on the claim being higher than the deductible. That is, they are divided by 1 – F (deductible).

The optimality of MLE is known for large samples, but nothing better is known in general; so it is typically used for small samples as well. However, for some particular distributions, small sample results are known. For instance, for the simple Pareto $F(x)=1 - (x/\theta)^{-\alpha}$, the MLE for α if θ is known is $1/\text{average}[\ln(x_i/\theta)]$. For a sample of size n, the MLE estimate is inverse gamma distributed[48] with scale parameter $n\alpha$ and shape parameter n. This has mean $n\alpha/(n-1)$. Thus, the MLE estimate of the simple Pareto α is biased upwards by a factor of $n/(n-1)$. Asymptotically, this washes out as the factor approaches unity, so the properties of MLE hold. But if the sample is small, the bias could have an impact.

Parameter Uncertainty

Also asymptotically, the covariance matrix of the parameters is the matrix inverse of the information matrix, which is the matrix of second derivatives of the negative loglikelihood with respect to the parameters at the maximum point. There, the first derivatives would all be zero and the second derivatives negative. The distribution of the parameters is asymptotically multivariate normal, with the MLE estimate as the mean and this covariance matrix.

In the simple Pareto case, this distribution is the inverse gamma, which is heavy-tailed, but eventually approaches the normal. The normal distribution has positive probability at negative values, while the inverse gamma does not.

---

48 Ln(x) is exponential, the sum of exponentials is gamma, with an inverse gamma reciprocal.

An approach we have found fruitful is to use a lognormal distribution for the parameter uncertainty for the parameters that are always positive, based on the covariance matrix from the information matrix. This also approaches the normal for large samples, but stays positive and has been found to be closer than the normal to the right distribution in other cases. A formal approach to this would be to reparameterize each distribution before fitting so that the new parameters are the exponentials of the old ones. Then the asymptotic theory would give joint lognormal distributions for the original parameters.

To help visualize parameter distributions, Figure 5.1.9 shows the joint normal density and its contours for a ballasted Pareto fit to a severity sample. The parameters are correlated, so a diagonal effect is apparent. Basically, there is some ambiguity between high mean with heavy tail and high mean with light tail for the ballasted Pareto sample used.

FIGURE 5.1.9: JOINT DISTRIBUTION OF PARETO PARAMETERS

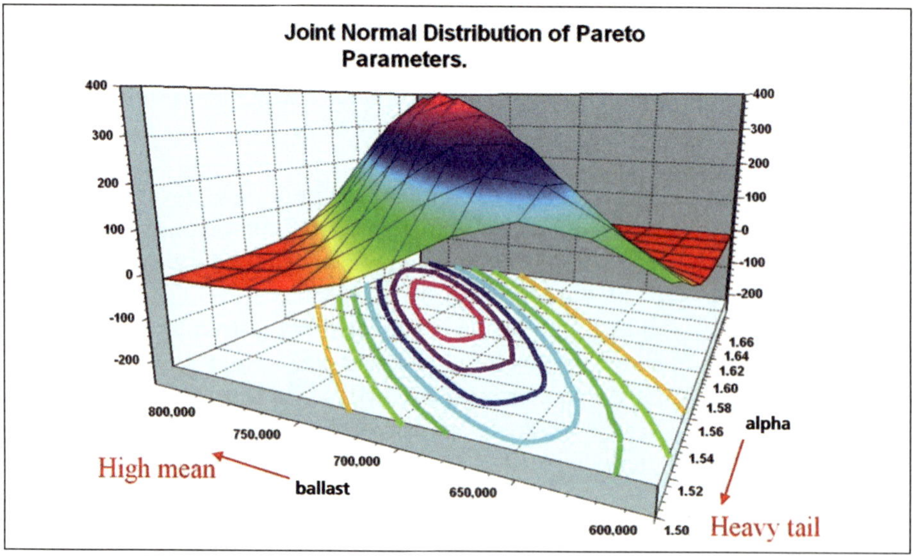

The delta method is a way to get a variance estimate for a function of the estimated parameters, such as the mean or a percentile of the distribution. The vector of derivatives of the function with respect to the parameters is needed. Then the covariance matrix of the parameters is multiplied on the left and on the right by that vector. The resulting scalar is the variance estimate. Asymptotically, a normal distribution can be assumed for the function, but for small samples a lognormal may be more appropriate. Because of the correlation of the parameters, some functions of the parameters might have a lower variance than the parameters themselves. Percentiles of the distribution are often in this category.

Comparing Fits

The loglikelihood function can also be used to compare fits of different distributions, as long as there is an appropriate adjustment for the number of parameters. The Akaike Information Criterion (AIC) is the starting point. This is defined as AIC = -2 log(L) + 2p, where p is the number of parameters. Maximizing (L) means minimizing AIC. It is often convenient to maximize –AIC/2. This is the loglikelihood minus the number of parameters – that is, you penalize each parameter by subtracting 1 from log(L). The AIC comes from information theory, and it represents an information distance between the model and the data. Taking its negative divided by 2 actually is the original interpretation of this statistic and gives a convenient way to compare models. Basically, each of the p parameters has to improve the loglikelihood by at least 1 to be worth keeping in the model.

Other information-theoretic work has extended the AIC. There is a suspicion that AIC understates the per-parameter penalty. The BIC (Schwartz Bayesian Information Criteria) is equivalent to penalizing each parameter by log($N^{1/2}$), where there are N points in the dataset. BIC penalizes additional parameters more for larger datasets. Our experience and some theory suggest that BIC may have gone too far. A compromise is the Hannan-Quinn Information Criterion (HQIC), which proposes a per-parameter penalty of log[log(N)]. For small samples (smaller than 40 times the number of parameters), the small sample correction for AIC, called AIC_C, has a fair amount of support. Here, the total penalty to the negative loglikelihood is Np/[N – p – 1]. This is inconvenient in that the per-parameter penalty depends on the number of parameters, but it appears to be the best supported measure for small samples. For large samples, the HQIC seems to be a reasonable compromise.

INFORMATION CRITERION	PENALTY TO LOG(L)
AIC	p log[e]
BIC	p log[√N]
HQIC	p log[log N]
AIC_C	p/[1 – (1+p)/N]

Bayesian Estimation

Bayes' Theorem follows directly from the definition of conditional distributions. That is, by definition, Pr(A&B) = Pr(A|B)Pr(B) = Pr(B|A)Pr(A). Thus, a single division shows that Pr(A|B) = Pr(B|A)Pr(A)/Pr(B). Since the conditional distribution of A has to integrate to 1, terms that do not involve A can be omitted and put in later by figuring what constant factor is needed to make the integral 1. Thus we can express Bayes' Theorem as Pr(A|B) ∝ Pr(B|A)Pr(A), where the curly little symbol stands for "is proportional to."

While the proportional form often simplifies the calculations of posterior distributions, it also leads to a whole new class of prior distributions, called "improper priors." The constant of proportionality is calculated as the reciprocal of the integral of Pr(B|A)Pr(A), which to work has to integrate to a finite number. But Pr(A) itself does not have to do so. If it doesn't, the prior is improper. An example is Pr(A) = 1 over an infinite range.

Usually, we are looking at the case where A is the parameter vector and B is the data. Then Pr(B|A) is the likelihood function at the parameters. Pr(A) is the prior distribution of the parameters. While it is not unusual to have some prior knowledge of the parameters of a distribution, there is a way to start a Bayesian analysis without such. This is by using so-called "non-informative" priors, which do not influence the estimation, but give a posterior distribution when Bayes' Theorem is applied. Non-informative priors are usually improper. The definition of non-informative is somewhat vague (but these are sometimes called vague priors) in that not influencing the estimation only makes sense in comparison to a specific estimation method.

As an example, consider the improper prior $f(\alpha) = 1/\alpha$ on $(0,\infty)$ for the α of the simple Pareto with θ known. Working through the calculation of the posterior, which is the likelihood function divided by α, finds that it is proportional to $\alpha^{N-1}e^{-\alpha N/b}$, where b is the MLE estimate of α, i.e., $b = 1/\text{average}[\ln(x_i/\theta)]$. This is just the gamma distribution for α, with shape parameter N and scale parameter b/N, so it has mean b. Thus the $1/\alpha$ prior is non-informative relative to MLE estimation of the simple Pareto. It turns out that the prior $1/\alpha^2$ gives the unbiased estimate (N–1)b/N, so it is non-informative relative to the bias-adjusted MLE. The prior distribution $1/\alpha$ is often non-informative relative to MLE for positive parameters. Its integral diverges in the region 0 to x and also in the region x to ∞, so it has an infinite pull up or down. On the other hand, $1/\alpha^2$ diverges on 0 to x, but not on x to ∞, so it has an overall downward pull on the parameter. For the simple Pareto that is just enough to compensate for the bias in MLE estimation.

Even though MLE is upwardly biased for the simple Pareto α, and a higher α gives a lighter-tailed distribution, the estimate of the expected cost of the losses above a given retention is also biased upwards in MLE. That arises because the excess cost is a highly nonlinear function of the parameter; and the estimates of α that are too low give higher excess costs sufficient to more than compensate for the estimates of α that are too high, even though those are enough to bias the parameter itself upward on the average. Correcting for the bias in the MLE estimate of α actually increases the bias in the estimate of excess losses.

Although it is customary to use the posterior mean as the parameter estimate, the median or mode could be used instead. The mean minimizes squared error, but in the end does that justify the mean? The median minimizes absolute error, and the mode minimizes a zero-one error function. For the simple Pareto with the $1/\alpha$ prior, the posterior mode is the bias-corrected estimate. Thus, that prior can be considered noninformative for the MLE if the posterior mode is used.

The prior $f(\alpha) = 1$ is improper and has infinite weight at both ends of the real line, so is usually a noninformative prior there (e.g., for the lognormal μ). But for parameters with positive support only, 1 exerts an upward pull on the posterior mean, so is not noninformative. This shows that just because a prior is improper does not mean that it is noninformative. It is useful to verify that the prior being used is noninformative in the specific estimation situation.

Robust Estimation

Given a sample from a Pareto distribution, MLE is the most efficient (lowest variance) method for estimating the parameters, asymptotically speaking. But if given a sample that may or may not be from a Pareto, in trying to find the best fitting Pareto to that sample, the efficiency falls apart. That is, estimating the right distribution is one of the conditions for MLE's optimality. Robust estimation looks for methods of estimation that will still be very efficient if you are in fact fitting the population distribution to a sample, but will still give reasonable results otherwise.

Two key concepts of robust estimation are the relative efficiency and the upper breakdown point. The relative efficiency of an estimation procedure is the relative sample size you would need to get the accuracy you get out of MLE, if in fact the sample were drawn from the distribution you are fitting. For instance, a relative efficiency of 98 percent would mean that if in fact you are sampling from the distribution you are fitting, you could get the same accuracy you are getting with your procedure if you had a sample 98 percent of the size of the sample you have and you used MLE.

The upper breakdown point is the lowest observation in the sample such that you could increase it and all larger observations to any degree and not change the estimate, expressed as the percent of the sample that is already that size or larger. For MLE, this is 0 percent.

Brazauskas and Serfling explore several classes of robust estimators. One is the generalized median, which is the median of the MLE estimators of all subsets of the data of a given size, such as three or four claims. For a particular example, they find an estimator that has a relative efficiency of 98 percent and an upper breakdown point of 7 percent and another with a relative efficiency of 88 percent and an upper breakdown point of 21 percent of the observations.

Robust estimation can be viewed as a treatment of outliers. The problem is that in many insurance and reinsurance applications, the largest claims are the most important to estimate; and so it seems undesirable to reduce their influence on the parameters. On the other hand, robust estimation does not remove the large points – it just allows them to be even larger without affecting the estimates.

Including Exposure Information and Multiple Deductibles

When there is a deductible, MLE estimates the parameters of the ground-up distribution by using conditional probabilities in the likelihood function. But when there are several different deductibles with different amounts of business written for each, including the exposure information can improve the estimates of the common ground-up parameters. This requires simultaneous MLE of the frequency and severity parameters, which otherwise break out into separate estimations.

Suppose the jth group has retention R_j, limit U_j, e_j exposure units, M_j claims at the limit and N_j other claims X_{ji}, i = 1, ... , N_j. For the case where ground-up frequency is Poisson in λ for a single exposure unit and the units are independent, the distribution of claims in the layer is Poisson in $\lambda_j = \lambda e_j S(R_j)$, where S is the severity survival function 1 – F, which has parameters θ.

The probability of observing the sample in a layer is:

$$L_j(\lambda,\theta) \propto \lambda_j^{N_j+M_j} e^{-\lambda_j} S(U_j|\theta)^{M_j} \prod_{i=1}^{N_j} f(X_{ji}) / S(R_j|\phi)^{M_j+N_j} \qquad [5.1.11]$$

The overall loglikelihood is the log of the product of these over the retention groups. That is:

$$l = \sum_j \left[(N_j + M_j)\ln(\lambda_j) - \lambda_j + M_j \ln S((U_j|\theta) - (M_j + N_j)\ln S(R_j|\theta) + \sum_{i=1}^{N_j} f(X_{ji}|\theta) \right]$$

$$[5.1.12]$$

Equation 5.1.12 could be broken out into frequency and severity components were it not for the fact that $\lambda_j = \lambda e_j S(R_j|\theta)$. Thus, λ and θ have to be estimated together. It is possible to solve for λ in terms of θ by taking the derivative of l with respect to λ:

$$\lambda = \Sigma_j(N_j+M_j)/\Sigma_j e_j S(R_j|\theta). \qquad [5.1.13]$$

Plugging 5.1.13 in for λ in 5.1.12 makes λ a function of θ only, which then can be maximized numerically.

As an example, suppose there are two groups of policies, with retentions of 1 million and 10 million; and each has 50 policies and one claim, with ground-up amounts of 2 million and 20 million, respectively. Suppose further that frequency is Poisson and severity is Pareto with $F(x) = 1 - (1+x/\theta)^{-1.5}$. Then:

$$1 = 2/\{50[1+1\theta)^{-1.5}+(1+10/\theta)-1.5\,]\} \text{ and}$$
$$\theta = 4.32 \text{ million is the MLE estimate, giving } \lambda = 0.0446. \qquad [5.1.14]$$

Thus about 4 1/2 claims are expected ground up, two of which are observed above the retentions. The expected excess claim counts λj are 1.63 and 0.37 for the two groups, and the median ground-up claim is $(2^{2/3}-1)\theta = 0.59\theta = 2.54$ million.

Compare this to the same claim experience for the same layers, but with exposures of 5 and 95, respectively. The MLE for θ is now 0.52 million with $\lambda=0.987$ and a median ground-up claim size of 0.3 million. Many more claims are imputed below the retention, and most claims are smaller. The expected excess claim counts are now 0.98 and 1.02 for the two layers, respectively.

Now suppose that there were 100 more exposures with retention of 50 million that had no claims. The estimate of θ now comes down to 0.44 million with a median claim size of 0.26 million, and λ is up to 1.15. Not having any claims above 50 million, despite having double the exposure, decreases the implied claim sizes. Thus, incorporating the exposure information can have a dramatic effect on the parameters.

Estimation with No Data

When there is very little or no data, writing insurance requires judgment and perhaps a degree of good fortune. When the demand is high and suppliers are few, the willing suppliers have sometimes been able to take a seemingly conservative position and succeed. Some legendary insurance institutions were built to some extent on succeeding in such undertakings. The failures have been relegated to the junk pile of history, so have not been well documented.

One way to formalize such judgments was provided by Reibesell [7]. His method was to have a base rate k for limit b, the base, and an increased limits factor of 1+z at twice the base. The judgments needed were then to set k and z. Each time the limit doubled, another factor of 1+z was to be applied. Thus, the increased limits factor at $2^r b$ is $(1+z)^r$.

Mack and Fackler [5] established a method for finding a distribution that agrees with these judgments. The distribution gives Reibesell's pricing rule as the expected costs, so in finance terms would be regarded as the transformed probabilities, not the loss probabilities. Using the notation ld(x) for log-base 2 of x, Mack and Fackler note that the increased limits factor at xb is $ILF(xb) = (1+z)^{ld(x)} = x^{ld(1+z)}$. The latter equality can be verified by taking ld of both sides. The ILFs are ratios of limited average severities (LAS). Thus $x^{ld(1+z)} = LAS(xb)/LAS(b) = LAS(xb)/k$. Setting $a = ld(1+z) < 1$ gives $LAS(xb) = kx^a$. Expressing losses in units of b (i.e., taking b = 1) gives $LAS(x) = kx^a$.

Mack and Fackler show that the severity that gives this is $G(x) = 1 - akx^{a-1}$ for x at or above some cutoff point u, and $G(x) = F(x)$ for x<u, where F satisfies the two equations:

$$LAS_F(u) = ku^a \text{ and} \qquad [5.1.15]$$
$$F(u) = 1 - aku^{a-1}.$$

Thus F matches G in probability at u and satisfies the Reibesell LAS formula at u. The resulting distribution satisfies Reibesell for x at u or above. Often, u can be set to a small fraction of the base, so the IFL rule works down to fairly small limits. Almost any distribution that starts at x=0 and has a free parameter can be found to solve the two equations for F, where u is the other variable to be found. For instance, if F(x) is the ballasted Pareto $1 - (1+x/\theta)^{-2}$, then it is possible to solve for u and θ in closed form:

$$u = [a^a/k]1^{/(a-1)}/a \text{ and} \qquad [5.1.16]$$
$$\theta = au/(1-a)$$

For instance, for a = 0.6 and k = 0.2, u = 0.064 and θ = 0.096. Thus Reibesell's rule holds down to 6.4 percent of b. Even lower values of u can be found if F(x) is a positive power distribution over a finite range (i.e., F(x) = $(x/θ)^β$). For these values of a and k, β = 9 gives u about 2 percent of b. However, with u so low, the discontinuity in the density of G at u is quite high.

5.2 Overview of Loss Reserve Risk Models

By Paul J. Brehm, FCAS, MAAA

Introduction

The stochastic nature of insured losses – both catastrophic and noncatastrophic – was covered in previous sections. In addition to being random in their frequency and severity, insurance losses are characterized by lags between the time the insured event happens and is reported and between the date reported and the date it is finally settled. These lags give rise to the need to recognize liabilities for unpaid losses and their associated loss adjustment expenses (hereinafter, simply "losses"). Since these lags, along with claim frequencies and severities, are stochastic, recorded liabilities for losses have substantial risk that the actual value realized will depart materially from the expectation. Actual results can vary from expectations due to the number of claims, the amount of the claims or the timing of payments.

In many countries, loss reserves are the single largest liability on the insurance industry's balance sheet. The delayed and stochastic nature of the timing and amount of insured loss payments not only makes the insurance industry unique, it effectively dominates or defines much of the financial management – and risk and opportunity management — of an insurance company. For example, insurers are typically hesitant to utilize a significant amount of debt in their capital structure, as their capital is already "leveraged" by reserves. Also, the characteristics of unpaid loss liabilities (e.g., cash flow, duration, volatility) heavily influence insurer investment policy.

This section deals with the topic of reserves for unpaid loss liabilities in two parts. First, there is a short synopsis of typical models used to measure the expected unpaid loss liability. Second, there is a discussion of some models used to estimate the second moment, or the volatility, of the unpaid loss liability. But first, a brief but necessary discussion of data requirements and notation is included.

Data

Actuaries will typically start their reserve analyses with aggregate claim data. Data elements may include paid loss amounts, case reserve amounts, incurred loss amounts, associated claim counts (reported, closed paid, outstanding, incurred, etc.) and the corresponding exposure information such as the actual insurance exposures and earned premiums. Analysis may be performed on data at a variety of levels, for instance, gross/ceded/net of reinsurance, gross/ceded/net of salvage and subrogation, with loss expense separated out or combined with losses.

Ideally, for analysis purposes, the data is grouped into "classes" that are both:

1. Homogenous – have similar claim characteristics (e.g., reporting lags, settlement or payment patterns, frequencies, severities, etc.); and
2. Credible – sufficiently voluminous or stable to allow for reliable predictions.

Actuaries often must sacrifice one of the above properties in order to have the other. Very often they have neither.

The aggregate data is organized by accident year (report year for claims-made coverages) or policy year, with accident year being the most typical. Each accident year is arrayed by sequential evaluations called development periods. We obviously have the opportunity to observe more development periods for older accident years. When the accident years are ordered from the oldest to the most recent, a triangular array of data is typically the result.[49] Figure 5.2.1 is an example of a loss triangle with m accident periods evaluated over n periods, including the notation conventions employed throughout this section.

FIGURE 5.2.1: LOSS TRIANGLE CONSTRUCTION

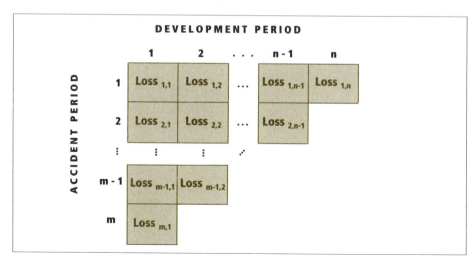

[49] In cases where data is missing, the shape will be other than a triangle. The models used to analyze the data generalize to these other shapes.

The losses in Figure 5.2.1's array are typically, though not exclusively, cumulative and will be assumed to be cumulative unless otherwise indicated.

In order to quantify the unpaid loss liability, one can envision the modeling exercise as filling in the lower half of the triangle and stretching it to the right as far as required for the accident periods to stop developing, a point referred to as "ultimate." Figure 5.2.2 is an example of how the loss triangle modeling exercise is completed.

FIGURE 5.2.2: LOSS TRIANGLE COMPLETION

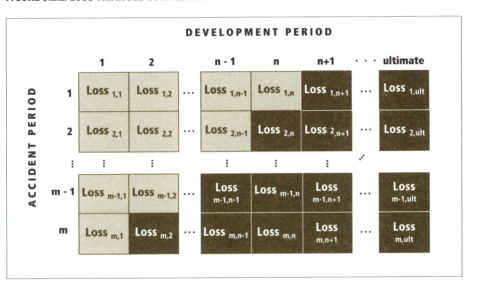

Thus actuaries often speak of triangles and completing or "squaring" the triangles (though technically, it is "rectangle-ing").

By estimating the ultimate valuation for each accident period for each class and subtracting from it its known, current valuation, the analyst can estimate the amount yet to be realized. The interpretation of the unrealized amount depends on the data being analyzed. Figure 5.2.3 is one example of a loss reserve data valuation.

FIGURE 5.2.3: RESERVE MODEL OUTPUTS, GIVEN INPUTS

Input Data	Output
Paid losses	Unpaid losses (total reserve estimate)
Incurred losses	Reserves other than case reserves
Paid claim counts	Unpaid claim counts
Reported claim counts	IBNR claim counts

Models of Point Estimates for Reserves

This section offers an overview of some of the typical reserve analysis models. The emphasis is on computational models in an enterprise risk analysis framework and is not intended as a thorough primer on reserve analysis. For a more in-depth treatment see, for example, "Foundations of Casualty Actuarial Science" [6].

Expected Loss Ratio Method

Perhaps the simplest method of estimating a required reserve for unpaid losses is the expected loss ratio method. Ultimate losses are simply defined as the product of period earned premium times the expected ultimate loss ratio. The difference between this estimate of ultimate losses and the losses paid to date is the estimated provision for unpaid losses.

This method is simple but is also potentially the least rigorous. Much demand is placed on the integrity of the estimate of the ultimate loss ratio. If the loss ratios used are the product of considerable thought and modeling, the method will be entirely appropriate. If, however, loss ratios are simply postulated (e.g., using a pricing target, regardless of current price adequacy), the result will be unreliable.

Link Ratio Models

Traditionally the most common model for estimating required loss reserves are link ratio methods, also referred to as chain-ladder or development factor methods. Link ratio models "normalize" the data triangles by dividing each development period entry, by accident period, in periods 2 through n by the column entry preceding it. The normalized ratios are called age-to-age development factors or link ratios.

Given an array of age-to-age development factors, the columns are typically averaged in some fashion in order to produce an estimate for the column development factors below the current diagonal. It seems every practitioner has her/his favorite method to average (or otherwise select) a representative factor, such as straight averages, weighted averages, geometric averages or medial averages. Consideration must also be given to the number of years used in the averaging. If the business underlying the data is stable, and the past is likely a good predictor of the future, then a long-term average is appropriate. If conditions have changed over time, it may argue for an average calculated over the nearer term.

It is computationally efficient to express the average or selected age-to-age development factors, f_j, according to the following equation (see Mack [12]):

$$f_j = \frac{\sum_{i=1}^{n-j} w_{ij} Loss_{ij}^\alpha \left(\frac{Loss_{i,j+1}}{Loss_{i,j}} \right)}{\sum_{i=1}^{n-j} w_{ij} Loss_{ik}^\alpha} \qquad [5.2.1]$$

Note that the expression within the parentheses in the equation is an observed age-to-age development factor for accident year i from development period j to j+1.

In formula 5.2.1, the w's are simply weights (between 0 and 1, inclusive) assigned to the accident period/development period experience. Thus, the w's can be used to exclude aberrant data points or restrict the experience period. The parameter α takes on the values of 0, 1 or 2. If $\alpha = 0$, the above formula for f_j simplifies to a straight average of the selected data points; $\alpha = 1$ is a geometric average; and $\alpha = 2$ calculates the development factor as the slope parameter in an ordinary least squares regression through the origin.

It is not always the case that the analyst believes that the losses or claims will no longer develop at the point where the observed triangle stops. When modeling long-tailed lines of insurance, a larger triangular array of data is required; or, if such data is unavailable or no longer applicable, ultimate losses are calculated from the final available development period (j = 10, above) with a "tail factor." There are a variety of models available to extrapolate tail factors beyond the development factors selected from the data. Mack [13], for example, recommends a linear extrapolation based on the model, as shown in Equation 5.2.2:

$$\ln\left(\hat{f}_j - 1\right) = a + bj + \varepsilon_j \qquad [5.2.2]$$

Extrapolated age-to-age factors (in our example for j=11, 12, ...) are calculated by fitting the equation with a regression model and using the regression parameters with subsequent values of j to calculate the tail f_j's. Tail f_j's are calculated until losses or claims stop developing; that is, when $\hat{f}_j = 1$. The tail factor is the product of these fitted values. There are a variety of other tail factor models in actuarial literature.

Bornhuetter-Ferguson

The Bornhuetter-Ferguson [1] model is particularly well-suited for longer tailed lines of insurance, for which data for less mature accident years are not necessarily predictive of ultimate values. This model's ultimate loss ratio estimate takes the current evaluation of loss and adds the expected remaining development given the development patterns and underlying loss ratios. Thus:

Ultimate = Losses-to-date + (Expected Loss)(1−1/development factor to ultimate) [5.2.3]

Since the link ratio estimate of ultimate is equal to losses-to-date times a development factor to ultimate ($d_j = \Pi f_j$), we can use a sneaky mathematical substitution in the above equation. By substituting link ratio ultimate/development factor (= losses to-date), the Bornhuetter-Ferguson ultimate becomes:

= Link ratio ultimate/d_j + (Expected Loss)(1−1/d_j) [5.2.4]

= (Link ratio ultimate)(1/d_j) + (Expected Loss)(1−1/d_j)

= (Link ratio ultimate)Z + (Expected Loss)(1−Z)

Where Z = (1/d_j)

Thus, the Bornhuetter-Ferguson estimate is a weighted average of the two previous models, where the weights are the inverse of the remaining development (percent of ultimate) and its complement. The closer the accident year is to its ultimate (based on expected development patterns), the more weight is given to link ratio estimates. The farther away from ultimate, the more weight is given to the expected loss estimate. In other words, the Bornhuetter-Ferguson methodology introduces a simple credibility calculation into loss reserving analysis.

Once again, the expected loss ratio plays a critical role in the accurate estimation of unpaid loss reserve requirements. The Bornhuetter-Ferguson method is expressed in general terms and does not specify the source of the expected loss ratios. A number of derivative methods add specificity. The most common is the Stanard-Buhlmann, or Cape Cod Method ([5], [15]), which calculates from the data triangle a single expected loss ratio for all years (after a suitable adjustment to a common level). Gluck [7] proposed the Generalized Cape Cod Method, which achieves a compromise between the Cape Cod and link ratio methods by allowing the expected loss ratio to drift over the accident years. Brehm [2] has recently published a methodology for deriving the expected loss ratio for the Bornhuetter-Ferguson calculation that utilizes the paid and incurred loss data simultaneously and incorporates claim counts, loss trend, premium and pricing information.

Loss Reserve Development and Calendar Time

All of the above models share a common assumption that runs throughout traditional loss reserve analysis: that losses for each accident year emerge based on a constant underlying development pattern. Within their structure, the models assume that trends have been constant throughout the historical period and will remain so (with certainty) throughout the projection period. The models reflect only the risk of misestimating the unchanging parameters. This conception allows no room for changing calendar-year influences (not even inflation)[50].

Practicing actuaries have long recognized this limitation. The most common techniques for addressing historical inconsistency have involved adjusting the data to a consistent basis (e.g., Berquist and Sherman [4]). Payment data can easily be corrected for a general inflation index, although this is rarely done in the United States. At a minimum, actuaries frequently rely on more recent observations of link ratios when the observations do not appear constant over time.

Historically, the constant pattern assumption appears to have been frequently violated in many data sets. Given this experience, there is considerable doubt whether it should ever be adopted, even when it cannot necessarily be rejected based on a specific data set.

Model Testing

Any model should be tested against the underlying assumptions required for the model to hold true. Reserving models are no different. Mack [12] shows that link ratio estimates will be optimal under three assumptions:

1. The expected value of the incremental losses in the next development period for a given accident period is a constant times the cumulative losses-to-date.
2. Cumulative losses for any two accident years are independent of each other for all accident years at all stages of development.
3. The variance of the next incremental observation is a function of the age of development and the cumulative losses-to-date.

The first assumption can be easily tested by simply looking at a graph of the incremental losses in a development triangle for a given column versus the cumulative losses in the column immediately prior. Figure 5.2.4 shows a graph of incremental versus cumulative losses for U.S. industry total commercial auto liability data, development period 5 versus 4.

---

[50] Zehnwirth deals with the calendar-year dimension; see page 206.

FIGURE 5.2.4: INCREMENTAL DEVELOPMENT AT T V; CUMULATIVE DEVELOPMENT AT T+1

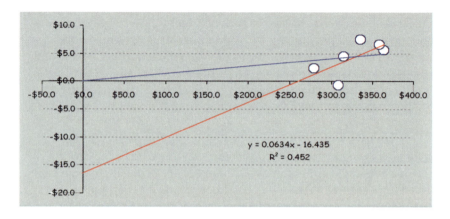

Mack's first assumption is equivalent to asserting the superiority of the blue line shown in Figure 5.2.4, a least squares regression through the origin, to other estimators. The red line in the figure shows the line of best fit when a non-zero intercept is included, and, in this case, it is statistically significantly different from zero. Thus, in this example, the first assumption does not hold.

Venter [16] covers each of Mack's assumptions and more and offers alternative models where the assumptions prove wrong. In particular, Venter offers tests of the residuals (actual triangle values minus predicted values) versus the previous cumulative value (the predictor) and versus time. The former is a test of linearity and constant error variance; the latter is a test of stability. Figure 5.2.5 shows the residuals using the paid data from the U.S. industry total commercial auto liability used in Figure 5.2.4 graphed against the respective prior cumulative paid loss. The graph exhibits what is known as heteroscedasticity, or nonconstant error variance. This heteroscedasticity is another violation of implicit modeling assumptions.

FIGURE 5.2.5: RESIDUALS VS. PRIOR CUMULATIVE PAID LOSSES

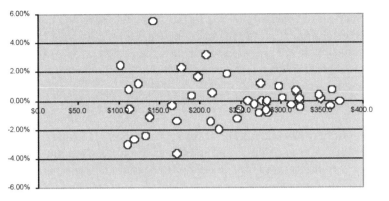

The models just described could be considered a subset of a bigger link ratio family of models. There are other members of the family, and there are other families. These models are beyond the scope of this introduction. However, additional models will be introduced as we move beyond the single point, deterministic estimate for unpaid losses.

Volatility (Stochastic) Models

Since reserves for unpaid losses are provisions for random amounts to be paid at random points in the future, they are, by definition, forward-looking forecasts. As such, and given their prominence on insurers' balance sheets, they represent a significant risk factor. Models of reserve volatility, then, are an integral component of the overall risk modeling effort; and appropriate management protocol regarding reserves is required as an integral piece of an enterprise-wide risk management process.

Models of unpaid loss volatility are relative newcomers to casualty actuarial science. While models to derive point estimates have been around since the 1930s, models to calculate the standard deviation of a reserve estimate began to surface in the 1980s and only gained popularity in the early 1990s. Perhaps this coincides with the rise of dynamic financial analysis (DFA), but equally likely is a product of a call for papers by the CAS Committee on the Theory of Risk in 1993. This call produced 10 papers, published in 1994 in the CAS Forum.

Venter [17] produced a thorough and convenient summary of the 10 papers in the same Forum. Venter notes that the models presented in 1994 fell into three classes: 1) models based on the variance of link ratios, 2) models based on collective risk theory (the convolution of a random frequency and a random severity) and 3) parametric models of development, typically in a regression or generalized least squares framework. Following is a brief description of a representative model from each category.

Mack[51] ([12], [13])

As mentioned above, Thomas Mack identified three assumptions that must hold true in order for link ratio or chain-ladder models to apply. He then proceeded to derive the formulas necessary to calculate the standard error of a reserve estimate for a single accident year and for all accident years combined.

Mack's variance formulas are mathematically tractable and easily executed in standard spreadsheet software. Using the notation introduced above, and again letting f_k equal the development factor from age k to k+1, the variance of an individual accident year (i) ultimate loss estimate is given by:

$$(s.e.R_i)^2 = Loss_{i,n}^2 \sum_{k=n+1-i}^{n-1} \frac{\gamma_k^2}{f_k^2}\left(\frac{1}{Loss_{i,k}} + \frac{1}{\sum_{j=1}^{n-k} Loss_{j,k}}\right) \quad [5.2.5]$$

where

$$\gamma_k^2 = \frac{1}{n-k-1}\sum_{j=1}^{n-k} Loss_{j,k}\left(\frac{Loss_{j,k+1}}{Loss_{j,k}} - f_k\right)^2 \quad [5.2.6]$$

The formula for the variance of the total reserve (the sum of all R_i) is given by:

$$(s.e.R)^2 = \sum_{i=2}^{n}\left\{(s.e.R_i)^2 + Loss_{i,j}\left(\sum_{k=i+1}^{n} Loss_{k,n}\right)\sum_{l=n+1-i}^{n-1}\frac{2\gamma_l^2/f_l^2}{\sum_{t=1}^{n-l} Loss_{t,l}}\right\} \quad [5.2.7]$$

Given the mean and variance of unpaid loss reserve estimates, Mack assumes that the values are distributed lognormally in order to derive a full distribution. Mack [12] deals only with the volatility that can be measured in the confines of the triangle, ignoring the volatility inherent in the tail for longer-tailed lines. Mack realized this shortcoming, as well, and authored a follow-up paper addressing the inclusion of tail factors and their volatility [13].

---

51 Mack's method is used in the recently introduced risk model employed by Fitch.

Hodes, Feldblum and Blumsohn [10]

Hodes, Feldblum and Blumsohn developed a simulation model based on the standard model. Despite the simulation approach, the method is easily executed with standard spreadsheet software.

The authors distinguish between process risk and parameter risk in their calculations. For process risk, age-to-age factors (f_j's) are assumed to be distributed lognormally with a known mean and standard deviation. The mean and variance are estimated from the observed f's, and the estimated parameters are used in a simulation, assuming independence.

However, the true distribution of development factors and the parameters are not known, so an adjustment is made for parameter risk according to Kreps [11]. The Kreps method proceeds as follows:

1. Given n = number of years available (or used) to calculate development factors, and σ = the standard deviation of the development factors, for a given development period (j);
2. Generate a standard normal random variable, z;
3. Simulate one Chi-squared random variable, χ^2, for each j, with parameter n+θ-1 (where θ is a scaling parameter, say, for example, 2);
4. Simulate a Student's-T variate - t(n+θ-2);
5. Calculate a revised standard deviation,
   σ' = t(n+θ-2) + z{n[1+t(n+Q-2)^2]/χ^2(n+θ-1)}$^{1/2}$;

The σ' is then used in the original process simulation for future development factors below the diagonal.

Repeated simulations of ultimate losses are used to define the variance and distribution of the loss reserve estimate.

Verrall and England (Bootstrapping) [18]

Bootstrap models, like the Hodes, Feldblum and Blumsohn model, also rely on simulation. Where the previous model simulates development factors, Verrall and England simulate data triangles with the same characteristics of the incremental paid and incurred triangles under review. Link ratio models are applied to the simulated triangles to estimate ultimate losses and reserve needs. By performing a large number of such simulations and calculations, distributions of ultimate losses and required reserves are estimated.

Murphy [14]

Murphy correctly noted that the calculation of development factors through some forms of averaging (straight averages, weighted averages, geometric averages) simply expresses the relationship between two consecutive cumulative columns. This relationship, if it is described by a single development factor, can be thought of as a regression through the origin of the latter cumulative on its predecessor (Mack's $\alpha=2$, above). With this construct in mind, Murphy goes on to generalize his regression models to include intercept parameters and also to accommodate different error structures, something the simple link ratio models do not accommodate. By converting the data triangle into a matrix, ordinary least squares regression can be used to complete the triangle.

Murphy uses the regression model statistics in recursive formulas to calculate the variance of the unpaid losses for individual accident years and for the reserve inventory as a whole. The formulas are, perhaps, a little more involved than Mack's, but are still entirely tractable and easy to implement in standard spreadsheet software.

As a side benefit, the regression construct relies on a set of explicit assumptions for estimating best linear unbiased estimates (BLUE). Murphy tests against these assumptions to identify the most appropriate model to use.

Murphy uses a t-distribution to compute confidence intervals. This requires the assumption that the variances are constant across development ages. Also, the calculation over multiple years requires an assumption of no correlation between development periods.

Hayne ([8], [9])

Hayne's 1989 paper [8] proposed the use of the collective risk model to measure the variability in loss reserves. The algorithm consists of estimating the frequency and the severity distributions of outstanding claims and then aggregating the two distributions across accident years to produce a distribution of unpaid losses. The distributions can be combined via simulation or Fourier transforms.

In his response to the above-mentioned call for papers, Hayne resurrected his collective risk model but included provisions for parameter uncertainty.

Zehnwirth [19]

Zehnwirth's contribution to the call for papers was a parametric model (though the model was developed years before the call). Zehnwirth also transforms the triangular data array into a regression matrix for computation. His method works with the logarithm of incremental loss data that has been normalized for volume differences over time by dividing by exposures.

Zehnwirth's model describes the patterns in the triangle with three types of variables, representing the three different time dimensions – accident period (α), development period (γ) and calendar period (i) – as shown in Figure 5.2.6.

FIGURE 5.2.6: TRIANGLE DIMENSIONS

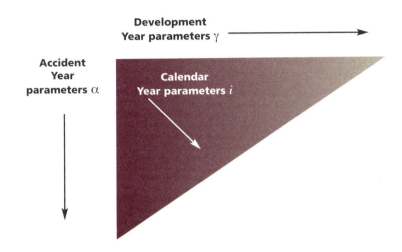

Once the α, γ, and i parameters are estimated, the triangle can be filled out; but the variance formulas cannot be derived in closed form. Zehnwirth uses conditional simulations to illustrate the distributions of each forecasted cell or any combination of cells (accident year, calendar year, entire reserve portfolio, etc.).

Like Murphy's regressions, Zehnwirth's model makes explicit assumptions in order to apply the least squares methodology. Considerable emphasis is placed on examining the residuals to test the appropriateness of the fitted model.

While technically elegant, the Zehnwirth model suffers from a few drawbacks:

1. Since model input is the natural log of incremental development, negative incremental development causes a problem. For example, any line of insurance that exhibits case reserve redundancy would make it difficult to utilize incurred loss data. Or, lines with a significant lag between a direct claim payment and a subsequent salvage or subrogation recovery (e.g., surety) are difficult to model even on a paid basis.
2. The model uses parameters in three dimensions to describe a two-dimensional data array. Thus, it is possible to develop a number of models that all fit reasonably well but yield very different answers. Considerable skill and practice are required.

3. The mathematics of Zehnwirth's model are considerably less tractable than, say, Mack's or Murphy's. While it is possible, implementation of this model in a spreadsheet package is not recommended.

Recall that the link ratio models share the common assumption that losses for each accident year emerge based on a constant underlying development pattern. Thus, the associated uncertainty measures specifically rely on the constant pattern assumption. Zehnwirth can reflect changes in calendar-year payment trends. While past trends may vary, Zehnwirth models future calendar-year trends as a single unchanging exponential parameter, with provision for uncertainty in the parameter value. There is no specific provision for unpredictable future change in the trend, although this could be incorporated.

The modeler must decide whether it is acceptable to model loss reserve development as independent of inflation or independent of other insurance trends. Each such assumption could significantly reduce the projected volatility in the enterprise risk model. In addition to observations based on the specific data set, this judgment requires common sense and an appreciation of the consequences.

Conclusion

Given the output of one of the above or similar models for the distribution of unpaid losses for a number of homogenous lines of business, the problem remains of trying to estimate the distribution of unpaid losses for the company as a whole. Such estimation requires knowledge, estimates or assumptions about the nature of the dependencies among the lines of business. At this writing, there are no generally accepted methods for estimating empirical correlation coefficients for unpaid loss distributions. Brehm [3] attempted to address this issue in the context of Zehnwirth's model. Zehnwirth himself has developed a model (currently unpublished) that simultaneously models all lines of business for a company and calculates the relevant correlations based on a two-stage methodology. The model first estimates the correlation in line model parameters, and the second stage measures any remaining correlation in the residuals.

In addition to dependency and aggregation issues, it would be desirable for modeling enterprise risk to have a descriptive (and stochastic) model of both future reserve development and payment timing. The modeler could develop a predicted mean and distribution of unpaid losses given the characteristics of the class of losses itself and given their relationship to prevailing economic variables such as inflation indexes. The said distribution would then be explicitly conditional on underlying economic scenarios and ideal for use in an enterprise risk model. Much work needs to be done on the relationship between the movement of reserve estimates and the economic environment, let alone the development of predictive models to explain and illustrate the relationship.

5.3 Reducing the Variance of Reserve Estimates

By Gary G. Venter, FCAS, MAAA

Introduction

Section 5.2 provided an overview of several popular models for modeling unpaid losses, both mean estimates and distributions. It would be a useful pursuit to seek a model or a class of models that not only calculate the mean and variance of reserve estimates but also represent those models that are minimum variance methods. There are three basic methods to reduce modeled error variance:

1. Find better-fitting models
2. Reduce the number of parameters
3. Use exposure information

This section will discuss a model that incorporates the first two of these methods. Incorporation of exposures is a generalization of the following model. Examples of the use of exposures can be found in Clark [1] and Taylor [6].

Poisson-Constant Severity Model

The link-ratio or chain-ladder family of models and the Bornhuetter-Ferguson (BF) approach exemplify two paradigms of loss reserving. In the former, losses emerging (paid or incurred) are proportional to losses already emerged. In the latter, loss emergence at any period is proportional to the ultimate losses for the year. Sometimes these have been called "conditional" and "unconditional" models, since the chain ladder's estimate of ultimate losses is a conditional expectation given the data. Especially when the ultimate losses are parameters of the model, the unconditional models can be called "multiplicative fixed-effects models," since each cell's expected loss is a product of row and column (and perhaps diagonal) factors. A convenient starting point for multiplicative fixed-effects model is the Poisson–Constant Severity Model (PCS). The PCS model postulates that each cell has an aggregate loss distribution consisting of a Poisson frequency and a constant severity – that is, all claims or payments in all cells are of the same size, b.

This, of course, is rarely the case; but the model has some advantages. First of all, aggregate claims distributions often have gamma-like tails, which the PCS model does as well. Second, its main appeal is that it gives the same reserve estimate as the chain-ladder, through the same calculation steps.

For maximum likelihood estimation (MLE) in the pure Poisson case, the agreement of methods was shown by Hachemeister and Stanard [2], although that finding was not published formally until Kremer [3] in German and Mack [4] in English. Renshaw and Verrall [5] extended previous results to the model with a Poisson aggregate and constant severity. A good presentation is Clark [1], who assumes a parameterized distribution for the payout pattern. He also discusses the Cape Cod version, for which all years are at the same level. None of the cited papers compare the resulting variance to that from Mack, however.

Modeling Approach

Giving the same answer as the chain-ladder is not a particularly useful criterion for evaluating models, but it starts from a familiar base. Thus PCS will start here. We employ the MLE approach, even though this abandons the nonparametric and regression frameworks. This sacrifices little, however, as adopting least-squares estimation is equivalent to MLE with a normal distribution assumption, as is regression.

There are some disadvantages to the PCS model. First of all, it assumes all observations are independent, which could easily fail. Second, it is not possible to estimate the severity parameter b by MLE, as the likelihood function is increasing in b so does not converge. Thus, b has to be assumed to be known in advance and in fact estimated separately later. Also, the PCS variance is proportional to its mean. Often, having the variance proportional to the square of the mean is thought to be more reasonable for loss models. The lognormal distribution has this property and also is a limiting case for products of random effects, via a multiplicative version of the central limit theorem, and so is a more logical distributional assumption. But start where you are, they say, so we will start with the PCS.

Comparing Models

Our stated goal is reducing the variance of reserve estimates, and so increasing their accuracy. The methods we explore for doing this are finding better-fitting models, reducing the number of parameters and using exposure information where available. Having a lower predictive variance is useful but not absolutely definitive as being the best model. Calculating variances can also be tedious. Thus, when searching for models, comparison of fits will be based on information-theoretic criteria, and variances only calculated for a few models. See Section 5.1 for a full discussion of information criterion such as Akaike (AIC), Hannan-Quinn (HQIC) and the small sample AIC (denoted by AIC_c).

Here we favor the AIC_c but also check the HQIC. However, since the PCS loglikelihood increases with b, as does the variance, worse-fitting models with a higher variance can have a higher loglikelihood. Thus, comparing loglikelihoods across PCS models requires fixing a value of b and using it for different models. The choice of b affects the scale of the loglikelihood and so the meaning of the parameter penalties, so these can be regarded as only general guidelines and not strict cutoffs for this model.

Modeling Details

The n+1 columns of a triangle are numbered 0, 1, ..., n and denoted by the subscript d, for delay. The rows are also numbered from 0 and denoted by w, for when. The last observation in each row of a typical full triangle then has w+d=n. The cumulative losses in cell w,d are denoted $c_{w,d}$ and the incrementals by $q_{w,d}$.

For the PCS model, a cell with frequency λ has mean loss of $b\lambda$ and variance $b^2\lambda$. Initially, we assume there is a separate parameter for each row and each column, so $b\lambda_{w,d} = U_w g_d$. Note that increasing each g by the same factor and dividing each U by that factor does not change the mean for any cell. We often adopt the convention that the g's sum to 1. Then U_w can be interpreted as the ultimate loss for year w and g_d the fraction that appears at lag d.

We apply this model to incremental losses, so that the observation $q_{w,d}/b$ is Poisson with mean $U_w g_d/b$. The loglikelihood function[52] can be shown to be a constant plus a weighted sum of these observed values minus the fitted means. The weight applied to each observed value is the log of its fitted mean, and the additive constant is $C = -\Sigma \ln \Gamma(1 + q_{w,d}/b)$. Thus:

$$l = C + \sum \left(\frac{q_{w,d}}{b} \ln \frac{U_w g_d}{b} - \frac{U_w g_d}{b} \right) \quad [5.3.1]$$

Taking derivatives, the MLE estimates can be expressed as:

$$g_d = \sum_{w=0}^{n-d} q_{w,d} \bigg/ \sum_{w=0}^{n-d} U_w \quad \text{and} \quad [5.3.2]$$

$$U_w = \sum_{d=0}^{n-w} q_{w,d} \bigg/ \sum_{d=0}^{n-w} g_d, \quad [5.3.3]$$

which do not depend on b.

---

[52] Note that we are not fitting just one Poisson distribution, but (n/2 +1)(n+1) of them, defined by 2n+1 row-column parameters plus b. But MLE applies to fitting multiple distributions with the same parameters. This is noted in the *Loss Models* textbook, for instance.

These can be put into a fixed-point iteration, starting with some values, then solving alternatively for the g's and U's until the results converge. If the resulting g's do not sum to 1, each is divided by the sum, and each U is multiplied by the same sum. However, with all the rows and columns getting their own parameters, starting at the upper right and working back can show that these estimates come from the chain-ladder calculation. Essentially, the U's are the last diagonal grossed up to ultimate by the development factors, and the g's are the factors converted to a distribution of ultimate. The fitted incrementals are then the g's applied to the U's and can be calculated by using the development factors to back cumulatives down from the last diagonal and then differencing to get the incrementals.

From the chain-ladder viewpoint, the fits so calculated use future information to predict the past, but this is essentially a different model. Sometimes incremental losses are better fit as a fraction of ultimate than as a factor times previous cumulative. The drawback is that there are more parameters needed. The chain ladder estimates each subsequent column conditionally on the current column and does not estimate the first column of the triangle. It requires the calculation of n parameters (factors) to do this. The PCS model does estimate the first column but uses 2n+1 parameters. Comparing the fits of the two models is thus a bit awkward. Perhaps comparing the estimated variances is the best way to do this. The process variances can be thought of as measuring the accuracy of the models, and the parameter variance is the parameter penalty.

Clark [1] discusses calculating the PCS variance. First, an estimate of b is needed. Since the variance of each cell is b times its mean, he suggests estimating b by the sum over the cells of the ratios of cell squared residual to cell fitted mean, all divided by (observations − parameters). That is, with N observations and p parameters, the estimate of b is:

$$\hat{b} = \frac{1}{N-p} \sum_{w,d} \frac{(q_{w,d} - U_w g_d)^2}{U_w g_d}$$

[5.3.4]

Then, the estimated variance of each projected incremental cell is the cell's mean times this b. For the reserve estimate, the variance is thus the reserve times b. But this assumes all the parameters are known. Since, in fact, they are estimated, there is another element of reserve variance usually called parameter variance. Clark suggests estimating the parameter variance by the delta method. The delta method (see *Loss Models*) starts with the usual covariance matrix of the parameters, calculated as the inverse of the MLE information matrix (matrix of 2nd derivatives of the negative loglikelihood with respect to the parameters). The delta method calculation of the parameter variance of a function of the parameters is the covariance matrix left and right multiplied by the vector of the derivatives of the function with respect to the parameters. In this case, the function of the parameters is the reserve. For the PCS model, the 2nd derivatives of the loglikelihood function with respect to the parameters are:

$$\frac{\partial^2 l}{\partial U_w^2} = -\sum_{d=0}^{n-w} \frac{q_{w,d}}{bU_w^2} ;$$ [5.3.5]

$$\frac{\partial^2 l}{\partial g_d^2} = -\sum_{w=0}^{n-d} \frac{q_{w,d}}{bg_d^2} ;$$

$$\frac{\partial^2 l}{\partial U_w \partial g_d} = -\frac{1}{b},$$

otherwise 0.

The derivative of the reserve with respect to g_d is $\Sigma_{w>n-d} U_w$ and with respect to U_w is $\Sigma_{d>n-w} g_d$.

However, with g_n set to $1-\Sigma_{d<n} g_d$, these have to be adjusted. First $\frac{\partial^2 l}{\partial U_0 \partial g_d} = 0$

Also now $\frac{\partial^2 l}{\partial g_d^2} = -\frac{q_{0,n}}{bg_n^2} - \sum_{w=0}^{n-d} \frac{q_{w,d}}{bg_d^2}$ and for $d \neq j$, $\frac{\partial^2 l}{\partial g_d \partial g_j} = -\frac{q_{0,n}}{bg_n^2}$.

The derivative of the reserve with respect to U_w is the same, but with respect to g_d it is now $-\sum_{w=1}^{n-d} U_w$.

Example

Following is an incremental development triangle from Taylor and Ashe [6], which has been used by Mack, Clark and many other authors.

FIGURE 5.3.1: TAYLOR AND ASHE DATA

357,848	766,940	610,542	482,940	527,326	574,398	146,342	139,950	227,229	67,948
352,118	884,021	933,894	1,183,289	445,745	320,996	527,804	266,172	425,046	
290,507	1,001,799	926,219	1,016,654	750,816	146,923	495,992	280,405		
310,608	1,108,250	776,189	1,562,400	272,482	352,053	206,286			
443,160	693,190	991,983	769,488	504,851	470,639				
396,132	937,085	847,498	805,037	705,960					
440,832	847,631	1,131,398	1,063,269						
359,480	1,061,648	1,443,370							
376,686	986,608								
344,014									

The data in Figure 5.3.1 was modeled with some of the models presented in Section 5.2, specifically, Mack, Hodes-Feldblum-Bluhmson (HFB), bootstrapping and Murphy (least squares multiplicative, or LSM). The triangle was modeled to the end of the available data, that is, no consideration was given to tail factors in estimating the mean or the variance. Figure 5.3.2 summarizes the results versus the PCS model. In this example the PCS is a discrete approximation to a continuous distribution and so is not exact. See Mack [7].

FIGURE 5.3.2: MODEL COMPARISON (VALUES IN THOUSANDS)

	MEAN	STD. ERR
Mack	18,681	2,475
HFB	19,460	2,628
Bootstrap	18,681	2,413
LSM	18,480	2,438
PCS 1	**18,681**	**2,827**

This first PCS model gives the same reserve estimate as the Mack and bootstrap models but a higher prediction standard error. The difference is due to the combination of a much better fit from the PCS model, indicated by an almost 50 percent reduction in process standard deviation, but a parameter standard deviation greater by almost 70 percent, owing to the number of parameters used in the model. This example is continued below, eliminating parameters from the PCS model to improve the variance estimate.

To illustrate the difference in fits, Figures 5.3.3 and 5.3.4 graph the delay 1 incremental losses as a function of the delay 0 losses, and as a function of the estimated ultimate losses. A factor times ultimate losses looks like a much better explanation of the incremental losses than does a factor times losses at 0.

FIGURE 5.3.3: DELAY 1 INCREMENTAL LOSSES VS. DELAY 0 LOSSES

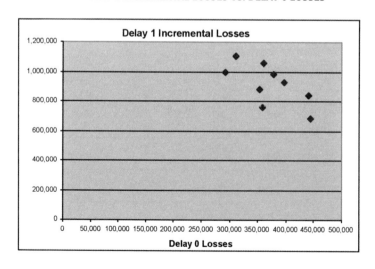

FIGURE 5.3.4: DELAY 1 INCREMENTAL LOSSES VS. ESTIMATED ULTIMATE LOSSES

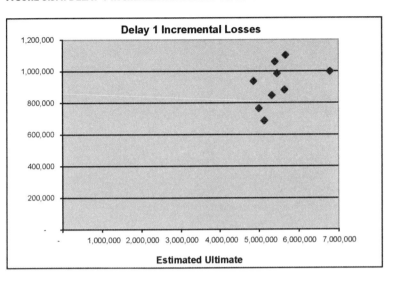

There are, of course, assumptions that would need to be verified for either model. For PCS, all of the observations are assumed to be independent; while for Mack's model, the rows should be independent. Both of these assumptions are violated when there are strong calendar-year (diagonal) effects, which there are in this triangle.

Diagonal effects can be a result of accelerated or stalled claim department activity in a calendar year. Such a departure would often be made up for in a later year or years, so more than one diagonal can be affected. A similar pattern can arise from inflation operating on calendar years. Inflation operating on year of origin is built into the factor approach, as each year gets its own level. But there can appear to be inflation by year of origin that is actually generated by calendar-year inflation. If the latter varies by year, a pattern of high and low residuals can be observed by diagonal. A large variation in residuals among diagonals would suggest that either calendar-year inflation or claim department variation is operating.

Figure 5.3.5 shows the residuals by diagonal for the PCS model. Diagonals 2, 3, 4, 6 and 7 are all suspicious, with 7 being the most problematic.

FIGURE 5.3.5: RESIDUALS BY DIAGONAL

DIAGONAL	AVERAGE RESIDUAL	FRACTION POSITIVE
0	87,787	1 of 1
1	35,158	1 of 2
2	(76,176)	0 of 3
3	(74,853)	1 of 4
4	100,127	4 of 5
5	(26,379)	2 of 6
6	103,695	5 of 7
7	(115,163)	1 of 8
8	(17,945)	3 of 9
9	38,442	6 of 10

A related issue is correlation of residuals between columns. This can be a result of diagonal effects that have not been modeled. Figure 5.3.6 shows the correlation of the PCS residuals from one column to the next for the first four columns. All the correlations are negative, and two are quite significant.

FIGURE 5.3.6: CORRELATION OF RESIDUALS

COLUMNS	0-1	1-2	2-3	3-4
Correlation	-21.5%	-89.5%	-48.9%	-85.4%
Significance	0.289	0.001	0.133	0.015

Incorporating Diagonal Effects

Factors can be put into the model for diagonal effects. Denoting the factor for the jth diagonal as h_j, then instead of the cell expected loss being given by $b\lambda_{w,d} = U_w g_d$, it becomes $b\lambda_{w,d} = U_w g_d h_{w+d}$. Still assuming that the λ's are Poisson means, the likelihood function becomes:

$$l = C + \sum \left(\frac{q_{w,d}}{b} \ln \frac{U_w g_d h_{w+d}}{b} - \frac{U_w g_d h_{w+d}}{b} \right) \qquad [5.3.6]$$

The unconstrained parameter estimates still have an iterative formulation:

$$g_d = \sum_{w=0}^{n-d} q_{w,d} \Big/ \sum_{w=0}^{n-d} U_w h_{w+d},$$

$$U_w = \sum_{d=0}^{n-w} q_{w,d} \Big/ \sum_{d=0}^{n-w} g_d h_{w+d} \quad \text{and} \qquad [5.3.7]$$

$$h_j = \sum_{w+d=j} q_{w,d} \Big/ \sum_{w+d=j} U_w g_d.$$

These converge a bit slowly, but 50 or so iterations will often suffice. This can be done in a spreadsheet without programming any functions. Again the g's can be made to sum to 1 and so represent a payout pattern, but with the calendar-year factors, the U's are then no longer the ultimate losses.

Two models with calendar-year effects were fit to the Taylor-Ashe data, adding diagonal parameters for the 7th diagonal and for the 6th and 7th. To compare the loglikelihoods, b was set at 37,183.5. This is the estimated value for another PCS model, discussed below. With this value, the maximum loglikelihood values for zero, one and two diagonal factors are:

-149.11, -145.92, -145.03.

With 55 observations, the HQIC penalty for an additional parameter is 1.388. According to this, the model with both diagonals is better than the one with no diagonal parameters but not as good as the one with only the 7th diagonal. The AIC_c reacts strongly to having so many parameters (up to 21) with only 55 observations and penalizes the first diagonal parameter by 2.5 and the second by 2.65. This says that the 2nd parameter is clearly not worth it, but the first one still is. The factors for the 6th and (in both models) 7th diagonal are 1.136 and 0.809.

Having the diagonal parameters corrects for random errors in the row and column parameter estimates. Recall that the chain ladder and original PCS reserves were 18,681,000. Adding one diagonal parameter increases this to 19,468,000, and having them both increases it further to 19,754,000. Thus, it appears that the original reserve estimates, made without consideration of diagonal effects, were too low.

Reducing the Number of Parameters

The number of parameters in the PCS model is uncomfortably high. There are a few methods available for reducing the number of parameters without materially hurting the goodness of fit. First, parameters that are fairly close to each other can be set as equal. Also, when things are changing systematically, a parameter for one year or delay could be set to the average of the parameters before and after it. More generally, several parameters in a row could be expressed as a trend, which could further reduce the number of parameters.

Reducing the parameters in these ways can eliminate distinctions that are not supported by the data. Every year gets its own level if the model allows it, but the differences between some years could be small compared to the variability in the possible parameters for each year. The same holds for the distribution by lag and the diagonal effects.

After reviewing some of these possibilities, we settled on the following model. Accident year 0 is low and gets a parameter U_0. Accident year 7 gets its own parameter, U_7, as it is high. All the other years get the same parameter, U_a, except year 6, which is a transition and gets the average of U_a and U_7. Thus, there are three accident-year parameters. The three-parameter case is between the original full-PCS and Cape Cod models, which get 10 and 1 accident-year parameters, respectively.

The fraction paid can be divided into high and low payment years with parameters g_a and g_b. Delay 0 is a low year, as things are just getting warmed up. Delays 1, 2 and 3 are where most of the action is, and all get g_b. Delays 5, 6, 7 and 8 are again low years getting g_a, but delay 4 is a transition and gets the average of g_a and g_b. Finally, delay 9 gets the leftovers, that is, $1 - 5.5g_a - 3.5g_b$. Thus, there are only two delay parameters. Clark suggested using parameterized distributions to describe the payout pattern. We tried Weibull and loglogistic distributions conditional on being less than or equal to 9. The loglogistic was better than the Weibull but not as good as the high-low model (all with two parameters) in terms of loglikelihood.

It was efficient enough to identify three of the diagonals as high or low diagonals, getting factors $1 + c$ or $1 - c$. The 7th diagonal was low and the 4th and 6th were high. Thus, only one diagonal parameter was used.

The loglikelihood for this six-parameter model is -146.66. This is not as good as the twenty-parameter model above, with a loglikelihood of -145.92, but it gets an HQIC penalty that is less by 19.4 and an AIC$_c$ penalty that is lower by 25.5. These clearly overwhelm the difference in loglikelihood of 0.74.

The estimated parameters and their standard errors are shown in Figure 5.3.7.

FIGURE 5.3.7: PARAMETERS AND ERRORS

PARAMETER	U_0	U_7	U_a	g_a	g_b	c
Estimate	3,810,000	7,113,775	5,151,180	0.0678751	0.1739580	0.1985333
Std Error	372,849	698,091	220,508	0.0034311	0.0056414	0.0568957

The parameter variances came from the information matrix. The second derivatives of the unconstrained loglikelihood with respect to U_w and g_d do not change with the inclusion of diagonal parameters. The other second partials are:

$$\frac{\partial^2 l}{\partial h_j^2} = -\sum_{w+d=j} \frac{q_{w,d}}{bh_j^2},$$

$$\frac{\partial^2 l}{\partial U_w \partial g_d} = -\frac{h_{w+d}}{b},$$

$$\frac{\partial^2 l}{\partial U_w \partial h_j} = -\frac{g_{j-w}}{b}, \qquad [5.3.8]$$

$$\frac{\partial^2 l}{\partial g_d \partial h_j} = -\frac{U_{j-d}}{b}.$$

To get the derivatives of the loglikelihood with respect to U_a, g_a, g_b and c, we use the chain rule on the sum of the derivatives of the loglikelihood with respect to the parameters shown in Equations 5.3.8. However, U_a and U_7 are now not independent, as they go into estimation of some of the same cells, and similarly for g_a and g_b. Appendix 1 summarizes the second partials of the loglikelihood for the six-parameter model.

The correlations of adjacent residuals improve a great deal with the diagonal parameters, as shown in Figure 5.3.8. This is still somewhat problematic, however, as the correlations are all negative and some are weakly significant. These correlations are still there after accounting for diagonal effects and thus might indicate some degree of actual serial correlation in accident-year payments. Perhaps ARIMA models could have a role in this modeling.

FIGURE 5.3.8: CORRELATION IN RESIDUALS

COLUMNS	0-1	1-2	2-3	3-4
Correlation	-0.9%	-58.1%	-50.7%	-74.1%
Significance	0.491	0.066	0.123	0.046

The reserve estimate from this model is 19,334,000, which is quite close to that of the twenty-parameter model. The prediction standard error (with $b = 37,183.5$) is down to 1,350,000, compared to 2,827,000 for the full PCS and 2,447,000 for the chain-ladder. The better fit from including calendar-year effects and the reduced number of parameters has decreased the standard error appreciably. The breakdown of the variance into parameter and process is shown in Figure 5.3.9.

FIGURE 5.3.9: PCS MODEL SUMMARIES

MODEL	ORIGINAL 19 PARAMETER	6 PARAMETER
Parameter Variance	7,009,527,908,811	1,103,569,529,544
Process Variance	982,638,439,386	718,924,545,072
Total Variance	7,992,166,348,198	1,822,494,074,616
Parameter Std Dev	2,647,551	1,050,509
Process Std Dev	991,281	847,894
Standard Deviation	2,827,042	1,349,998

There is a decrease in the process standard deviation of 15 percent, probably coming from recognizing the diagonal effects, and a 60 percent reduction in the parameter standard deviation in going from 19 to 6 parameters, for a total decrease in the prediction standard error of more than 50 percent. Figure 5.3.10 shows the final PCS model results appended to the original results in Figure 5.3.2.

FIGURE 5.3.10: MODEL COMPARISON (VALUES IN THOUSANDS)

	MEAN	STD. ERR
Mack	18,681	2,475
HFB	19,460	2,628
Bootstrap	18,681	2,413
LSM	18,480	2,438
PCS 1	18,681	2,827
PCS Final	19,334	1,350

Testing the Variance Assumption

In the PCS model, the variance of each cell is b times its mean. For many loss processes, the variance is proportional to the square of the mean. If that assumption holds for a particular loss triangle, then the PCS standardized residuals (residuals divided by modeled standard deviation) would probably tend to be larger in absolute value for the cells with the larger means. A plot of standardized residuals versus fitted values would be a way to demonstrate this variance property. These are graphed in Figure 5.3.11 for the six-parameter model. This effect does not appear. However, the positive residuals have more extreme values than do the negative residuals, which could be indicative of a more highly skewed model.

FIGURE 5.3.11: RESIDUALS VS. FITTED VALUES

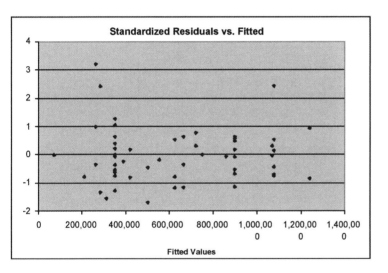

There is a possible analogue to the PP-plot as well. A PP-plot for a probability distribution fitted to data compares the empirical cumulative probability to the fitted cumulative probability at each sample point. Here we are fitting 55 Poisson distributions, each of which has a sample of 1, namely $q_{w,d}/b$. The typical empirical probability for the pth observation out of a sample of N is $p/(N+1)$, so this would be 1/2 for each of our 55 observations. But we could start with the fitted probability at each observation and rank these 55 fitted values from 1 to N and then assign the empirical probability of rank/(N+1) to each. This gives something like a PP-plot and is shown in Figure 5.3.12 for the six-parameter model.

FIGURE 5.3.12: PP-LIKE PLOT

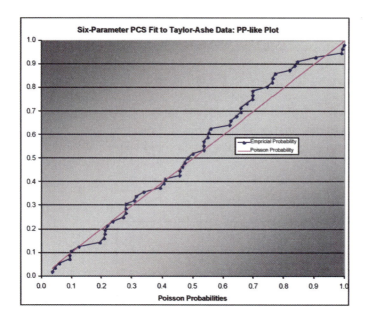

The fit is not too bad, but is better below the median than above. Above the median, there are more observations below most of the probability levels than the Poisson would predict, as shown by the empirical probabilities being higher than the Poisson probabilities. That is a bit surprising, in that usually we would expect observed data to have more large observations than the Poisson. Overall, this graph would be supportive of the distributional assumption.

Conclusion

When given one parameter for each row and column, the PCS model matches the chain-ladder reserve calculation, but can have very different fitted values for the history in the triangle. It seems to have more parameters, so a better fit would be expected; but the variance calculation reflects the parameter uncertainty, so the chain-ladder can easily give a lower variance. The fit and assumptions of both models can be strained by calendar-year effects, but these can be modeled with their own parameters in either model. It should be possible in most cases to reduce the number of parameters in the models through the use of trends, combination of similar parameters, etc. Although not discussed here, calendar-year parameters can be introduced and delay parameters can be reduced in the chain-ladder paradigm. The PCS model allows for eliminating some accident-year parameters, which can be reduced even to a single parameter as in the Cape Cod case. In the example here, three levels sufficed for 10 years. Many other possible models have not been considered here and may give better fit to this data. In summary, getting a better fit by recognizing calendar-year effects and then reducing the number of parameters in the model can decrease both the process and parameter variances of the reserve estimate.

Addendum: 1 – 2nd Partials for Six-Parameter Model of Taylor-Ashe Data

These can be written in terms of the following unconstrained second partials:

$$\frac{\partial^2 l}{\partial U_w^2} = -\sum_{d=0}^{9-w} \frac{q_{w,d}}{bU_w^2} \quad ; \quad \frac{\partial^2 l}{\partial g_d^2} = -\sum_{w=0}^{9-d} \frac{q_{w,d}}{bg_d^2} \quad ; \quad \frac{\partial^2 l}{\partial h_j^2} = -\sum_{w+d=j} \frac{q_{w,d}}{bh_j^2} \quad ;$$

$$\frac{\partial^2 l}{\partial U_w \partial g_d} = -\frac{h_{w+d}}{b} \quad ; \quad \frac{\partial^2 l}{\partial U_w \partial h_j} = -\frac{g_{j-w}}{b} \quad ; \quad \frac{\partial^2 l}{\partial g_d \partial h_j} = -\frac{U_{j-d}}{b}.$$

For this model, $U_1 = \ldots = U_5 = U_8 = U_9 = U_a$ and $U_6 = 1/2\,[U_a + U_7]$. Also $g_0 = g_5 = g_6 = g_7 = g_8 = g_a$; $g_1 = g_2 = g_3 = g_b$, $g_4 = 1/2\,[g_a + g_b]$; and $g_9 = 1 - 5.5g_a - 3.5g_b$. Finally, $h_7 = 1 - c$ and $h_6 = h_4 = 1 + c$, o.w. $h_j = 1$. For notation sake here, let $W_a = \{1,2,3,4,5,8,9\}$, $G_a = \{0,5,6,7,8\}$, $G_b = \{1,2,3\}$, $C = \{4,6,7\}$, $h_j = 0$ for $j>9$ and $U_w = g_d = 0$ for w or d < 0.

From these we get, in terms of the unconstrained partials,

$$\frac{\partial^2 l}{\partial U_a^2} = \tfrac{1}{4}\frac{\partial^2 l}{\partial U_a^2} + \sum_{w \in W_a} \frac{\partial^2 l}{\partial U_w^2} \quad ; \quad \frac{\partial^2 l}{\partial U_7^2} = \text{unconstrained value} + \tfrac{1}{4}\frac{\partial^2 l}{\partial U_6^2}$$

$$\frac{\partial^2 l}{\partial g_a^2} = \tfrac{1}{4}\frac{\partial^2 l}{\partial g_4^2} + \sum_{d \in D_a} \frac{\partial^2 l}{\partial g_d^2} + 5.5^2\,\frac{q_{0,9}}{bg_9^2} \quad ; \quad \frac{\partial^2 l}{\partial g_b^2} = \tfrac{1}{4}\frac{\partial^2 l}{\partial g_4^2} + \sum_{d \in D_b} \frac{\partial^2 l}{\partial g_d^2} + 3.5^2\,\frac{q_{0,9}}{bg_9^2}$$

$$\frac{\partial^2 l}{\partial c^2} = \sum_{j \in C} \frac{\partial^2 l}{\partial h_j^2}$$

$$\frac{\partial^2 l}{\partial U_a \partial U_7} = \tfrac{1}{4}\frac{\partial^2 l}{\partial U_6^2} \quad ; \quad \frac{\partial^2 l}{\partial g_a \partial g_b} = \tfrac{1}{4}\frac{\partial^2 l}{\partial g_4^2} + (3.5)(5.5)\frac{q_{0,9}}{bg_9^2}$$

$$\frac{\partial^2 l}{\partial U_0 \partial g_a} = -\sum_{d \in D_a} \frac{h_d}{b} - \tfrac{1}{2}\frac{h_4}{b} + 5.5\frac{h_9}{b} \quad ; \quad \frac{\partial^2 l}{\partial U_0 \partial g_b} = -\sum_{d \in D_b} \frac{h_d}{b} - \tfrac{1}{2}\frac{h_4}{b} + 3.5\frac{h_9}{b}$$

$$\frac{\partial^2 l}{\partial U_7 \partial g_a} = -\frac{h_7}{b} - \frac{h_6}{2b} \quad ; \quad \frac{\partial^2 l}{\partial U_7 \partial g_b} = -\frac{2}{b}$$

$$\frac{\partial^2 l}{\partial U_a \partial g_a} = -\sum_{d \in D_a, w \in W_a} \frac{h_{w+d}}{b} - \tfrac{1}{2}\left(\sum_{d \in D_a} \frac{h_{6+d}}{b} + \sum_{w \in W_a} \frac{h_{4+w}}{b}\right)$$

$$\frac{\partial^2 l}{\partial U_a \partial g_b} = -\sum_{d \in D_b, w \in W_a} \frac{h_{w+d}}{b} - \tfrac{1}{2}\left(\sum_{d \in D_b} \frac{h_{6+d}}{b} + \sum_{w \in W_a} \frac{h_{4+w}}{b}\right)$$

$$\frac{\partial^2 l}{\partial U_0 \partial c} = -\frac{g_a + g_b}{2b} \quad ; \quad \frac{\partial^2 l}{\partial U_7 \partial c} = \frac{g_a + g_b}{2b} \quad ; \quad \frac{\partial^2 l}{\partial U_a \partial c} = -\frac{3g_a + 9g_b}{2b}$$

$$\frac{\partial^2 l}{\partial g_a \partial c} = -\frac{1}{2}\frac{U_0 + U_a - U_7}{b} \quad ; \quad \frac{\partial^2 l}{\partial g_b \partial c} = -\frac{1}{2}\frac{U_0 + 7U_a - U_7}{b}$$

The diagonals are 1 in the projection period, so the unconstrained derivative of the reserve with respect to g_d is still $\Sigma_{w>n-d} U_w$ and with respect to U_w is $\Sigma_{d>n-w} g_d$. Thus

$$\frac{\partial R}{\partial g_a} = \sum_{d=0}^{n}\left(\sum_{w=n+1-d}^{n} U_w \frac{\partial g_d}{\partial g_a}\right) \text{ and } \frac{\partial R}{\partial U_a} = \sum_{w=0}^{n}\left(\sum_{d=n+1-w}^{n} g_d \frac{\partial U_w}{\partial U_a}\right), \text{ etc.}$$

■ ■

5.4 Approaches to Modeling the Underwriting Cycle

BY JOHN A. MAJOR, ASA, MAAA

Introduction

Since the firm exists within, and is conditioned by, its competitive environment, it is important that competitive risks be considered in an ERM framework. This chapter is written for the analyst considering how to embark upon a project to model or otherwise analyze the property-casualty underwriting cycle. It reviews the research literature and outlines several possible modeling approaches. The first section introduces the cycle. The second section discusses the numerous theories of its causes. The subsequent sections introduce three approaches to modeling the cycle and discuss each of them in turn.

The Phenomenology of the Underwriting Cycle

"Price competition is inevitable in insurance markets," write Stewart et al. [29],[53] "because entry into the business is easy [and] insurers have not been able to patent, copyright or franchise their product." Therefore, most competition is on price. Yet, despite its commodity nature, insurance is also complex. Even with the extensive financial reporting that firms in the United States do, basic economic concepts such as quantity and price are difficult to assess from outside the firm. Premiums can rise and fall; but so can limits and retentions, terms and

---

[53] This is a "must read" for anyone who wants to understand the underwriting cycle.

conditions and, therefore, expectations of loss. It is the ratio between premiums and expected losses that defines "price" as an economist would understand it. While an accountant can accurately report premiums to the penny, reporting loss expectations is the domain of actuarial judgment.

Stewart et al. define the property-casualty underwriting cycle as "the recurring pattern of increases and decreases in insurance prices and profits." See Figure 5.4.1. In the United States, this cycle can be traced back as far as the beginnings of fire insurance in the 19th century. Each line of insurance, as it arose and developed, exhibited similar fluctuating behavior (but not necessarily to the same degree). Not really a cycle in the sense of a regular, predictable pattern, the underwriting cycle appears to be more the result of a dynamical system with feedback and/or external shocks but slow adjustment and possibly inadequate damping (momentum and overshoot). Typically, each line of business has its own cycle; the dominance of the automobile line tends to imprint the industry aggregate statistics with its own six-year cyclical character. Of course, common economic and societal shocks, and the recent (in historical terms) prevalence of multiline companies (each of which has a single pool of capital supporting multiple lines), cause linkages between the cycles across lines of business as well.

FIGURE 5.4.1: COMBINED RATIO, U.S. PROPERTY-CASUALTY INSURANCE INDUSTRY (INCLUDES STATE FUNDS)

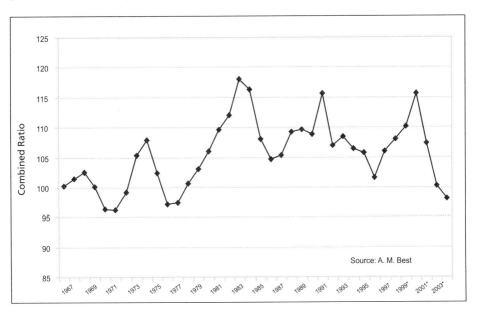

Stewart et al. describe the evolution of a line of insurance business as following four stages:

1. Emergence — A new line of business arises. Statistical experience data is thin or nonexistent. Demand grows quickly, but pricing is erratic and price wars set in. Eventually, there is a crisis of solvency, with a sudden price correction and a shakeout of weaker competitors. A period of profitability follows, which eventually brings in more competition; and the cycle repeats.
2. Control — Eventually, stabilization is reached by collective coercive control. Rating bureaus and state insurance departments regulate price changes.
3. Breakdown — Due to technological and social changes, the control regime breaks down. New types of competitors, not under control, take business away.
4. Reorganization — This resembles a return to the conditions of the first phase, as a new "version" of the old line of business, or a new configuration of the marketplace, emerges.

Stewart et al. characterized 1990 as experiencing a great deal of disruption in the commercial lines. They write:

> Most commercial lines are mature, with participants struggling to hold onto share. There is one important exception: commercial general liability. After stabilizing early and remaining stable for a long time, general liability has again become a new, emerging line with all the disruptions of that initial stage.
>
> Competition in the mature markets and competition in the new general liability market are feeding on each other. Insuring capacity sloshes back and forth between them. That has led to cyclicality in both markets, but it has been far more violent in the liability market. Understanding the coexistence, even the symbiosis, of those two kinds of market also helps explain why the total commercial insurance market can have too much capacity and too little capacity at the same time.

Hartwig [19] reports that the post-September 11, 2001 market hardening is over and that softening has set in again.

Theories of the Cycle
Each stage in Stewart's taxonomy has its own distinct dynamics and cyclical characteristics. The emergence and reorganization stage dynamics are driven primarily by competitive factors. Control stage dynamics are driven primarily by statistical data lags. Breakdown stage dynamics mix the two.

Many researchers have theorized and attempted to quantify the cycle. Often, they focused on one line or group of lines of business, in one relatively narrow historical period, in only one stage. (No one has created a mathematical model of the evolution from one stage to another.) It is not surprising then, that the literature is replete with contradictory findings. Three main themes can be discerned.

Institutional Factors
Pricing involves forecasting based on historical results; therefore, there are time lags. Papers exemplifying this explanation include Venezian [32], Cummins and Outreville [5], Lamm-Tennant and Weiss [23], and Chen et al. [3]. Venezian's paper is noteworthy as an early explanation, often referred to as the "actuaries are dumb" theory because it assumes naïve regression-style extrapolation in ratemaking. Cummins and Outreville, however, show that reporting and regulatory delays could cause the second order autoregression[54] Venezian observed even under the assumption that actuaries behave as rationally as possible.

Competition
Not all competitors have the same view of the future, with a "winner's curse" (Thaler [31]) phenomenon pushing the group towards lower rates, even if all participants are behaving rationally (and they may not be). Examples of this reasoning include Feldblum [8], Harrington and Danzon [17] and Harrington [18]. Feldblum, writing as an insider, is detailed in his explanation of competitive mechanisms. He depicts firms' underwriting strategies as alternating between (a) aggressive growth and (b) price maintenance, with the change in strategy announced in *National Underwriter*. Dowling [7] characterizes the cycle as consisting of four phases: cheating (in terms of optimistic reserve assumptions), pain, fear and restoration.

Supply and Demand, Capacity Constraints and Shocks
Since insurance needs capital to support it, any shock that reduces capital, such as a natural catastrophe, will reduce capacity and therefore raise prices as supply becomes constricted. Declining profits may be exacerbated by antiselection as more favorable business exits first. Capital market frictions (costly external capital) mean that capital cannot be replaced quickly (another source of delay). Papers include Winter ([34], [35]), Gron ([13], [14]), Niehaus and Terry [27] and Cummins and Danzon [4].

---

54 See the section on technical modeling on page 230 for an explanation of autoregressive models.

Economic Linkages

Profitability for an insurer is linked to investment income, and cost of capital is linked to the wider economy. Expected losses in some lines of business are affected by inflation, GNP growth or unemployment. Therefore, variation in the economic background has an effect on profitability. Examples include Wilson [33], Doherty and Kang [6], Haley [15], Grace and Hotchkiss [12] and Madsen et al. [26]. Madsen et al. focus in particular on the "optionality" nature of insurance and hypothesize an economy-wide "price of risk" that the insurance industry is seen to ignore or contradict in its pricing behavior.

All of the Above

Fung et al. [10] test the predominant theories for underwriting cycles by sophisticated statistical methods and find that no single theory can explain underwriting cycles completely. Schnieper [28] constructs a model that incorporates all three types of theories.

Approaches to Modeling the Cycle
Selection of Variables

This section assumes the objective is a model of aggregate industry behavior.

The first question is, what is the criterion variable? Clearly, the concern is price: If a firm cannot compete at the prevailing price, it will either lose money or lose business. Yet, price is multidimensional. Conceptually, it may be possible to define price as the premium required to cover a standard risk (e.g., a certain model of car garaged in a certain location and driven for a certain number of miles by a driver of a certain age with a clean accident record), but in practice, this is generally impossible.[55] Instead, most analyses focus on some sort of profitability measure, usually based on the loss ratio or combined ratio, possibly with adjustments for the time value of money.

There are many potential predictor variables. Depending on one's theory of the cycle, they may include:

- Previous time period values of the profitability variable and its components (premiums, losses, expenses).
- Other internal financial variables such as reserves and reserve development, investment income, catastrophe losses, total capital and capital flows (dividends and new investment) and reinsurance cessions.
- Regulatory/ratings variables, especially upgrades and downgrades.
- Reinsurance sector financials.
- Econometric variables such as inflation, unemployment and GNP.
- Financial market variables such as interest rates and stock market returns.

---

55 There are exceptions; the Medical Liability Monitor reports premiums for standard policies.

Competitor Intelligence

For more detailed insight into the state of the underwriting cycle, competitor analysis techniques (Youngman [36]) may be used. Sources of information include the firm's own agents and field staff, customer surveys (especially at renewal time), trade publications, news scanning, rate filings and the Internet. Of particular note is Dowling & Partners' *IBNR Weekly* and Advisen, Ltd.'s *RIMS Benchmark Survey*.

Beware of legal issues, however. This is not industrial spying; it is legitimate data gathering.[56] Also, one needs to be aware of antitrust issues. Consult your in-house or external counsel, as appropriate, for guidance prior to conducting these activities.

What is sought here are leading indicators that can foretell the "turn" – the change in industry behavior from one mode to the other. See the section below on soft approaches for more on competitor analysis.

Styles of Modeling

We may distinguish three "styles" of seeking enlightenment about the underwriting cycle. They are (1) "soft" approaches, (2) behavioral modeling and (3) technical modeling. They vary in multiple dimensions:

- Data quantity, variety and complexity: soft > behavioral > technical
- Recognition of human factors: soft > behavioral > technical
- Mathematical formalism and rigor: technical > behavioral > soft

Depending on the style and intellectual assets of the firm doing the analysis, and the specific goals of the exercise, one of these approaches may work better than the others. The two extremes, soft approaches and technical modeling, will be discussed first in the following two sections, respectively, with the intermediate behavioral modeling approach addressed last in the subsequent section. It should be noted that technical and behavioral models are not distinct categories, but poles in a continuum. Even the simplest technical model has some sort of underlying (if naïve) theory, and even the most heavily theory-based behavioral model will be subject to some sort of fitting or validation against observed data.

Soft Approaches

Soft approaches represent a human approach to human issues. They start with an intensive focus on data gathering and intelligence, as discussed above. Analysis techniques include scenarios, the Delphi method and formal competitor analysis. The objective is to give human analysts insight into the complex social reality that is the state of the underwriting cycle.

---

56 As a former supervisor once wisely advised, "Don't do anything you wouldn't mind reading about on the front page of the newspaper."

A scenario (Schwartz [30]) is a detailed written statement describing a possible future state of the world. Scenarios are used to "stake out" a space of possible futures and to organize systematic thinking about the future and how one might prepare for or respond to contingencies. Simulation (especially catastrophe) modelers sometimes describe simulated outcomes as "scenarios," but here they are intended to be many fewer in number, much richer in content and processed by minds rather than computers.

The Delphi method (Helmer-Hirschberg [20], Linstone and Turoff [24]) is a method of obtaining expert consensus on an issue. It was developed by the Rand Corporation during the Cold War. Participants are all given the same core background material and asked for their opinions in a carefully designed questionnaire. The answers are collated and then summaries are returned to the participants to allow them to reconsider their opinions, or articulate their reasons for disagreeing. The process repeats until convergance and consensus emerge.

Scenarios and Delphi work together naturally. A Delphi process can create a set of scenarios spanning the likely future; and, in turn, a set of scenarios can form the input to a Delphi assessment about the likelihood of, and best response to, each.

Competitor analysis looks within the industry and attempts to discern the state, motives and likely behavior of individual competing firms. It starts with a database of competitor information, including key financials as well as news items and behavioral metrics. Over time, the distinction between normal and abnormal statistics and behavior become evident. For predicting turns in the underwriting cycle, the key is seeing unusually profitable or distressed financial conditions reproduced over a large number of firms.

Technical Modeling

Technical modeling is at the other extreme from soft modeling. Here the focus is on a small number of industry financial statistics – possibly only one – and there is at best a rudimentary theory underlying the model. Data is king, and statistical analysis is the royal road.

The basic method is time series analysis (Box et al. [2]) and the basic model is *autoregressive* ("AR"). Let X_t represent the key variable, say the industry-combined ratio in the general liability line of business, in year t. An AR(n) model is of the form:

$$X_t = a + \sum_{i=1}^{n} b_i \cdot X_{t-i} + \sigma \cdot \varepsilon_t \qquad [5.4.1]$$

where ε_t are independent and identically distributed unit normal random disturbances. Most researchers have found that n = 2 or 3 is sufficient to model the cycle. Formal statistical tests determine the most appropriate value of n and the coefficients a, b_i, and σ.

For example, an AR(2) model fit to the data of Figure 5.4.1 is:

$$CR_t = 38 + 0.957 \cdot CR_{t-1} - 0.318 \cdot CR_{t-2} + 3.83 \cdot \varepsilon_t \qquad [5.4.2]$$

and produces the forecasts shown in Figure 5.4.2. The open boxes are one-step-ahead forecasts based on the previous history and give a sense of the accuracy of the fit. The solid boxes extrapolate into 2005 and 2006, with the solid curves around them indicating a 90 percent prediction interval.

A generalization of this procedure known as VARMAX handles multiple simultaneous variables and exogenous (external) regressors as well.

A more sophisticated approach is to hypothesize a more general factor model.[57] An example might be:

$$Z_t = a + b \cdot Z_{t-1} + \sigma \cdot \varepsilon_t$$
$$X_t = c + d \cdot (Z_{t-1} - X_{t-1}) + \tau \cdot \delta_t \qquad [5.4.3]$$

where the ε and δ are not necessarily distributed as normals and Z is not observable. If, for example, b were a small negative number and d were (relatively) large and positive, this would represent X as randomly varying around a long-term moving average determined by Z. Such a model is not as straightforward to fit as an AR model and may require techniques such as Generalized Method of Moments (Hansen [16]) or Efficient Method of Moments (Gallant and Tauchen [11]).

---

[57] Factor models are intended to be continuous-time models; here we render them in discrete time. An AR model can be represented as a factor model by treating each lag of the variable as a distinct, different variable.

FIGURE 5.4.2: AR(2) FORECASTS OF INDUSTRY-COMBINED RATIOS

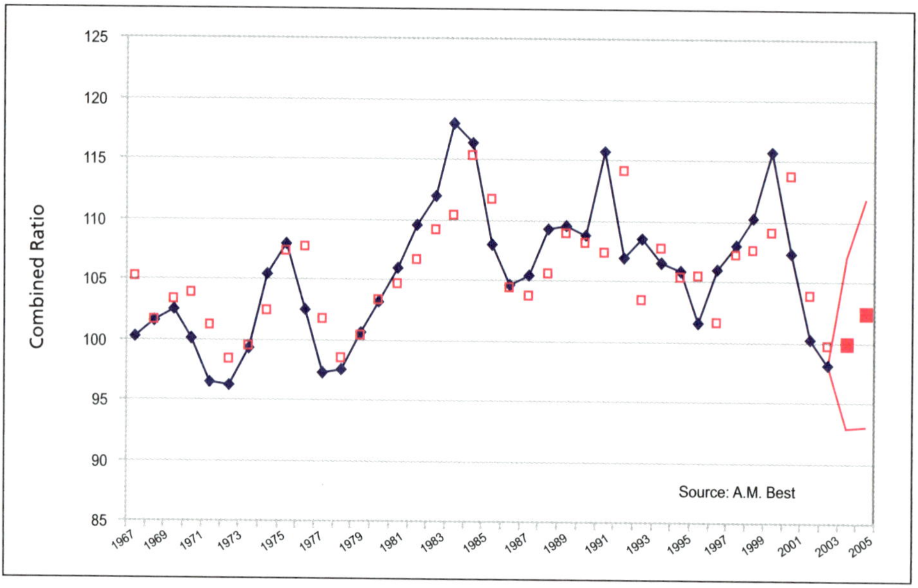

Once parameter values have been fitted to the data, a technical model can be used to simulate future possible values of the criterion variable. These can be used to generate probability forecasts or as direct inputs to a larger ERM or strategic planning model of the firm.

Econometric Modeling

Econometric or behavioral modeling occupies a middle ground between the soft methods' concern for structural insight and technical modeling's concern for statistical validity. Here the models consist of components that, individually, have meaningful interpretations motivated by economic and behavioral theory.

Like the soft methods, behavioral modeling can occur at either the aggregate industry level or at the level of individual firms. Firm-level modeling is more complicated because multiple entities and their interactions need to be tracked. Typically, models for individual behaviors are simpler than aggregate models, but their interactions lead to "emergent" behavior on the part of the collective. Interested readers should pursue Alkemper and Mango [1].

The remainder of this section outlines an example of an aggregate industry approach.

Supply and Demand

Most econometric models revolve around supply and demand, two relationships between price P and quantity Q that determine the price and quantity that "clears the market." In drawing graphs, the convention is to place quantity on the horizontal axis and price on the vertical axis.

The supply curve slopes up to the right, signifying that in order to bring more to the market, the price must go up. Figure 5.4.3 shows examples. The supply curve may change over time. In particular, there are several forces that operate on the supply curve for insurance. On the one hand, competitive (new entrants) and technological (cost-saving) forces tend to push the curve down and to the right. On the other hand, restrictions in available capital tend to push the curve up and to the left (Gron [13]).

FIGURE 5.4.3: SUPPLY CURVES

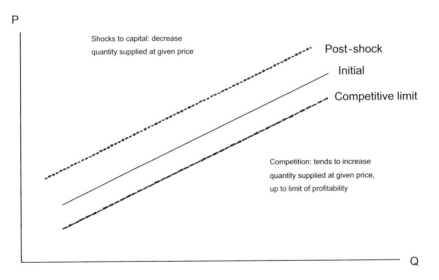

The demand curve slopes down to the right, signifying that in order to sell more, the price must go down. Figure 5.4.4 shows examples. (It should be emphasized that Figure 5.4.4 shows demand for the industry as a whole. Individual firms face flatter demand curves because of competition between firms.) The demand curve, too, may change over time. As the industry capital increases, there is a general increase in "quality" as measured by default probability. If buyers recognize quality, then they are likely to demand more when the quality is higher because they are, in effect, getting more for their money. Conversely, after a shock loss and reduction of capital, demand is likely to go down somewhat, in recognition of an overall lowering of quality (Cummins and Danzon [4]).

FIGURE 5.4.4: DEMAND CURVES

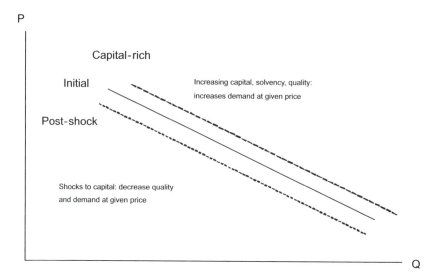

The interaction of supply and demand curves determines the price and quantity observed in the marketplace. This is illustrated in Figure 5.4.5. A change in the conditions underlying the curves themselves will change the curves and therefore the point at which they intersect.

FIGURE 5.4.5: EQUILIBRIUM SHIFT FOLLOWING A SHOCK LOSS

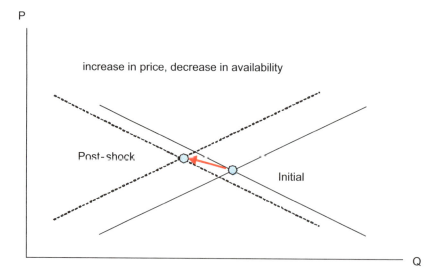

Because only the equilibrium can be observed, estimating supply and demand curves is quite challenging (Intriligator [22], Froot and O'Connell [9]). Bringing in other considerations may help. For example, Gron [14] hypothesizes a particular shape for the supply curve, shown in Figure 5.4.6.

FIGURE 5.4.6: GRON SUPPLY CURVE

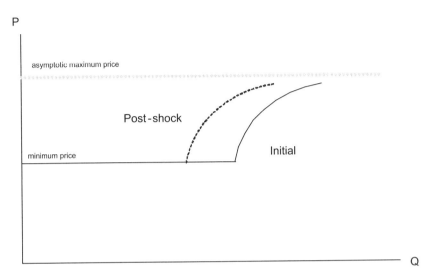

There is a minimum price, reflective of expected losses and marginal costs of writing the business, below which policies will not be sold. Up to a certain quantity, all business sells at this price. Such behavior is termed "perfectly elastic" because the supply stretches without requiring higher prices. At some point, however, a capacity threshold is reached and in order to take on more business, the industry must acquire more risk capital – and therefore charges for it. This causes an upward slope to the supply curve. At the extreme right, there is an asymptotic approach to a price so high that the premium itself contributes enough capital. Shocks manifest themselves by shifting the supply curve right and left. Competitive drift manifests by lowering the minimum price threshold.

Capital Flows

An important element in many models of the cycle is the amount of capital available to support business, and the dynamics of its ebb and flow. Capital rises and falls naturally according to the level of profitability, with retained earnings adding to capital stocks and operating losses drawing down capital. Additionally, capital can enter and exit the firm from outside. Capital infusions are likely to occur when capacity is limited and profit expectations are high. Sudden withdrawal of capital corresponds to firms exiting the business, either voluntarily or as a result of financial distress.

Figure 5.4.7 is an example of a nonlinear relationship between profitability and capital flows. Generally, the relationship is positive, with high profits drawing capital in and low profits pushing capital out. In the center, there is a "normal" region where steady dividends are paid out to shareholders. At some critical threshold, profits are high enough to cause a sudden surge of new capital for existing firms and new firms entering the market. The precise location, shape and level of this discontinuity are themselves subject to random influences.

FIGURE 5.4.7: CAPITAL FLOWS

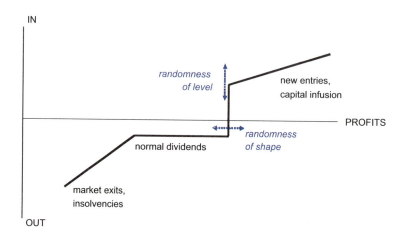

Assembling the Components

In order to build an econometric model of the industry that exhibits an underwriting cycle, the following relationships need to be taken into account:

- How economic factors influence the supply and demand curves (Grace and Hotchkiss [12], Doherty and Kang [6]).
- How capital influences the supply and demand curves (Harrington and Danzon [17], Gron [13], [14]).
- How the current level of prices and losses influence the supply curve, possibly with a delay (Cummins and Outreville [5], Cummins and Danzon [4], Lamm-Tennant and Weiss [23]).
- How the supply and demand curves jointly determine price and quantity.
- How premiums and losses affect capital stock directly.
- How profitability affects external capital flows (Schnieper [28]).

Figure 5.4.8 is a schematic of a possible architecture for an econometric model of the industry. Solid lines indicate a direct relationship, dotted lines a relationship with a time lag and the dashed line a nonlinear relationship. Plus and minus signs indicate the direction of the influence; for example, an increase in the demand curve – all else being equal – will increase the equilibrium price.

Some boxes represent exogenous, random factors. These include insurance experience (shock losses and core losses) and economic factors (interest rates, inflation, cost of capital). These components will need to be developed outside of the model, but will no doubt be of use elsewhere in a larger ERM model.

FIGURE 5.4.8: ARCHITECTURE OF AN ECONOMETRIC MODEL

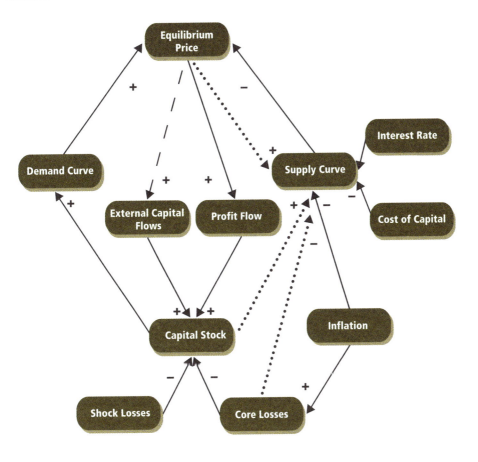

Such a model is implemented as a set of interlinked equations. The key output is the average market price level (equilibrium price) that sets the benchmark against which the firm must compete. As with the technical models, a behavioral/econometric model can be used to simulate an empirical distribution of possible future outcomes and should be validated against historical experience.

Conclusion

This section reviewed the phenomenon of the underwriting cycle and discussed several approaches to its analysis and modeling. The "cycle" is not really a cycle so much as the behavior of a complex dynamical system. Like all markets, this system is very much connected with human perceptions, desires and bounded rationality (Kahneman [21]).

In order to be useful for ERM, underwriting cycle forecasts (whether computed from a mathematical model or agreed upon by a panel of experts) are not ends in themselves. They need to feed into the firm's demand and retention models, that is, models of how existing and prospective buyers of insurance will react to the difference between the firm's pricing and the alternatives available to them in the marketplace. (See, for example, MacMahon [25].) While they may be informed by or use the demand components of the cycle model, the construction and use of such market models are outside the scope of this chapter.

Financial Risk Models

6.1 Reinsurance Receivable Risk: Willingness to Pay

By Richard Shaw, FIA

Introduction

Credit risk refers to the risk of loss if another party fails to meets its financial obligations or fails to meet them in a timely fashion. Credit risk arises either as:

- Investment credit risk, for example, from holdings of non-government bonds

- Insurance-related credit risk, associated with reinsurance recoveries, reinsurance receivables and, where material, premium debtors and other balances with intermediaries or banks

Credit losses related to the insurance exposure arise from either the default of a company's reinsurer(s) or nonpayment ("dispute" risk) of balances due. The concept of "willingness to pay" addresses this latter risk.

Regulatory Developments

Historically, credit risk calculations have been considered only in light of "bad debt" provisions within a company's balance sheet. However, the topic has gained far more importance and a higher profile with the developments of the various risk-based capital regimes within both the UK and Continental Europe, in particular, the FSA's Individual Capital Assessment Standards regime (ICAS) and the current Solvency II Solvency Capital Requirement (SCR) proposals.

Such developments have led to some companies considering alternative risk solutions such as securitization to mitigate the financial impact of such changes.

Within the ICAS regime, companies are now required to model their business in aggregate such that there is enough capital equivalent to a 99.5 percent probability of survival (or a 0.5 percent ruin probability) over one year. Similar principles adhere in Europe under the Solvency II framework.

Calculation of Credit Risk Losses

Companies often assume that the capital number arising from the insurance-related component of the credit risk is a small number; but for many companies that may not be the case, especially if previously highly rated reinsurers have experienced rating downgrades over time.

When modeling credit risk exposure, one typically considers:

- Exposure for each reinsurer and their respective credit ratings
- Default probabilities over time
- Credit rating migration over time
- The amount and timing of recoveries (e.g., the different projected time horizons for recoveries on paid claims, case reserves and IBNR)
- Loss given default, as it is very unlikely in the event of default that there would be no loss recovery at all
- Correlation default among reinsurers
- Changing exposure over time – the runoff of existing reinsurance balances increased by reinsurance exposures arising from new business
- More complex considerations like the increased risk of reinsurance failure in extreme loss scenarios where the correlation between insurance and credit risk varies by insurance loss amount

The lack of credible historical data and the complexities of modeling the likelihood and impact of reinsurer default lead to less refined models than those used to model the underlying insurance risk.

Most companies have focused on the factors listed above and have not looked further into the more subtle issue of willingness to pay, as this aspect of credit risk is less tractable and more complex in practice. However, these companies could be missing a key component of credit risk.

Willingness to Pay – The Missing Piece
Willingness to pay addresses the risk that even though a reinsurer is able to pay (reflected in its claims-paying-ability rating), it may not be willing to pay or do so in a timely manner.

Non-payment of reinsurance recoveries may occur if claims are disputed by the reinsurer, and such amounts are an obvious loss. Also of importance is the timing of recoveries, as the deferral of payments could become a cash-flow issue for a company that faces large immediate cash-flow commitments on its insurance liabilities.

The development of a statistical predictive model to estimate losses arising from the willingness to pay risk is complex, as there are many factors that influence the risk of loss. Examples of such factors include:

- Line(s) of business
- Age of asset
- Reinsurer (e.g., location, rating, strength of relationship with insured)

It is important to avoid the potential double-counting of risk factors that may be already included within a reinsurance company's credit rating. Understanding what is either already explicitly or implicitly included within a company's credit rating is important if one is to minimize this risk.

The availability of data is also an issue in developing a statistical predictive model, because certain risk factors, for example, the strength of the insurer/reinsurer relationship, can only be captured in a "soft" manner (i.e., qualitatively).

Willingness to Pay – Preliminary Work

Guy Carpenter, in conjunction with a leading rating agency and insurance entity, has participated in preliminary work being conducted by a third-party risk modeling company with respect to the willingness to pay risk.

Work to date has explored some of the issues previously described through modeling a sample of existing portfolios of reinsurance recoverables. This initial work has been very beneficial in providing participants with a greater understanding of the risk drivers, while at the same time, exploring ideas not typically considered within the insurance/reinsurance industry. Examples being the use of:

- Diversity ratings that take account of the distribution of reinsurance recoveries among reinsurers in a portfolio
- Dominance ratings that measure the extent of dominance of reinsurance recoveries by particular reinsurers, segments or other such groupings

Willingness to Pay – The Industry Benefits

Considering willingness to pay offers a number of potential benefits to insurers, runoff companies and rating agencies such as:

- The identification of high-risk recoveries
- The ability to comparatively rate reinsurance recoverable portfolios
- Quantification of the missing piece of credit risk capital
- A predictive indicator of reinsurance company default
- An increase in the understanding of the dynamics of loss due to reinsurance failure
- Additional analytical perspective on the risks associated with the sale and purchase of books of reinsurance recoverables

6.2 Investment Market Risk

By Gary G. Venter, FCAS, MAAA

Introduction

Investment market risk for an insurer is the risk arising from financial markets. Invested assets are a big part of this risk, but for a multinational insurer, foreign exchange risk is also significant.

Modeling Approaches

There are several levels of modeling of market risks. Investment funds or investment departments that are charged with trading in such markets might have very detailed models of price movements throughout the trading day. A very simplified stochastic model, at the other extreme, might take a random draw from a normal distribution of outcomes once a year. For much of enterprise risk analysis, something between these extremes is typically needed.

Usually, a stochastic scenario generator of market price movements is desired, and a fair degree of realism in the distribution of possible outcomes is sought. At a minimum, the model should be able to quantify the risk inherent in a buy-and-hold strategy or, more generally, "buy and hold until cash flow demands require a sale." A more demanding requirement would be to show the risk and return from specified mechanized investment strategies, such as "hold until certain market conditions occur." This approach might still incorporate a longer-term perspective than the trading models would require.

Accounting standards also enter in. If assets are held at amortized values unless sold, a more simplified asset model might suffice.

Here we will assume that stochastic generators that capture the statistical properties of price movements for key asset classes are desired, with prices to be simulated at convenient discrete intervals. The remainder of this section discusses issues related to modeling these price movements.

Bond Models

Insurers' assets are invested in bonds, stocks and various real estate-related instruments. Pretty good bond models are available, but modeling gets more difficult for the other financial instruments.

For government bonds, it is important to use arbitrage-free models, not because there are never any arbitrage opportunities in the bond market, as in fact there might be some from time to time. Rather, it is important because having arbitrage strategies possible in a set of simulated scenarios will show these strategies as optimal and will show other similar strategies as close to optimal. Arbitrage opportunities in the market usually do not last for very long and may not still be there after running the model. Thus, having them in the model can create inappropriate priorities.

A useful test for evaluating bond models is their ability to capture actual aspects of the market. Examples of bond models and a testing methodology are discussed in Venter [10]. Some features of bond markets are:

1. Very high autocorrelation of interest rates
2. Higher volatility with higher interest rates
3. Long-term mean reversion
4. Short-term reversion to a temporary mean
5. Stochastic volatility
6. Stochastic yield spreads
7. Lower spreads with higher short-term rates

Bond models that capture these effects are known. For instance, the model of Andersen and Lund [1] was tested in Venter [10] with additional factors added for stochastic changes in the shape of the yield curve. Their model is a three-factor short-rate model which includes processes for the short-term rate, its volatility and reversion to a moving temporary mean.

Hibbert, Mowbray and Turnbull [6] present a simpler model that does not include stochastic volatility but which does have most of the other features and appears to test reasonably well. Bond modeling is an ongoing area of research, however, with new models and testing procedures arising frequently, e.g., see Driessen, Klaassen, and Melenberg [4], who test models by their ability to price options.

A good starting point for bond models is stochastic models of the short-term rate. These models are often expressed in the form of instantaneous changes in the short-term rate r using Brownian motion, denoted by Z. Brownian motion is a continuous-time process for which changes over time are normally distributed with variance proportional to time. For instance, Cox, Ingersoll and Ross [2] (CIR) provide a model of the motion of the short-term rate that has been widely studied. In the CIR model, the instantaneous change dr follows the following process defined in terms of change in time, dt, and change in Brownian motion, dZ:

$$dr = a(b - r)dt + sr^{1/2}dZ \quad [6.2.1]$$

Here b is the level of mean reversion. If r is above b, then the time trend component is negative, and if r is below b, it is positive. Thus, the trend is always towards b. The speed of this mean reversion is expressed by a. Note that the volatility depends on r itself, so higher short-term rates would be associated with higher volatility. Also, if $r=0$, there is no volatility, so the trend takes over. With $r=0$, the trend would be positive, so r would move to a positive value. The mean reversion combined with rate-dependent volatility thus prevents negative interest rates.

If this model were discretized it could be written:

$$r_t - r_{t-1} = a(b - r_{t-1}) + sr_{t-1}^{1/2}\varepsilon_t, \quad [6.2.2]$$

where ε_t, is a standard normal residual.

This is a fairly standard autoregressive model, so the CIR model can be considered a continuous analogue of an autoregressive model.

One controversial aspect of the CIR model is the power of 1/2 on r in the last term. There has been a lot of empirical work on what the power should be, with values greater than 1/2 but less than 1 gaining favor. More problematic is the fact that the volatility of the Brownian motion portion is strictly dependent on the short-term rate r. It seems that the volatility actually displays some random behavior beyond that of r.

Models of the short-term rate can lead to models of the whole yield curve. This is done by modeling the prices of zero-coupon bonds with different maturities all paying $1. If $P(T)$ is the current price of such a bond for maturity T, the implied continuously compounding interest rate can be shown to be $-\ln[P(T)]/T$. $P(T)$ itself is calculated as the risk-adjusted discounted expected value of $1. Here "discounted" means continuously discounted by the evolving interest rate r, and "expected value" means that the mean discount is calculated over all possible paths for r. This can be expressed as:

$$P(T) = E^* [exp(-\int r_t dt)] \quad [6.2.3]$$

Where r_t is the interest rate at time t, the integral is over the time period 0 to T, and E^* is the risk-adjusted expected value of the results of all such discounting processes.

If E were not risk adjusted, P(T) could be estimated by many instances of simulating the r process to time T over small increments and then discounting back over each increment. The risk-adjusted expected value is obtained by using a risk-adjusted process to simulate the r's. This process is like the original process, except that it tends to produce higher r's over time. These higher rates provide a reward for bearing the longer-term interest rate risk. Increasing the trend portion of the diffusion process produces the adjusted process. In the CIR model, the trend is increased by λr, where λ is called "the market price of risk."

In the case of the CIR model, a closed form solution exists which simplifies the calculation. The yield rate for a zero coupon bond of maturity T is given by Y(T) = A(T) + rB(T) where:

$$A(T) = -2(ab/s^2 T) \ln C(T) - 2aby/s^2$$
$$B(T) = [1 - C(T)]/yT$$
$$C(T) = (1 + xye^{T/x} - xy)^{-1}$$
$$x = [(a-\lambda)^2 + 2s^2]^{-1/2}$$
$$y = (a - \lambda + 1/x)/2.$$

[6.2.4]

Note that neither A nor B is a function of r, so Y is a linear function of r (but not of T, of course). Still the yield spreads $Y(T_1) - Y(T_2)$ are linear functions of r, and as the three-month rate is as well, the spreads are strictly linear in the three-month rate. This is in contrast to the historical data, which shows a dispersion of the yield spreads around what seems to be a linear function of the three-month rate.

In general terms, the problem with the CIR model is that it produces some deterministic behavior that is stochastic in reality.

The Andersen and Lund (AL) [1] model adds in more stochastic behavior:

$$dr = a(b - r)dt + sr^k dZ_1 \quad k>0$$
$$d\ln s^2 = c(p - \ln s^2)dt + v dZ_2$$
$$db = j(q - b)dt + wb^{1/2} dZ_3$$

[6.2.5]

Here there are three independent standard Brownian motion processes, Z_1, Z_2 and Z_3. The volatility parameter s^2 now also varies over time, but via a mean reverting geometric Brownian motion process (i.e., Brownian motion on the log).

The reverting mean b itself is stochastic but reverts to a long-run mean q. In fact, b follows a CIR process. In total, there are eight parameters: a, c, j, k, p, q, v and w and three varying factors r, b and s. This is thus labeled a three-factor model. The power k on r in the stochastic term is a parameter that can be estimated.

In their estimation procedure, AL found all the parameters were significant for U.S. Treasury rates. Thus stochastic volatility and reverting to a stochastic mean can help explain real behavior of interest rates. AL suggest modeling the yield curve by using market-price-of-risk factors for both r and b. Venter [10] showed that these factors themselves need to be stochastic to get realistic representations of the yield-curve risk.

The Hibbert, Mowbray, and Turnbull [6] model is intermediate in complexity between AL and CIR. It keeps stochastic mean reversion but not stochastic volatility, and does not have the volatility depend on the level of the interest rate at all. In the AL notation, the HMB model is:

$$dr = a(b - r)dt + sdZ_1$$
$$db = j(q - b)dt + wdZ_3 \qquad [6.2.6]$$

This is actually a special case of an earlier model of Hull and White [7]. HMB suggest using a market price of risk only for r and not for b. This model ignores aspects of the interest rate process that are known to be significant, but is simpler than AL and may be sufficient for ERM for insurers if its limitations are recognized.

Share Prices

For shares, the models are also developing rapidly. A starting point is geometric Brownian motion, for which the log of the process is Brownian motion. The idea is that in the long run, growth should be exponential. Models like Black-Scholes option pricing assume this, for instance. To test share price change models, comparisons can be made between model-implied option price estimates and the prices for actual options. Option prices are higher for longer-term and far out-of-the-money options, relative to shorter-term and at-the-money options than the Black-Scholes model would predict. In practice, this model is used in options trading along with a volatility sheet which adjusts the volatility to be used based on term and distance from current price. In other words, the Black-Scholes model is not really what the prices are based on.

Multi-factor models like those used for bonds are an alternative. Perhaps a geometric Brownian motion, plus another stochastic process for volatility, could be used. Fouque, Papanicolaou and Sircar [5] use this approach.

The next level of sophistication for share prices is Lévy processes, discussed briefly in Section 2.6, which allow for jumps and heavier tails, and can get the right relationship between at-the-money and out-of-the money option prices. It appears, however, that if these models are calibrated to short-term volatility levels, they actually have too much volatility for longer terms. There might be some way to correct for this discrepancy using mean reversion, like in the bond models. Schoutens [9] uses a Lévy process, which, with stochastic time compression, can fit options prices fairly well.

There are other ways to model jumps and heavy tails. For instance, Kou [8] uses jumps with different exponential tails in both directions, along with geometric Brownian motion to model stock options.

Another possibility that shows some promise is regime-change models, which postulate a few or a continuum of geometric Brownian motion processes that prices could follow, and a mechanism for shifting from one process to another under various conditions.

There are likely to be better proprietary models that never get published, as information is valuable in share trading. Share price modeling is an evolving area, and selecting the best model involves choosing which compromises to make. If equity portfolios are not too large, even simpler approaches may suffice for evaluating risk in buy and hold strategies. A regression on bond prices, for instance, could be used to simulate an equity index and maintain relationships with bonds.

Real Estate

Detailed models of real estate instruments are even less developed in the public domain. There are a variety of such instruments with subtly different risks. Funds that trade in these securities develop sophisticated models, which the market tends to sort out. Perhaps at this point, simply simulating from a selected distribution is all that can be done without getting into the very detailed mechanics, although this approach would miss correlations with other assets.

Foreign Exchange

Foreign exchange (f/x) risk is a market risk that can affect several asset and liability accounts. It is typically modeled in conjunction with asset classes, as it is related to interest rates and inflation, but changes in exchange rates are applied to both the asset and liability accounts in modeling.

One theory of f/x movement is that it is a stochastic process with drift that, on average, equalizes government bond returns across currencies. Thus, a country with lower bond returns would have a higher expected growth in the value of its currency, so investments in bonds in different countries would be equivalent.

However, a good deal of bond investment still appears to be local, so this theory has not performed well historically. In fact, the opposite has often been observed – countries with higher interest rates have often had higher currency value growth.

Thus, if you wanted to build a model that links interest rates and f/x movement, you have had to choose between facts and theory. However, the increasing globalization of markets may be changing this dynamic.

Correlation is also a key issue in f/x modeling. For instance, regions like Australia and New Zealand, or Sweden and Switzerland and the UK, have some tendency to move together, with lower correlations among regions. Some work has been done on using t-copulas to model this, but different pairs of currencies appear to need different degrees of freedom. The grouped t-copula of Daul et al. [3] is a promising alternative.

Correlations in modeling f/x is an area where continued attention to model development will be important.

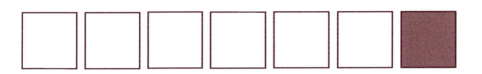

Chapter References

Additional references can be found at http://ERMBook.guycarp.com.

Section 1.2

[1] Miller, Kent. "A Framework for Integrated Risk Management in International Business." *Journal of International Business Studies* (Second Quarter, 1992).

Section 1.3

[1] Kreps, Rodney E. "Continuous Distributions." Instrat® Working Paper, Guy Carpenter & Co. Inc. (1998).

[2] Venter, Gary G. "Transformed Beta and Gamma Distributions and Aggregate Losses." Proceedings of the Casualty Actuarial Society LXX (1983) pp. 156-193.

[3] ____. "Tails of Copulas." Proceedings of the Casualty Actuarial Society LXXXIX (2002) pp. 68-113.

[4] ____. "Fit to a t - Estimation, Application and Limitations of the t-copula." ASTIN Colloquium Scientific Papers (2003). Available online at http://www.astin2003.de/03_call_03.shtml.

[5] ____. "A Survey of Capital Allocation Methods with Commentary." ASTIN Colloquium Scientific Papers (2003). Available online at http://www.astin2003.de/03_call_03.shtml.

Section 2.1

[1] Kalkbrener, Michael. "An Axiomatic Approach to Capital Allocation." *Mathematical Finance,* vol. 15, no. 3 (July 2005) pp. 425-437.

[2] Mango, Donald F. "Capital Consumption: An Alternative Methodology for Pricing Reinsurance." *Casualty Actuarial Society Forum* (Winter 2003), Ratemaking Call Paper Program, pp. 351-378. Available online at http://www.casact.org/pubs/forum/03wforum/03wf351.pdf.

[3] ____. "Insurance Capital As a Shared Asset." *ASTIN Bulletin,* 35 (2), (November 2005). Available online at www.casact.org/library/astin/vol35no2/471.pdf.

[4] Merton, Robert, and Andre Perold. "Theory of Risk Capital in Financial Firms." *Journal of Applied Corporate Finance,* vol. 6, no. 3 (Fall 1993) pp. 16-32.

[5] Meyers, Glenn, Frederick Klinker, and David Lalonde. "The Aggregation and Correlation of Insurance Exposures." *Casualty Actuarial Society Forum* (Summer 2003), DFA Call Paper Program, pp. 15-82. Available online at http://www.casact.org/pubs/forum/03sforum/03sf015.pdf.

[6] Myers, Stewart C., and James A. Read. "Capital Allocation for Insurance Companies." *Journal of Risk and Insurance,* 68:4 (2001) pp. 545-580. Available online at www.aib.org/RPP/Myers-Read.pdf.

[7] Spetzler, Carl S. "The Development of a Corporate Risk Policy for Capital Investment Decisions." *IEEE Transactions on Systems Science and Cybernetics,* vol. SSC-4, no. 3 (September 1968) pp. 279-300.

[8] Venter, Gary G. "Capital Allocation: An Opinionated Survey." *Casualty Actuarial Society Forum* (Summer 2003) pp. 279-306. Available online at http://www.casact.org/pubs/forum/03sforum/03sf279.pdf.

[9] Venter, Gary G., John Major, and Rodney E. Kreps. "Marginal Decomposition of Risk Measures." *ASTIN Bulletin* (2006).

[10] Walls, Michael R. "Combining Decision Analysis and Portfolio Management to Improve Project Selection in the Exploration and Production Firm." *Journal of Petroleum Science and Engineering,* 44 (2004) pp. 55-65. Available online at www.econbus.mines.edu/walls-pubs.htm.

Section 2.2

[1] Mango, Donald F. "Capital Consumption: An Alternative Methodology for Pricing Reinsurance." *Casualty Actuarial Society Forum* (Winter 2003), Ratemaking Call Paper Program, pp. 351-378. Available online at http://www.casact.org/pubs/forum/03wforum/03wf351.pdf.

[2] Merton, Robert, and Andre Perold. "Theory of Risk Capital in Financial Firms." *Journal of Applied Corporate Finance,* vol. 6, no. 3 (Fall 1993) pp. 16-32.

Section 2.4

[1] CAS Valuation, Finance, and Investment Committee. "Interest Rate Risk: An Evaluation of Duration Matching as a Risk-Minimizing Strategy for Property/Casualty Insurers." *Casualty Actuarial Society Forum* (Summer 2002).

[2] Venter, Gary G. and others. "Implications of Reinsurance and Reserves on Risk of Investment Asset Allocation." *Casualty Actuarial Society Forum* (Summer 1998) pp. 221-272.

Section 2.5

[1] Epermanis, Karen, and Scott E. Harrington. "Market Discipline and Reaction to Ratings Changes in U.S. Property-Liability Insurance Markets." University of South Carolina (March 2001).

[2] Froot, Kenneth, Gary G. Venter, and John Major. "Capital and Value of Risk Transfer." AFIR Colloquium, Boston (November 2004). Available online at http://www.actuaries.org/AFIR/colloquia/Boston/Froot_Venter_Major.pdf.

[3] Phillips, Richard D., J. David Cummins, and Franklin Allen. "Financial Pricing of Insurance in the Multiple-Line Insurance Company." *The Journal of Risk and Insurance,* vol. 65, no. 4 (1998) pp. 597-636.

[4] Sommer, David W. "The Impact of Firm Risk on Property-Liability Insurance Prices." *The Journal of Risk and Insurance,* vol. 63, no. 3 (1996) pp. 501-636.

Section 2.6

[1] Asmussen, S., and M. Taksar. "Controlled Diffusion Models for Optimal Dividend Pay-out." *Insurance: Mathematics and Economics,* 20:1 (1997) pp.1-15.

[2] Asmussen, S., B. Højgaard, and M. Taksar. "Optimal Risk Control and Dividend Distribution Policies: Example of Excess-of Loss Reinsurance for an Insurance Corporation." *Finance and Stochastics,* 4:3 (2000) pp. 299-324.

[3] Avram, F., Z. Palmovski, and M. R. Pistorius. "On the Optimal Dividend Problem for a Spectrally Negative Lévy Process." Working Paper, King's College, London (2006).

[4] Azcue, P., and N. Muler. "Optimal Reinsurance and Dividend Distribution Policies in The Cramér-Lundberg Model." *Mathematical Finance*, 15 (2005) 261ff.

[5] Bather, J. A. "Diffusion Models in Stochastic Control Theory." *J. Royal Statistical Society A.*, 132 (1969) pp. 335-352.

[6] Bäuerle, N. "Approximation of Optimal Reinsurance and Dividend Payout Policies." *Mathematical Finance*, 14:1 (2004) 99ff.

[7] Belhaj, M. "Optimizing Dividend Payments When Cash Reserves Follow a Compound Process." Stochastic Finance International Conference, Lisbon, Portugal (2004).

[8] Bellman, Richard E. *The Theory of Dynamic Programming*. Santa Monica, California: The RAND Corporation, 1954.

[9] Black, F., and M. Scholes. "The Pricing of Options and Corporate Liabilities." *Journal of Political Economy*, 81:3 (1973) pp. 637-654.

[10] Blazenko, G. W., G. Parker, and A. D. Pavlov. "Financial Risk Theory for a Regulated Insurer." Working Paper, Simon Fraser University (2004).

[11] Borch, K. "The Theory of Risk." *The Journal of the Royal Statistical Society*, Series B, 29:3 (1967) pp. 432-467.

[12] _____. "Objectives and Optimal Decisions in Insurance." Transactions of the 20th International Congress of Actuaries, Tokyo, 3:4 (1976) pp. 33-441.

[13] _____. "A Theory of Insurance Premiums." *The Geneva Risk and Insurance Review*, 10 (1985) pp. 192-208.

[14] _____. "Risk Theory and Serendipity." *Insurance Mathematics and Economics*, 5(1), (1986) pp. 103-112.

[15] Cadenillas, A., S. Sarkar, and F. Zapatero. "Optimal Dividend Policy with Mean-Reverting Cash Reservoir." To appear in *Mathematical Finance* (2006).

[16] Cai, J., H. Gerber, and H. Yang. "Optimal Dividends in an Ornstein-Uhlenbeck Type Model with Credit and Debit Interest," *North American Actuarial Journal*, 10:2 (2006) pp. 94-119.

[17] Chen, R., B. Logan, O. Palmon, and L. Shepp. "Dividends vs. Reinvestments in Continuous Time: A More General Model." Working Paper, Rutgers University (2003).

[18] Choulli, T., M. Taksar, and X. Y. Zhou. "A Diffusion Model for Optimal Dividend Distribution for a Company with Constraints on Risk Control." *SIAM Journal on Control and Optimization*, 41:6 (2003) pp. 1946-1979.

[19] Cont, Rama, and Peter Tankov. *Financial Modelling with Jump Processes*. New York: Chapman & Hall, 2004.

[20] Cramér, H. "On the Mathematical Theory of Risk." Skandia, Jubilee Volume, Stockholm (1930).

[21] Culp, C. *The ART of Risk Management: Alternative Risk Transfer, Capital Structure, and the Convergence of Insurance and Capital Markets*. New York: Wiley, 2002.

[22] Daykin, C., T. Pentikainen, and E. Pesonen. *Practical Risk Theory for Actuaries*. London: Chapman and Hall, 1994.

[23] De Finetti, B. "Su un' impostazione alternativa della teoria colletiva del rischio." Transactions of the XVth International Congress of Actuaries 2 (1957) pp. 433-443.

[24] Decamps, J. P., and S. Villeneuve. "Optimal Dividend Policy and Growth Option to Expand." IDEI Working Paper, no. 369, Institut d'Économie Industrielle (IDEI), Toulouse, France (2005).

[25] Dickson, D., C. M. and H. Waters. "Some Optimal Dividends Problems." *ASTIN Bulletin*, 34(1), (2004) pp. 49-74.

[26] Doherty, N. *Corporate Risk Management: A Financial Exposition*. New York: McGraw-Hill, 1985.

[27] ____. *Integrated Risk Management: Techniques and Strategies for Reducing Risk*. New York: McGraw-Hill, 2000.

[28] Froot, K. "Risk Management, Capital Budgeting and Capital Structure Policy for Insurers and Reinsurers." NBER Working Papers 10184, National Bureau of Economic Research, Inc. (2003).

[29] Froot, K., and J. Stein "Risk Management, Capital Budgeting and Capital Structure Policy for Financial Institutions: An Integrated Approach." *Journal of Financial Economics*, 47 (1998) pp. 55-82.

[30] Froot, K., D. Scharfstein, and J. Stein. "Risk Management: Coordinating Corporate Investment and Financing Policies." *Journal of Finance*, 48 (1993) pp. 1629-1658.

[31] Gerber, H. "Games of Economic Survival With Discrete- and Continuous-Income Process." *Operations Research*, 20 (1972) pp. 37-45.

[32] Gerber, H., and E. Shiu. "Optimal Dividends: Analysis with Brownian Motion." *North American Actuarial Journal*, 8:1 (2004) pp. 1-20.

[33] ____. "On Optimal Dividend Strategies in the Compound Poisson Model." *North American Actuarial Journal*, 10:2 (2006) pp. 76-93.

[34] Guo, Xin, Jun Li, and Xun Yu Zhou. "A Constrained Nonlinear Regular-Singular Stochastic Control Problem, with Applications." *Stochastic Processes and Their Applications*, 109 (2004) pp. 167-187.

[35] Hipp, C. "Optimal Dividend Payment Under a Ruin Constraint: Discrete Time and State Space." Working Paper, University of Karlsruhe, Germany (2003).

[36] Højgaard, B. "Optimal Dividend Pay-out with the Option of Proportional Reinsurance in the Diffusion Model." *Insurance: Mathematics and Economics*, 20:2 (1997) p. 151.

[37] ____. "Optimal Dynamic Premium Control in Non-life Insurance. Maximizing Dividend Pay-outs." *Scandinavian Actuarial Journal*, 2002:4 (2002) pp. 225-245.

[38] Højgaard, B., and M. Taksar. "Optimal Proportional Reinsurance Policies for Diffusion Models." *Scandinavian Actuarial Journal*, 1998:2 (1998) pp. 166-180.

[39] ____. "Optimal Proportional Reinsurance Policies for Diffusion Models with Transaction Costs." *Insurance: Mathematics and Economics*, 22:1 (1998) pp. 41-51.

[40] ____. "Controlling Risk Exposure and Dividends Payout Schemes: Insurance Company Example." *Mathematical Finance*, 9:2 (1999) pp. 153-182.

[41] _____. "Optimal Risk Control for a Large Corporation in the Presence of Returns on Investments." *Finance and Stochastics*, 5:4 (2001) pp. 527-547.

[42] _____. "Optimal Dynamic Portfolio Selection for a Corporation with Controllable Risk and Dividend Distribution Policy." *Quantitative Finance*, 4:3 (2004) pp. 315-327.

[43] Hubalek, F., and W. Schachermayer. "Optimizing Expected Utility of Dividend Payments for a Brownian Risk Process and a Peculiar Nonlinear ODE." *Insurance Mathematics & Economics*, 34:2 (2004) pp. 193-225.

[44] Itô, K. "On Stochastic Differential Equations." Memoirs of the American Mathematical Society, 4 (1951) pp. 1-51.

[45] Jeanblanc-Picqué, M., and A. Shiryaev. "Optimization of the Flow of Dividends." Uspekhi Mathem. Naut. 50, 25-46 (in Russian), translated in Russian Mathematical Surveys, 50 (1995) pp. 257-277.

[46] Kushner, Harold J., and Paul Dupuis. *Numerical Methods for Stochastic Control Problems in Continuous Time, Second edition*. New York: Springer-Verlag, 2001.

[47] Løkka, A., and M. Zervos. "Optimal Dividend and Issuance of Equity Policies in the Presence of Proportional Costs." Working Paper, King's College, London (2005).

[48] Major, J. A. "A Brief History of the de Finetti Optimal Dividends Problem." Working Paper, Guy Carpenter & Co. Inc. (2006).

[49] _____. "On a Connection Between Froot-Stein and the de Finetti Optimal Dividends Models." Working Paper, Guy Carpenter & Co. Inc. (2006).

[50] Merton, R. C. "Lifetime Portfolio Selection Under Uncertainty: The Continuous-Time Case." *Review of Economics and Statistics*, 51 (1969) pp. 247-257.

[51] _____. "An Intertemporal Capital Asset Pricing Model." *Econometrica*, 41:5 (1973) pp. 867-887.

[52] _____. "On the Pricing of Corporate Debt: The Risk Structure of Interest Rates." *Journal of Finance*, 29 (1974) pp. 449-470.

[53] Miller, M. H., and F. Modigliani. "Dividend Policy, Growth, and the Valuation of Shares." *Journal of Business*, 34 (1961) pp. 235-264.

[54] Milne A., and D. Robertson. "Firm Behaviour Under the Threat of Liquidation." *Journal of Economic Dynamics and Control*, 20:8 (1996) pp. 1427-1449.

[55] Miyasawa, K. "An Economic Survival Game." *Journal of Operations Research Society of Japan*, 4 (1962) pp. 95-113.

[56] Mnif, M., and A. Sulem. "Optimal Risk Control and Dividend Policies Under Excess of Loss Reinsurance." *Stochastics: An International Journal of Probability and Stochastic Processes*, 77:5 (2005) pp. 455-476.

[57] Modigliani, F. and M. H. Miller. "The Cost of Capital, Corporation Finance, and the Theory of Investments." *American Economic Review*, 48 (1958) pp. 261-297.

[58] Morill, J. "One-Person Games of Economic Survival." *Naval Research Logistics Quarterly*, 13 (1966) pp. 49-70.

[59] Øksendal, Bernt, and Agnès Sulem. *Applied Stochastic Control of Jump Diffusions*. New York: Springer-Verlag, 2005.

[60] Paulsen, J. "Optimal Dividend Payouts for Diffusions with Solvency Constraints." *Finance and Stochastics*, 7:4 (2003) pp. 457-473.

[61] Paulsen, J., and H. Gjessing. "Optimal Choice of Dividend Barriers for a Risk Process with Stochastic Return on Investments." *Insurance: Mathematics and Economics*, 20:3 (1997) pp. 215-223.

[62] Peura, S. "Essays on Corporate Hedging." Academic dissertation, University of Helsinki (2003).

[63] Porteus, E. L. "On Optimal Dividend, Reinvestment, and Liquidation Policies for the Firm." *Operations Research*, 25:5 (1977) pp. 818-834.

[64] Radner, R., and L. Shepp. "Risk vs. Profit Potential: a Model for Corporate Strategy." *Journal of Economic Dynamics and Control*, 20 (1996) pp. 1373-1393.

[65] Rochet, J., and S. Villeneuve. "Liquidity Risk and Corporate Demand for Hedging and Insurance." IDEI Working Paper, no. 254, Institut d'Économie Industrielle (IDEI), Toulouse, France (2004).

[66] Ross, S. "The Arbitrage Theory of Capital Asset Pricing." *Journal of Economic Theory*, 13:3 (1976).

[67] Schoutens, Wim. *Lévy Processes in Finance: Pricing Financial Derivatives*. New York: Wiley, 2003.

[68] Sethi, S. P., and M. I. Taksar. "Optimal Financing of a Corporation Subject to Random Returns." *Mathematical Finance*, 12:2 (2002) pp. 155-172.

[69] Shubik, M., and G. L. Thompson. "Games of Economic Survival." *Naval Research Logistics Quarterly*, 6 (1959) pp. 111-123.

[70] Takeuchi, K. "A Remark on Economic Survival Games." *Journal of Operations Research Society of Japan*, 4 (1962) pp. 114-121.

[71] Taksar, M. "Incorporating the Value of Bankruptcy into the Optimal Risk/Dividend Control of a Financial Corporation." Proceedings of the 4th International Conference on Optimization: Techniques and Applications, Perth, Australia (1998) pp. 1247-1254.

[72] ____. "Optimal Risk and Dividend Distribution Control Models for an Insurance Company." *Mathematical Methods of Operations Research*, 51:1 (2000) pp. 1-42.

[73] Taksar, M., and X. Y. Zhou. "Optimal Risk and Dividend Control for a Company with a Debt Liability." *Insurance: Mathematics and Economics*, 22:1 (1998) pp. 105-122.

[74] Venter, Gary G. "Measuring Value in Reinsurance." *Casualty Actuarial Society Forum* (Summer 2001).

[75] Waldmann, K-H. "On Optimal Dividend Payments and Related Problems." *Insurance Mathematics and Economics*, 7:4 (1988) pp. 237-249.

[76] Yong, J. and X. Zhou. *Stochastic Controls: Hamiltonian Systems and HJB Equations*. New York: Springer, 1999.

[77] Zajic, T. "Optimal Dividend Payout Under Compound Poisson Income." *Journal of Optimization Theory and Applications*, 104:1 (2000) pp. 195-213.

Section 3.2

[1] Klugman, S., H. Panjer, and G. Wilmont. *Loss Models: From Data to Decisions*, Second edition. New York: John Wiley and Sons, 1998.

Section 3.3

[1] Belguise, Olivier, and Charles Levi. "Tempêtes: Etude des Dépendances Entre les Branches Automobile et Incendie à l'Aide de la Théorie des Copulas." *Bulletin Francais d'Actuariat*, vol. 5 (2002) pp. 135-174.

[2] Kreps, Rodney E. "A Partially Co-monotonic Algorithm for Loss Generation." ASTIN Colloquium (2000).

[3] Venter, Gary G. "Tails of Copulas." Proceedings of the Casualty Actuarial Society LXXXIX (2002) pp. 68-113.

Section 4.1

[1] Basel Committee on Banking Supervision. "International Convergence of Capital Measurement and Capital Standards – A Revised Framework." November 2005, Part 2, Section V-A. Available online at www.bis.org/publ/bcbs118.pdf.

[2] Basel Committee on Banking Supervision. "Sound Practices for the Management and Supervision of Operational Risk." July 2002. Available online at www.bis.org/publ/bcbs91.pdf.

[3] Davies, Jonathan, and Michael Haubenstock. "Building Effective Indicators to Monitor Operational Risk." *The RMA Journal* (May 2002) pp. 40-43.

[4] Hoskisson, R., M. Hitt, and C. Hill. "Managerial Incentives and Investment in R and D in Large Multiproduct Firms." *Organization Science*, 3 (1992) pp. 1-17.

[5] Jensen, M. "Agency Costs of Free Cash Flow, Corporate Finance, and Takeovers." *American Economic Review*, 76 (1986) pp. 323-329.

[6] Jensen, M., and W. Meckling. "Theory of the Firm: Managerial Behavior, Agency Costs, and Ownership Structure." *Journal of Financial Economics*, 3 (1976) pp. 305-360.

[7] Verheyen, Mark. "Operational Risk Management in a Property/Casualty Insurance Company." Casualty Actuarial Society Spring Meeting presentation (2005). Available online at www.casact.org/education/spring/2005/handouts/verheyen.ppt.

Section 4.2

[1] Baird, Inga Skromme, and Howard Thomas. "Toward a Contingency Model of Strategic Risk Taking." *Academy of Management Review,* vol. 10, no. 2 (1985) pp. 230-243.

[2] Basel Committee on Banking Supervision. "International Convergence of Capital Measurement and Capital Standards – A Revised Framework." November 2005, Part 2, Section V-A. Available online at www.bis.org/publ/bcbs118.pdf.

[3] Hertz, David B., and Howard Thomas. "Decision and Risk Analysis in a New Product and Facilities Planning Problem." *Sloan Management Review,* 24, 2 (Winter 1983).

[4] Knight, F. H. *Risk, Uncertainty and Profit*. New York: Harper and Row, 1921.

[5] Miller, Kent D. "A Framework for Integrated Risk Management in International Business." *Journal of International Business Studies,* vol. 23, issue 2 (1992) pp. 311-331.

[6] Shoemaker, Paul J. H. "Scenario Planning: A Tool for Strategic Thinking." *Sloan Management Review,* 36, 2 (Winter 1995) pp. 29-40.

[7] Slywotzky, Adrian J., and John Drzik. "Countering the Biggest Risk of All." *Harvard Business Review* (April 2005).

Section 5.1

[1] Brazauskas, V., and R. Serfling. "Robust and Efficient Estimation of the Tail Index of a Single-Parameter Pareto Distribution." *North American Actuarial Journal,* 4(4), (2000) pp. 12-27.

[2] Heckman, Philip E., and Glenn G. Meyers. "The Calculation of Aggregate Loss Distributions from Claim Severity and Claim Count Distributions." PCAS LXX (1983) pp. 22-61.

[3] Hogg, R., and Stuart Klugman. *Loss Distributions.* John Wiley and Sons, 1984.

[4] Klugman, S., H. Panjer, and G. Wilmont. *Loss Models: From Data to Decisions, Second edition.* New York: John Wiley and Sons, 1998.

[5] Mack, T., and M. Fackler. "Exposure Rating in Liability Reinsurance." Blätter of the DGVFM (German Association for Mathematics of Insurance and Finance), vol. XXVI, 2 (2003).

[6] McDonald, J. "Some Generalized Functions for the Size Distribution of Income." *Econometrica,* vol. 52, issue 3 (1984) pp. 647-663.

[7] Riebesell, P. *Introduction to Property-Liability Insurance Mathematics (Einführung in die Sachversicherungsmathematik).* Berlin, 1936.

[8] Venter, Gary G. "Transformed Beta and Gamma Distributions and Aggregate Losses." PCAS LXX (1983) pp. 156-193.

Section 5.2

[1] Bornhuetter, Ron, and Ron Ferguson. "The Actuary and IBNR." Proceedings of the Casualty Actuarial Society, vol. LIX (1972) pp. 181.

[2] Brehm, Paul. "A Least Squares Method of Producing Bornhuetter-Ferguson Initial Loss Ratios." *Casualty Actuarial Society Forum* (Fall 2006) p. 441.

[3] _____. "Correlation and Aggregation of Unpaid Loss Distributions." *Casualty Actuarial Society Forum* (Fall 2002) p. 1.

[4] Berquist, J., and R. Sherman. "Loss Reserve Adequacy Testing: A Comprehensive, Systematic Approach." Proceedings of the Casualty Actuarial Society, vol. LXIV (1977) p. 123.

[5] Buhlmann, H. "Estimation of IBNR Reserves by the Methods Chain Ladder, Cape Cod, and Complementary Loss Ratio." Unpublished (1983).

[6] Casualty Actuarial Society. "Chapter 5 Loss Reserving." *Foundations of Casualty Actuarial Science* (2001).

[7] Gluck, S. "Balancing Development and Trend in Loss Reserve Analyses." Proceedings of the Casualty Actuarial Society, vol. LXXXIV (1997) pp. 482-532.

[8] Hayne, Roger. "Application of Collective Risk Theory to Estimate Variability in Loss Reserves." Proceedings of the Casualty Actuarial Society, vol. LXXVI (1989) p. 77.

[9] _____. "A Method to Estimate Probability Level for Reserves." *Casualty Actuarial Society Forum* (Spring 1994) p. 297.

[10] Hodes, Douglas, Shalom Feldblum, and Gary Blumsohn. "Workers Compensation Reserve Uncertainty." Proceedings of the Casualty Actuarial Society, vol. LXXXVI (1999) pp. 263-392.

[11] Kreps, Rodney. "Parameter Uncertainty in (Log) Normal Distributions." Proceedings of the Casualty Actuarial Society, vol. LXXXIV (1997) pp. 553-580.

[12] Mack, Thomas. "Measuring the Variability of Chain Ladder Reserve Estimates." *Casualty Actuarial Society Forum* (Spring 1994) p. 101.

[13] _____. "The Standard Error of Chain Ladder Reserve Estimates: Recursive Calculation and Inclusion of a Tail Factor." *ASTIN Bulletin,* vol. 29:2 (1999) pp. 361-366.

[14] Murphy, Daniel. "Unbiased Loss Development Factors." *Casualty Actuarial Society Forum* (Spring 1994) p. 183.

[15] Stanard, J. "A Simulation Test of Prediction Errors of Loss Reserve Estimation Techniques." Proceedings of the Casualty Actuarial Society, vol. LXXII (1985) pp. 124-153.

[16] Venter, Gary G. "Testing the Assumptions of Age-to-Age Factors." Proceedings of the Casualty Actuarial Society, vol. LXXXV (1998) p. 807.

[17] _____. "Introduction." *Casualty Actuarial Society Forum* (Spring 1994) p. 91.

[18] Verrall, Richard, and Peter England. "Analytic and Bootstrap Estimates of Prediction Errors in Claims Reserving." *Insurance: Mathematics and Economics,* vol. 25 (1999) pp. 281-293.

[19] Zehnwirth, Ben. "Probabilistic Development Factor Models with Applications to Loss Reserve Variability, Prediction Intervals and Risk Based Capital." *Casualty Actuarial Society Forum* (Spring 1994) p. 447.

Section 5.3

[1] Clark, D. R. "LDF Curve-Fitting and Stochastic Reserving: A Maximum Likelihood Approach." *Casualty Actuarial Society Forum* (Fall 2003) pp. 41-92.

[2] Hachemeister, C., and J. Stanard. "IBNR Claims Count Estimation with Static Lag Functions." ASTIN Colloquium, Portimao, Portugal (1975).

[3] Kremer, E. *Einfuhrung in die Versicherungsmathematik*. Gottingen: Vandenhoek & Ruprecht, 1985.

[4] Mack, T. "A Simple Parametric Model for Rating Automobile Insurance or Estimating IBNR Claims Reserves." *ASTIN Bulletin*, 21:1 (1991) pp. 93-109.

[5] Renshaw, A., and R. J. Verrall. "A Stochastic Model Underlying the Chain Ladder Technique." *British Actuarial Journal*, 4:90 (1998) pp. 3-23.

[6] Taylor, G., and F. Ashe. "Second Moments of Estimates of Outstanding Claims." *Journal of Econometrics*, 23 (1983) pp. 37-61.

[7] Mack T. *Schadenversicherungsmathematik, Second edition*. Karlsruhe, Germany: Verlag Versicherungswirtshaft, 2002.

Section 5.4

[1] Alkemper, J., and D. F. Mango. "Concurrent Simulation to Explain Reinsurance Market Price Dynamics." *Risk Management*, 6 (November 2005) pp. 13-17.

[2] Box, G., G. Jenkins, and G. Reinsel. *Time Series Analysis: Forecasting & Control*, Third edition. New York: Prentice-Hall, 1994.

[3] Chen, R., K. Wong, and H. Lee. "Underwriting Cycles in Asia." *Journal of Risk and Insurance*, 66 (1999) pp. 29-47.

[4] Cummins, J. D., and P. Danzon. "Price, Financial Quality and Capital Flows in Insurance Markets." *Journal of Financial Intermediation*, 6 (1997) pp. 3-38.

[5] Cummins, J. D., and F. Outreville. "An International Analysis of Underwriting Cycles In Property-Liability Insurance." *Journal of Risk and Insurance*, 54 (1987) pp. 246-262.

[6] Doherty, N. A., and H. B. Kang. "Interest Rates and Insurance Price Cycles." *Journal of Banking and Finance,* 12 (1988) pp. 199-214.

[7] Dowling, V. J. "An Analyst's Perspective: The State of the Industry." 8th Annual Roundtable, American Re-Insurance Company (2002).

[8] Feldblum, S. "Underwriting Cycles and Business Strategies." *Casualty Actuarial Society Forum* (Spring 1990).

[9] Froot. K. A., and P. G. J. O'Connell. "On the Pricing of Intermediated Risks: Theory and Application to Catastrophe Reinsurance." NBER Working Papers 6011, National Bureau of Economic Research, Inc. (1997).

[10] Fung, H-G., G. C. Lai, G. A. Patterson, and R. C. Witt. "Underwriting Cycles in Property and Liability Insurance: An Empirical Analysis of Industry and By-Line Data." *Journal of Risk and Insurance,* 65:4 (1998) pp. 539-561.

[11] Gallant, A. R., and G. E. Tauchen. "Which Moments to Match." *Econometric Theory,* 12:4 (1996) pp. 657-681.

[12] Grace M. F., and J. L. Hotchkiss. "External Impacts on Property-Liability Insurance Cycle." *Journal of Risk and Insurance,* 62 (1995) pp. 738-754.

[13] Gron, A. "Property-Casualty Insurance Cycles, Capacity Constraints and Empirical Tests." Ph.D. Thesis, Boston: Massachusetts Institute of Technology (1990).

[14] _____. "Capacity Constraints and Cycles in Property-Casualty Insurance Markets." *Rand Journal of Economics,* 25 (Spring 1994) pp. 110-127.

[15] Haley, J. D. "A Cointegration Analysis of the Relationship Between Underwriting Margins and Interest Rates: 1930-1989." *The Journal of Risk and Insurance,* 60:3 (1993) pp. 480-493.

[16] Hansen, L. P. "Large Sample Properties of Generalized Method of Moments Estimators." *Econometrica,* 50:4 (1982) pp. 1029-1054.

[17] Harrington, S. E., and P. Danzon. "Price-Cutting in Liability Insurance Markets." *Journal of Business,* 67 (1994) pp. 511-538.

[18] Harrington, S. E. "Tort Liability, Insurance Rates, and the Insurance Cycle." Brookings-Wharton Papers on Financial Services (2004) pp. 97-138.

[19] Hartwig, R. P. "The Insurance Cycle Is Alive and Well and Ready to Kill Your Company: Are Actuaries to Blame?" Presentation to Casualty Actuarial Society Ratemaking Seminar, New Orleans, Louisiana (2005). Available online at https://www.casact.org/education/ratesem/2005/handouts/hartwig.ppt.

[20] Helmer-Hirschberg, Olaf. *Analysis of the Future: The Delphi Method.* Santa Monica, California: The RAND Corporation, 1959.

[21] Kahneman, D. "Maps of Bounded Rationality: Psychology for Behavioral Economics." *The American Economic Review,* 93:5 (2003) pp. 1449-1475.

[22] Intriligator, M. D. *Econometric Models, Techniques, and Applications.* New York: Prentice-Hall, 1978.

[23] Lamm-Tennant, J., and M. A. Weiss. "International Insurance Cycles: Rational Expectations/Institutional Intervention." *Journal of Risk and Insurance,* 64 (1997) pp. 415-439.

[24] Linstone, H. A., and M. Turoff, eds. *The Dephi Method: Techniques and Applications.* New Jersey Institute of Technology, 2002. Available online at www.is.njit.edu/pubs/delphibook/.

[25] MacMahon, B. E. "The Implications of Market Return Pricing Strategies Upon Profit and Required Surplus." Casualty Actuarial Society Discussion Paper Program 2 (1992) pp. 759-818.

[26] Madsen, C. K., S. Haastrup, and H. W. Pedersen. "A Further Examination of Insurance Pricing And Underwriting Cycles." Presented at 15th AFIR Colloquium, Zurich, Switzerland (1992). Available online at www.actuaries.org/AFIR/Colloquia/Zurich/Madsen_Haastrup_Pedersen.pdf.

[27] Niehaus, G., and A. Terry. "Evidence on the Time Series Properties of Insurance Premiums and Causes of the Underwriting Cycle." *Journal of Risk and Insurance,* 60 (1993) pp. 466-479.

[28] Schnieper, R. "Modelling the Underwriting Cycle." Presented at 15th AFIR Colloquium, Zurich, Switzerland (2005).

[29] Stewart, B. D., R. E. Stewart, and R. S. L. Roddis. "A Brief History of Underwriting Cycles." *Cycles and Crises in Property-Casualty Insurance: Causes and Implications for Public Policy.* Kansas City, Missouri: National Association of Insurance Commissioners (1991). Available online at www.stewart economics.com/Cycle%20History.pdf.

[30] Schwartz, Peter. *The Art of the Long View: Planning for the Future in an Uncertain World.* New York: Currency Doubleday, 1991.

[31] Thaler, R. H. *The Winner's Curse: Paradoxes and Anomalies of Economic Life.* Princeton, New Jersey: Princeton University Press, 1992.

[32] Venezian, E. "Ratemaking Methods and Profit Cycles in Property and Liability Insurance." *Journal of Risk and Insurance,* 52 (1985) pp. 477-500.

[33] Wilson, W. C. "The Underwriting Cycle and Investment Income." *CPCU Journal,* 34 (1981) pp. 225-232.

[34] Winter, R. A. "Solvency Regulation and the Property-Liability Insurance Cycle." *Economic Inquiry,* 29 (1991) pp. 458-471.

[35] _____. "The Dynamics of Competitive Insurance Markets." *Journal of Financial Intermediation,* 3 (1994) pp. 379-415.

[36] Youngman, Ian. *Competitor Analysis in Financial Services.* CRC Press, 1998.

Section 6.2

[1] Andersen, T., and J. Lund. "Stochastic Volatility and Mean Drift in the Short Rate Diffusion: Sources of Steepness, Level and Curvature in the Yield Curve." Working Paper, Northwestern University (1997).

[2] Cox, J., J. Ingersoll, and S. Ross. "A Theory of the Term Structure of Interest Rates." *Econometrica,* 53 (March 1985) pp. 385-408.

[3] Daul, S., E. De Giorgi, F. Lindskog, and A. McNeil. "The Grouped t–Copula with an Application to Credit Risk." *RISK,* 16 (2003) pp. 73-76.

[4] Driessen, Joost, Pieter Klaassen, and Bertrand Melenberg. "The Performance of Multi-Factor Term Structure Models for Pricing and Hedging Caps and Swaptions." University of Amsterdam Faculty Papers (2002). Available online at www1.fee.uva.nl/fm/PAPERS/Driessen/multifactor_models.pdf.

[5] Fouque, J., G. Papanicolaou, and K. R. Sircar. *Derivatives in Financial Markets with Stochastic Volatility*. Cambridge University Press, 2000.

[6] Hibbert, John, Philip Mowbray, and Craig Turnbull. "A Stochastic Asset Model & Calibration for Long-Term Financial Planning Purposes." Technical Report, Barrie & Hibbert Limited (2001). Available online at www.barrhibb.com.

[7] Hull, J., and A. White. "Numerical Procedures for Implementing Term Structure Models II: Two-Factor Models." *Journal of Derivatives* (Winter 1994).

[8] Kou, S. "A Jump Diffusion Model for Option Pricing with Three Properties: Leptokurtic Feature, Volatility Smile, and Analytical Tractability." Econometric Society in Its Series Econometric Society World Congress 2000 Contributed Papers (2002). Available online at http://fmwww.bc.edu/RePEc/es2000/0062.pdf.

[9] Schoutens,W. "The Meixner Process in Finance." EURANDOM Report 2001-002, EURANDOM, Eindhoven (2000).

[10] Venter, Gary G. "Testing Distributions of Stochastically Generated Yield Curves." *ASTIN Bulletin* (2004).

Index

A

ABM (agent-based modeling), 171–172
Accumulated risk, 73–78
Accumulation risk, 45, 47
Actuarial risk modeling, 25
Adequacy models, for capital
  (see Capital adequacy models)
Aftermath, of catastrophes, 19
Agency theory, 155–156
Agent-based modeling (ABM), 171–172
Age-to-age factor (see Link ratio)
Aggregate data, 198
AIC (see Akaike Information Criterion)
Akaike Information Criterion (AIC),
  191, 212
AL (Andersen and Lund) model, 250
Allocation:
  capital (see Capital allocation)
  of costs, 41–42
  of risk, 35–36
ALM (see Asset-liability management)
Alpha (α) parameters, 181–182
Alternative minimum taxes (AMTs), 51
A.M. Best, 46, 147–148
A.M. Best's Capital Adequacy Ratio
  (BCAR), 48
AMTs (alternative minimum taxes), 51
Andersen and Lund (AL) model, 250
Annual reporting, 131
"The Application of Strategic Models to
  Non-Life Insurance Markets" (GIRO),
  161–162
APRA (Australian Prudential Regulation
  Authority), 145
AR (autoregressive) model, 232–233
Arbitage-free pricing, 84, 248
As-if loss reserves, 73–74
Assessment:
  of cycle management performance,
    151
  of risks, by company, 7
Asset classes, 15

Asset risks, 15–16
Asset-liability management (ALM),
  49–55
  future research for, 55
  in insurance industry, 49
  modeling approach to, 52–54
  reinsurance in, 49
Asset-liability models, 49–55
Association of British Insurers
  Operational Risk Insurance
  Consortium (ORIC), 147
Australia Internal Model Based
  Method, 3
Australian Prudential Regulation
  Authority (APRA), 145
Autoregressive (AR) model, 232–233
Avoidance, default, 19

B

Baird, Inga Skromme, 163, 164
Ballasted Pereto distributions, 114, 186
Banking industry:
  99th percentile of, 20
  operational risk in, 156–157
Bankruptcy cost, 88
Basel Committee on Banking
  Supervision, 2, 144–145, 162–163
Basel I, 2, 148
Basel II, 2, 3
Bather, J. A., 91
Bayes' Theorem, 191
Bayesian estimation, 191–193
Bayesian Information Criteria (BIC), 191
BCAR (A.M. Best's Capital
  Adequacy Ratio), 48
Behavioral modeling
  (see Econometric modeling)
Benefit measures, 79
Berkshire Hathaway, 153–154
Best's Capital Adequacy Ratio (BCAR), 48
Best's rating agency, 3
Beta (β) parameters, 182–183, 186–187

Beta transformations, 177–181
B-F model/method (see Bornhuetter-Ferguson model)
BIC (Schwartz Bayesian Information Criteria), 191
Black, F., 84
Black & Scholes, 84
Black-Scholes options pricing, 33, 251
Blazenko, G. W., 85
Bond models, 16, 248–251
Book value, 26
Bootstrap models, 207, 216
Borch, K., 82
Bornhuetter-Ferguson (BF) model, 149, 202–203, 211
Branding, 164, 165
Brazauskas, V., 194
Breakdown points, 193, 228
Break-even point, 41
Brehm, Paul, 202–203
"Bridging model," 149
Brownian motion, 82, 97, 248–251
Buffett, Warren, 155
Business disruption, 145
Business risks:
   of ERM, 10
   operational, 145

C

Calendar time:
   influences by, 131
   loss reserve risk models and, 203
Calendar-year effects, 217, 219
Canadian Dynamic Capital Adequacy Test, 3
Canadian Minimum Capital Test, 46
Capacity constraints, 229
Cape Cod (Stanard-Buhlmann) Method, 202
Capital:
   cost allocation, 41–42
   economic, 31
   flows of, 237–238
   in insurance, 229
   reinsurance and, 48, 56, 68–73
   required, 34–35, 69–70
   setting requirements for, 19–21
   sources of, 48
Capital adequacy models:
   leverage ratios, 43–44
   of regulatory (rating) agencies, 42–49
   from regulatory and rating agencies, 42–49
   risk-based, 44–47
   scenario testing for, 47–48
   strategy evaluation for, 48–49
Capital allocation, 41–42
   in internal risk model, 29–30
   models, 34–36
CARRMEL, 3
CAS Committee on the Theory of Risk, 205
CAS Forum, 205
Casualty Actuarial Society Valuation, Finance, and Investment Committee (CFIC), 51
Catastrophe(s), 121–124
   aftermath of, 19
   copulas for, 121–124
   natural, 14
   PML for, 2
Catastrophe insurance, 97
Catastrophe (cat) models:
   history of, 2
   underwriting for uncertainty in, 14
Catastrophic losses, 121–124
CBA (see Cost benefit analysis)
CDFs (cumulative distribution functions), 74–75
Certainty equivalent, 25
CFIC (Casualty Actuarial Society Valuation, Finance, and Investment Committee), 51
Chain-ladder family (models), 211, 219
Chief Risk Officer (CRO), 3, 144
CIR (Cox, Ingersoll and Ross) model, 248–250

Claims:
    risk indicators in, 158
    Six Sigma for, 159
Coefficient of variation (CV), 108
Collective risk model, 130
Co-measures, 36–37
Commercial lines, 228
Commitment, resource, 103
Committee of Sponsoring Organization of the Treadway Commission (COSO), 157
Communications, for IRM, 106
Competition and competitors:
    analysis of, 232
    intelligence of, 231
    in mature markets, 229
    over price, 226
    in SRM, 164–166
    in underwriting cycle, 229
Comptroller of Currency (OCC), 162
Conditional models, 211
Confidence, in model, 9
Continuous Distributions, 11
Control Self-Assessment (CSA), 157, 160
Controls:
    in business evolution, 228
    for IRM, 107
Copulas, 18, 118–123
    for catastrophe loss, 121–124
    dependencies and, 118–129
    describing, 121–123
    fitting, to data, 126–129
    Frank copula, 119–120
    Gumbel copula, 120
    heavy right tail (HRT) copula, 120–121
    joint Burr distribution and, 120–121
    modeling for, 118–123
    multivariate, 125–126
    normal copula, 121
    t-copula, 125, 126
"Corner office risk," 150

Corporate decision making:
    evolution of, 24–26
    with internal risk model (IRM), 26–30
    under uncertainty, 24–26
Corporate risks, 4–6
Cost benefit analysis for, 28
    in internal risk model, 27–29
    tolerance of, 27–29
Correlation (see Dependencies)
Correlation assessment, 104
COSO (Committee of Sponsoring Organization of the Treadway Commission), 157
Cost allocation, 41–42
Cost benefit analysis (CBA):
    for corporate risk, 28
    for mitigation, in internal risk model (IRM), 30
Covariance adjustment, 46
Cox, Ingersoll and Ross (CIR) model, 248–250
Cramér-Lundberg model, 81
Credible data, 198
Credit risks, 244–245
    exposure to, 245
    loss calculation for, 244–245
    origin of, 244
Critical risks, 7
CRO (see Chief Risk Officer)
CSA (see Control self-assessment)
Cumulative distribution functions (CDFs), 74–75
Customers, in SRM, 164, 166
CV (coefficient of variation), 108
Cycle management, 150–152
    for IRM, 107
    naïve, 151
    operational risk and, 150–152
    performance assessment for, 151
    performance improvement via, 151–152
    for volatility, 166

D

Data:
  aggregate, 198
  estimation with, 196–197
  fitting, from copulas, 126–129
  homogenous, 198
  in loss reserve risk models, 198–200
Davies, Jonathan, 158
De Finetti, B., 81, 82
De Finetti-Lévy Asset Value of Optimized Risk, Equity, and Dividends (see FLAVORED models)
Decision analysis, 24
Decision making:
  corporate, 24–30
  strategic, 8, 164
Decomposition, of risk measures, 41
Deductibles, multiple, 194–195
Default:
  avoidance, 19
  value of, 33
Deficiencies, reserve, 148–150
Delivery, operational risk in, 145
Delphi method, 232
Delta method, 190
Dependencies (correlation):
  assessment of, 104
  copulas and, 118–129
  inflation and, 17–18
  for IRM, 105
  modeling for, 17–18
  sources of, 17
  tail, 17
Dependent losses, 117–118
Determinalistic project analysis, 25
DFA (see Dynamic financial analysis)
DFA models (see Internal risk model)
Diagnostic stage, 7
Diagonal effects, 218–219
DIL (direct incurred loss), 139
Direct incurred loss (DIL), 139
Direct paid loss (DPL), 139
Discounting:
  on short-term rate, 249
  timeline for, 131

Distributions:
  Bayesian estimation for, 191–193
  exposure information for, 194–195
  fit comparisons for, 191
  frequency, 187–188
  loss distribution, 189
  for model risk, 115–116
  parameter uncertainty in, 189–190
  robust estimation for, 193–194
  severity, 176
  (see also specific types, e.g.: Ballasted Pereto distributions)
Dividends, optimal, 82
Doherty, N., 84
Dowling, V. J., 229
DPL (direct paid loss), 139
Dynamic Capital Adequacy Test, 47
Dynamic financial analysis (DFA), 25
  in FLAVORED models, 81
  history of, 2
  IRM (see Internal risk model)
  NAIC and, 2
  volatility models and, 205
Dzrik, John, 164, 165

E

Econometric modeling (behavioral modeling), 234–240
  capital flows in, 237–238
  supply and demand in, 235–237
Economic linkages, 230
Economic value added (EVA®), 30
Education:
  for IRM, 106
  of owner, on operational risk, 153–155
Efficient Method of Moments, 233
ELR (see Expected loss ratio)
Emergence, of businesses, 228
Emergent properties, 171
Emerging Market Country Products and Trading Activities (OCC), 162, 163
Employment practices, as operational risk, 144

England, Peter, 207
Enterprise Risk Management (ERM):
   defined, 4
   historical context of, 2–4
   overview, 48
   process of, 6–7
Enterprise risk models, 8–21, 42
   for bonds, 16
   capital requirements in, 19–21
   corporate decision making using, 24–30
   for dependencies, 17–18
   for equities, 16
   for foreign exchange, 16
   macro-economic model in, 111
   risks in, 10–16
   underwriting risk in, 10–16
Entropy martingale transform, 42
EPD (see Expected policyholder deficit)
Equities:
   investments into, 51
   modeling for, 16
ERM (see Enterprise Risk Management)
Errors:
   forecasting, 149
   squared, 126
   strategic, 165
Estimation:
   Bayesian, 191–193
   for distributions, 191–194
   for frequency distribution parameters, 113
   of loss distribution, 189
   with no data, 196–197
   parameter uncertainty risk and, 113–115
   of parameters, 189
   robust, 193–194
Estimation risks, 12
   in insurance modeling, 108
   underwriting for, 12
ETNB (extended truncated negative binomial), 188
EU (European Union), 3

European index, 140
European Union (EU), 3
EVA® (economic value added), 30
Event(s), 132–133
Event generators, 133
Event risks, 13
Excess of loss (XOL) reinsurance, 97
Excess tail value at risk (XTV@R), 33, 39
Execution, operational risk in, 145
Expectation management, 102
Expected loss ratio (ELR), 149, 200
Expected policyholder deficit (EPD), 33, 40
Expert opinion, 104
Exposure:
   for distributions, 194–195
   growth of, 38
Extended truncated negative binomial (ETNB), 188
External fraud, 144

F

Fackler, M., 14
"Failed Promises: Insurance Company Insolvencies" (Congressional Report), 147
Feldblum, S., 229
Finance theory, 83–86
   disconnect with, 83–84
   later models of, 84–86
Financial engineering, 84
Financial risks, 5
Financial Services Authority (FSA), 3, 145
de Finetti-Lévy Asset Value of Optimized Risk, Equity, and Dividends (see FLAVORED models)
Firm-level modeling, 234
Fit comparisons, 191
Fitch rating agency, 3
FLAVORED models, 80–99
   dynamic financial analysis in, 81
   early forms of, 81–83
   example problem, 92–97

finance theory and, 83–86
Froot models and, 86–90
   history of, 81
   for proportional reinsurance, 91–92
   risk management evaluation with, 90
   solution methodology of, 97–99
   Vanilla model and, 90–91
Forecasting errors, 149
Foreign exchange (f/x):
   investment market risk for, 252–253
   modeling for, 16
   movement of, 253
Foresight Insurance, 151–153
Frank copula, 119–120
Fraud, 144
Frequency distributions, 113, 187–188
Frontier charts, 66
Froot, Kenneth:
   on financial engineering paradigm, 84
   on FLAVORED models, 90
Froot models, 80, 86–90
   FLAVORED models and, 86–90
   going-concern, 87–90
   simplified, 86–87
FSA (Financial Services Authority), 3, 145
Fung, H-G., 230
F/x (see Foreign exchange)

G

GAAP accounting-based metrics, 51
Gamma distributions, inverse, 187
Gamma function, 176
Gaussian distribution, inverse, 176
General Insurance Research Organization (GIRO), 161
Generalized Cape Cod Method, 202
Generalized Method of Moments, 233
Generalized moments, 34
GIRO (General Insurance Research Organization), 161
GIRO Working Party, 161–162
Gluck, Spencer, 202
Goford, Jeremy, 150

Going-concern Froot models, 87–90
Google Scholar, 83
Government bonds, 248
Gumbel copula, 120
Guy Carpenter, 4, 246

H

Hachemeister, C., 212
Hamilton-Jacobi-Bellman (HJB) equation, 97
Hannan-Quinn Information Criterion (HQIC):
   BIC and, 191
   in Instrat®, 115
Hartwig, R. P., 228
Haubenstock, Michael, 158
Hayne, Roger, 208
Hayne's model, 208
Hazard risk:
   insurance, 5
   reinsurance and, 55
Heavy Right Tail (HRT) copula, 18, 118, 120–121
Heckman, P., 187
Hertz, David B., 164, 165
HFB (see Hodes-Feldblum-Blumsohn's model)
Hibbert, Mowbray and Turnbull model, 248, 251
HIH Royal Commission, 147, 148
HJB (Hamilton-Jacobi-Bellman) equation, 97
Hodes-Feldblum-Blumsohn's (HFB) model, 207, 216
Homogenous data, 198
HQIC (see Hannan-Quinn Information Criterion)
HR (human resources), 156
HRT copula (see Heavy Right Tail copula)
Human resources (HR), 156

I

IAIS (International Association of Insurance Supervision), 3
ICAS (see Individual Capital Adequacy Standards)
IIA (Institute of Internal Auditors), 157
Incentive programs:
  disadvantages of, 156
  in insurance industry, 156
  for management, 155–156
  for underwriters, 152
Incomplete markets, 33
Indifference, 28
Individual Capital Adequacy Standards (ICAS), 3, 244
Industry, in SRM, 164, 165
Inefficiency, in IRM implementation, 105
Inflation:
  dependencies and, 17–18
  trend model for, 110–111
Information matrix, 113
Initial scope, 103
Inputs, 103, 107
Institute of Internal Auditors (IIA), 157
Instrat®:
  for dependent losses modeling, 117
  HQIC in, 115
Insurance:
  capital in, 229
  for catastrophes, 97
  hazard risk, 5
  modeling for, 108
  modeling risks in, 108
Insurance hazard risk, 5
Insurance industry:
  99th percentile of, 20
  asset-liability management in, 49
  incentives in, 156
  liabilities of, 49–50
  regulatory and rating agency modeling in, 2–3
Insurance Regulatory Information System (IRIS) tests, 43
Insurers, 4
  failure of, 148
  KRIs for, 158
  operational risk in, 147–148
  profitability for, 230
  strategic risk examples for, 165–167
  value of, 19
Intellectual property, 152
Internal control, 157, 158
Internal enterprise-wide risk models, 2
Internal fraud, 144
Internal risk model (IRM), 26–30, 102–107
  capital allocation, 29–30
  corporate decision making with, 26–30
  corporate risk in, 27–29
  corporate risk tolerance, 27–29
  cost benefit analysis (CBA) for mitigation, 30
  impact of, 106
  implementation of, 102–107
  integration of, 107
  maintenance of, 107
  parameter development for, 103–105
  scope of, 102–103
  staffing for, 102–103
  validation/testing of, 104
Internal sell, 105
International Association of Insurance Supervision (IAIS), 3
Inverse Gamma distributions, 187
Inverse Gaussian distribution, 176
Inverse Weibull distributions, 186
Investment market risk, 15, 247–253
  bond models for, 248–251
  for foreign exchange, 252–253
  modeling approaches for, 247
  for real estate, 252
  for share prices, 251–252
IRIS (Insurance Regulatory Information System) tests, 43
IRM (see Internal risk model)
IT failure risk, 156

J

Joint Burr distribution, 120–121

K

Key risk indicators (KRIs), 158
Klugman, Stuart, 176
Knight, F. H., 163
Kou, S., 252
Kreps, Rodney, 11, 117
Kreps method, 207
KRIs (key risk indicators), 158

L

Labeling, 31
LAE (loss adjustment expense), 139
Lawsuits, 157
Lemur Insurance, 148–150
Leverage ratios, 43–44
Lévy process, 83, 252
Liabilities:
    asset risk and, 15
    of insurance industry, 49–50
Likelihood function, 189
Line of business (LOB), 168–169
Link estimates, 203
Link ratio (age-to-age factor), 200–201
Link ratio models, 200–201
Liquidity management, 86
LOB (line of business), 168–169
Loglogistic distributions, 186
Løkka, A., 85
Loss(es):
    of credit, 244–245
    dependent, 117–118
    directly incurred, 139
    directly paid, 139
    simulation of, 130
    unpaid, 197–199
Loss adjustment expense (LAE), 139
Loss distribution, 189
"Loss Distributions", 176
Loss expenses (see Loss reserves)
Loss frequency, 11
Loss reserves (loss expenses), 14–15, 73–74, 197

Loss reserves risk models, 197–210
    calendar time and, 203
    data in, 198–200
    point estimate models, 200–203
    testing, 203–205
    volatility (stochastic) models, 205–210
Loss triangle modeling, 199

M

Mack, Thomas, 203, 204, 206–207
Mack's variance formula, 206–207
Macro-economic model, 111
Madsen, C. K., 230
Maintenance, of IRM, 107
Management, 155
Management incentives, 156
Mango, Donald F., 30
Manufacturing, 156–157
Marginal method, for risk decomposition, 37–38
Marginal risk attribution, 37–38
Market, incomplete, 33
Market price, of risk, 28
Market risk
    (see Investment market risk)
Market value, 26
    decision making and, 26
    reinsurance and, 78–79
    of risks, 41
McDonald, J., 176, 177
M-curve, 82, 95
Mean-variance efficient investment frontier, 16
Medical Liability Monitor, 230
Merton, Robert, 30, 41, 84
Metrics (risk), 52
Meyers, Glenn, 187
Miller, Kent D., 7, 163, 164
Mitigation, 30
MM1 copula, 126, 127
MM2 copula, 127
Model risks:
    in insurance modeling, 108
    parameter uncertainty and, 115–116

Model(s) and modeling, 24–99
  actuarial risk, 25
  for asset-liability management, 49–55
  bond, 248–251
  for bonds, 16
  bootstrap, 216
  Bornhuetter-Ferguson model, 202–203
  for capital allocation, 34–36
  confidence in, 9
  for copulas, 118–123
  corporate decision making using, 24–30
  for dependencies, 17–18, 117–129
  for dependent losses, 117–118
  econometric, 232–234
  enterprise risk model, 24–30 (See also Enterprise risk models)
  for equities, 16
  FLAVORED, 80–99
    for foreign exchange, 16
    goal of, 116
    for insurance, 108
    internal enterprise-wide risk models, 2
    internal risk model, 26–30, 102–107
    for investment market risk, 247
    link ratio models, 200–201
    loss reserve risk models, 197–210
    loss triangle, 199
  Murphy's model, 216
    for operational risk, 159–160
    for parameter uncertainty, 108–116
    parameterized models, 55
    point estimate models, 200–203
    Poisson-constant severity model, 211–212
    regime-change models, 252
    from regulatory and rating agencies, 42–49
    regulatory and rating agency modeling, 2–3
  for reinsurance value measure, 55–79
  for reserve estimates, 212–218
  for risk measures, 31–34
  simulation, 130–138
  Standard & Poor's, 46
  technical modeling, 232–234
  uncertainty, for catastrophes, 14
  unconditional models, 211
  for underwriting cycle, 232–234
  volatility (stochastic) models, 205–210
Modeling (see Models and modeling)
Modeling approach, to ALM, 52–54
Modeling software, for IRM, 105
Modigliani & Miller theorem, 83–85
Moment-based risk measures, 32
Monitoring, solvency, 43, 47
Moody's rating agency, 3
Multiple deductibles, 194–195
Multivariate copulas, 125–126
Murphy, Daniel, 209
Murphy's model, 208, 216

N

National Association of Insurance Commissioners (NAIC), 2
National Indemnity, 155
Natural catastrophes, 14
Negative moments, 182
Negligence, 145
99th percentile, 20
Normal copula, 18, 121

O

Office of the Comptroller of Currency (OCC), 162
Operation Riskdate eXchange Association (ORX), 147
Operational risks, 6, 10, 144–160
  agency theory for, 155–156
  in banking, 156–157
  control self-assessment (CSA) for, 157

cycle management and, 150–152
defined, 6
definition of, 144–147
general, 156–157
in insurers, 147–148
of intellectual property, 152
key risk indicators (KRIs) for, 158
in manufacturing, 156–157
modeling for, 159–160
overreaction to, 152
owner education on, 153–155
reserve deficiencies and, 148–150
in Six Sigma, 158–159
underwriter incentives and, 152
Opinion leaders, 105
Optimal dividends, 82
"Optionality," 230
ORIC (Association of British Insurers Operational Risk Insurance Consortium), 147
ORX (Operation Riskdate eXchange Association), 147
Outliers, 194
Outputs, 103, 107
Overhead expense ratio, 153
Overreaction, 152
Owners, 153–155

P

Parameter(s):
 for internal risk model (IRM), 103–105
 in PCS model, 220
 reduction of, 220–222
 for reserve estimates, 220–222
 of severity distributions, 181–186
Parameter risks, 11
 estimation risk, 12
 event risks, 13
 impact of, 108–109
 parameter uncertainty and, 108–109
 projection risks, 12, 109–113
 systematic risks, 13
 underwriting for, 11
Parameter uncertainty, 108–116

in distributions, 189–190
 estimation risk and, 113–115
 model risk and, 115–116
 models for, 108–116
 parameter risk and, 108–109
 projection models for, 116
 projection risk and, 109–113
Parameterized models, 55
Pareto distributions:
 ballasted, 114, 186
 MLE for, 193
 for risk analysis, 114
 simple, 187
 uniform, 187
Pay, willingness to (see Willingness to pay)
PCS model (see Poisson-constant severity model)
PDFs (probability density functions), 74–75
Pension funding, 156
People failure, 150
Performance assessment, 151
Performance improvement, 151–152
Perold, Andre, 30, 41
PETNB (Poisson extended truncated negative binomial), 188
Peura, S., 84, 85
Physical assets, 145
Pilot testing, 106
Plan estimates, 168
Planning, 167–171
PML (probably maximum loss), 2
Point estimate models:
 Bornhuetter-Ferguson model, 202–203
 expected loss ratio method in, 200
 link ratio models, 200–201
 loss reserve risk models, 200–203
Poisson distributions, 187
Poisson extended truncated negative binomial (PETNB), 188

Poisson-constant severity (PCS) model:
   for comparisons of, 216–217
   parameters in, 220
   for reserve estimates, 211–212
Portfolio concepts, 28
Positive moments, 181
PP-plot, 223
Practical models, 69, 70
Premiums, 153
Price competition, 226
Pricing, 229
   arbitage-free, 84, 248
   Black-Scholes options pricing, 33
   competition with, 226–227
   for government bonds, 248
   in incomplete markets, 33
   investment market risk for, 251–252
   of risk, 28
   share, 251–252
Pricing risks, 11
Priority, 105, 106
Probabilistic reality, 15
Probability density functions (PDFs), 74–75
Probability distributions, 223
Probability levels, 31–33
Probability transforms, 33–34
Probably maximum loss (PML), 2
Process management, 145
Production, risk indicators in, 158
Production incentives, 156
Professional Practices Pamphlet, 157
Profitability, risk-adjusted, 21
Projection models, 116
Projection risks, 12, 109–113
   in insurance modeling, 108
   modeling for, 108
   parameter uncertainty and, 109–113
   trend model for, 109–113
   underwriting for, 12
Projects, in SRM, 164, 166
Property-casualty underwriting cycle, 227
Property-liability companies, 15

Proportional reinsurance, 91–92
Prototypical events, 132
"Pure insurance risk," 149

Q
Quarterly reporting, 131

R
Random mode (event generator), 133
RAROC (Risk-Adjusted Return on Capital), 29
Rating agency, modeling by (see Regulatory and rating agency modeling)
RBC (see Risk-based capital)
Real estate, 252
Receivable risk, 244–246
Regime-change models, 252
Regulatory and rating agency modeling, 2–3
   A.M. Best, 46
   for Basel Committee, 2
   Best's rating agency, 3
   capital adequacy models of, 42–49
   Fitch rating agency, 3
   in insurance industry, 2–3
   leverage ratios, 43–44
   scenario testing for, 47–48
   strategy evaluation for, 48–49
Reibesell, P., 14
Reinsurance:
   accumulated risk and, 73–78
   in ALM, 49
   as capital, 68–73
   capital and, 56
   for capital source, 48
   comparisons for, 62–68
   cost of, 69
   excess of loss, 97
   FLAVORED models for, 91–92
   hazard risk for, 55
   market value and, 78–79
   proportional, 91–92
   purchasing, by corporations, 48

Six Sigma for, 159
stability measures for, 57–62
value measurement for, 55–79
Reinsurance receivable risk, 244–246
Relative efficiency, 193
Renewals, 19
Reorganization, 228
Reporting relationship, 103
Reputational risks, 157
Required capital, 34–35, 69–70
Research:
   for asset-liability management (ALM), 55
   on strategic risk, 163–165
Reserve(s):
   as-if, 73–74
   conflagration of, 149
   deficiencies of, 148–150
Reserve estimates:
   diagonal effects for, 218–219
   model comparisons for, 212–213
   model details for, 213–218
   modeling approach for, 212
   parameter reduction for, 220–222
   Poisson-constant severity (PCS) model, 211–212
   testing, 223–224
   testing variance assumption for, 223–224
   variance of, 211–226
Reserve uncertainty, 15
Reserves risk, 14–15, 47
Resource commitment, 103
Responsive mode (event generator), 133
Return on equity (ROE), 69
Risk(s):
   accumulated, 73–78
   allocation of, 35–36
   analysis of, 7–8, 25, 164–165
   assessment of, by company, 7
   asset risks, 15–16
   business, 10
   "corner office risk," 150
   corporate, 4–6, 27–29
   critical, 7
   definitions of, 163
   double-counting of, 246
   estimation, 108
   estimation risk, 12, 113–115
   event risks, 13
   financial, 5
   hazard, 5, 55
   investment market risk, 15
   IT failure risk, 156
   of lawsuits, 157
   marginal, 37–38
   market price of, 28
   market value of, 41
   model, 108
   model risk, 115–116
   operational risk, 144–160
   operational risks, 6, 10
   parameter risks, 11–13, 108–109
   pricing, 11
   projection, 108
   projection risks, 12, 109–113
   "pure insurance risk," 149
   reputational, 157
   reserve risks, 14–15, 47
   severity trend risk, 74
   speculative, 5
   strategic, 6, 161–172
   systematic risks, 13
   tolerance of, 27–29
   underwriting for, 10–16
Risk attribution, marginal, 37–38
Risk capital, 29–30
Risk decomposition, 37–38
Risk indicators, 158
Risk management:
   forms of, 8
   market value of (see FLAVORED models)
   modern texts on, 83
   (see also Enterprise Risk Management (ERM))
Risk measures:
   co-measures and, 36–37

decomposition of, 41
exponential, 40
generalized moments as, 34
marginal impact of, 38–39
models for, 31–34
moment-based, 32
probability transforms and, 33–34
standard deviation of, 39–40
tail-based, 32–33
variance and, 39
V@R in, 39
Risk metrics, 52
Risk models:
  goal of, 116
  internal enterprise-wide, 2
Risk-Adjusted Capital (RORAC), 29–30
Risk-adjusted performance measurement, 21
Risk-adjusted profitability, 21
Risk-Adjusted Return on Capital (RAROC), 29
Risk-based capital (RBC), 2
Risk-based capital adequacy models, 42, 44–47
Robust estimation, 193–194
Rochet, J., 86
ROE (return on equity), 69
RORAC (Risk-Adjusted Capital), 29–30
Ruin theory, 82

S

Safety, 144
Scalability, 38
Scenario planning (SP):
  for asset risk modeling, 15
  strategic risk and, 167–171
Scenario testing, 47–48
Scharfstein, D., 84
Scheduled mode (event generator), 133
Schnieper, R., 230
Scholes, M., 84
Schwartz Bayesian Information Criteria (BIC), 191
Scope, of internal risk model, 102–103

SCR (solvency capital requirement), 3
SDE (stochastic differential equation), 83
Seasonality, 131
Serfling, R., 194
Sethi, S. P., 85
Severity distributions, 176
  alpha (α) parameter for, 181–182
  beta (β) parameter for, 182–183, 186–187
  beta transformations, 177–181
  estimating parameters for, 113
  math background for, 176–177
  parameters, 113, 181–186
  tau (τ) parameter for, 183–187
  theta (Θ) parameter for, 186–187
  underwriting for, 11
Severity model:
  Poisson-constant, 211–212
  trend, 110–111
Severity trend, 74, 110–111
Severity trend risk, 74
Share prices, 251–252
Shareholder value, 19
Shocks, 229, 237
Short-term treasuries, 50
Simple Pareto distributions, 187
Simplified Froot models, 86–87
Six Sigma, 158–159
Slywotzky, Adrian J., 164, 165
Soft approaches, 231–232
Solvency capital requirement (SCR), 3
Solvency I, 43
Solvency II, 44, 47
Solvency monitoring, 43, 47
SP (see Scenario planning)
SPC (Statistical Process Control), 158
Speculative risks, 5
Spetzler, Carl S., 24, 28
"Squaring," 199
SR (see Strategic risk)
SRM (see Strategic risk management)
SSE (sum of squared errors), 126
Stability measures:

for reinsurance, 57–62
surplus and, 68–69
tools for, 68
Staffing:
for internal risk model, 102–103
risk indicators for, 158
risks in, 156
Stagnation, in SRM, 164, 166
Stanard, J., 212
Stanard-Buhlmann (Cape Cod) Method, 202
Standard & Poor's:
ERM program, 3
models of, 46
Standard deviation:
of risk measures, 39–40
as volatility measure, 59
Statistical Process Control (SPC), 158
Stein, J., 84
Stewart, B. D.:
on line of insurance business, 228
on pricing, 226–227
on property-casualty underwriting, 227
Stochastic differential equation (SDE), 83
Stochastic generators, 247
Stochastic models (see Volatility models)
Stop-loss, 41, 59
Strategic decision making, 8, 164
Strategic error, 165
Strategic risk (SR), 6, 161–172
definition of, 161–164
elements of, 164
history of, 161–163
for insurers, examples, 165–167
OCC definition of, 162, 163
research on, 163–165
scenario planning and, 167–171
Strategic risk management (SRM), 163, 164
Strategy: for capital adequacy models, 48–49

GIRO Working Party definition of, 162
testing, 170–171
Sum of squared errors (SSE), 126
Supply and demand:
in econometric modeling, 235–237
in underwriting cycle, 229, 235–237
Surplus, stability and, 68–69
System failures, 145
Systematic risks, 13

T

Tail dependencies, 17
Tail value at risk (TV@R), 20
as business unit contribution measure, 36
calculating, 34
for EPD, 33
scalability of, 38
Tail-based risk measures, 32–33
Taksar, M. I., 85
Tau (τ) parameters, 177, 178, 183–187
t-copula, 125, 126
t-distribution, 208
Technical modeling, 232–234
Technology, in SRM, 164, 165
Testing:
of loss reserve risk models, 203–205
for reserve estimates, 223–224
Theoretical models, for required capital, 69
Theories, of underwriting cycle, 229
Theta (Θ) parameters, 186–187
Thomas, Howard, 163–165
Threshold values, 70
Time series, trend model as, 111–113
Timeline:
formulation of, 130–131
for IRM, 103
Timeline simulation, 130–138
basics of, 131–133
essence of, 130
examples of, 135–138
operation of, 133–134
in practice, 131–133

properties of, 130–131
Tolerance:
   of corporate risk, 27–29
   of risks, by firms, 28
Total Quality Management (TQM), 158
"Toward a Contingency Model of Strategic Risk Taking" (Baird and Thomas), 163
TQM (Total Quality Management), 158
Transaction processing, 145
Transformed Beta and Gamma Distributions and Aggregate Losses (Venter), 11
Treasuries, short-term, 50
Trend lines, 109
Trend model:
   for inflation, 110–111
   for projection risk, 109–113
   for severity, 110–111
   as time series, 111–113
"True economics," 52
TV@R (see Tail value at risk)

U

UK Enhanced Capital Ratio, 46
Uncertainty:
   categories of, 7
   corporate decision making under, 24–26
   models for, 108–116
   parameter (see Parameter uncertainty)
   reserve, 15
Unconditional models, 211
Underwriting:
   for asset risk, 15–16
   for catastrophe modeling uncertainty, 14
   in enterprise risk models, 10–16
   for estimation risk, 12
   for event risk, 13
   incentives for, 152
   for loss frequency, 11
   operational risk and, 152
   for parameter risk, 11
   for pricing risk, 11
   for projection risk, 12
   for reserves risk, 14–15
   risks in, 10–16
   for severity distributions, 11
   Six Sigma for, 159
   strategies for, 229
   for systematic risk, 13
Underwriting cycle:
   capacity constraints in, 229
   capital flows in, 237–238
   competition in, 229
   competitor intelligence and, 231
   components of, 238–239
   econometric modeling for, 232–234
   economic linkages in, 230
   institutional factors of, 229
   modeling approaches to, 226–240
   modeling styles for, 231
   phenomenology of, 226–228
   shocks in, 229
   soft approaches to, 231–232
   supply and demand in, 229, 235–237
   technical modeling for, 232–234
   theories of, 229
   variable selection for, 230
Uniform Pareto distributions, 187
Unpaid losses, 55, 197–199
Updating, for IRM, 107
Upper breakdown points, 193

V

Validation, for IRM, 105
Value:
   to shareholder, 19
   threshold, 70
Value at risk (V@R), 20, 33
   at 99th percentile, 20
   for economic capital, 31–32
   in risk measures, 39
Value of default option, 33
Vanilla model, 90–91
Variable selection, 230

Variance, 36
    of reserve estimates, 211–226
    risk measures and, 39
Variance assumption, 223–224
Variation, coefficient of, 108
VARMAX, 233
Venter, Gary:
    on bond markets, 248
    on liabilities, 50–51
    on model testing, 204
    on reinsurance, 55
    on severity distributions, 11, 176
    on volatility models, 206
Verheyen, Mark, 148, 158
Verrall, Richard, 207
Verrall and England's model, 207
Villeneuve, S., 86
Volatility:
    management of, 166
    measures of, 59
Volatility (stochastic) models, 205–210
    bootstrap models, 207
    Hayne's model, 208
    Hodes, Feldblum, and Blumsohn's model, 207
    Mack's variance formula, 206–207
    Murphy's model, 208
    Verrall and England's model, 207
    Zehnwirth's model, 208–210
V@R (see Value at risk)

W

Walls, Michael R., 28
Wang transform, 33
Weibull distributions, inverse, 186
Weighted excess tail value at risk (WXTV@R), 34
Weighted tail value at risk (WTV@R), 34
Weighted value at risk (WV@R), 34
Willingness to pay, 244–246
    discussed, 245–246
    industry benefits of, 246
    preliminary work for, 246
"Winner's curse," 229
Workplace safety, 144
WTV@R (weighted tail value at risk), 34
WV@R (weighted value at risk), 34
WXTV@R (weighted excess tail value at risk), 34

X

XOL (excess of loss) reinsurance, 97
XTV@R (see Excess tail value at risk)

Z

Zehnwirth, Ben, 203, 208
Zehnwirth's model, 208–210
Zervos, M., 85

About the Authors

PAUL J. BREHM
Paul Brehm is a Managing Director of the Instrat® unit at Guy Carpenter & Company, LLC. Paul has more than 20 years of experience in product pricing, forecasting, reserving, reinsurance, catastrophe modeling and portfolio management.

Paul is a Fellow of the Casualty Actuarial Society (CAS) and a member of the American Academy of Actuaries. He has chaired the CAS Valuation, Finance and Investment Committee, and was an original member of its ERM Committee.

Paul has authored a number of articles relating to pricing, reserving, risk transfer and financial models. He earned a B.S. in economics from the University of Minnesota.

SPENCER M. GLUCK
Spencer Gluck is a Senior Vice President in the Instrat® unit at Guy Carpenter & Company, LLC. Spencer has 30 years of industry experience and has worked with many lines of business as well as complex alternative risk transfer and capital markets transactions.

Spencer is a Fellow of the Casualty Actuarial Society (CAS) and a member of the American Academy of Actuaries. He has authored articles on reserving and risk transfer in the *Proceedings of the Casualty Actuarial Society* and the *CAS Forum*. He earned a B.A. in mathematics and an M.A. in education from Cornell University.

RODNEY E. KREPS
Rodney Kreps was a Managing Director and Chief Actuary in the Instrat® unit at Guy Carpenter & Company, LLC before retiring in 2006.

Rodney is a Fellow of the Casualty Actuarial Society (CAS) and was a previous chair of the CAS Committee on the Theory of Risk. He has written several papers for the association's journal, including two that have won CAS's prestigious Dorweiler Prize: "Investment-Equivalent Reinsurance Pricing" (1998) and "Riskiness Leverage Models" (2005).

Rodney earned a B.S. from Stanford University and a Ph.D. in theoretical physics from Princeton University. He also acquired tenure as an associate professor of physics at Princeton.

JOHN A. MAJOR
John Major is a Senior Vice President at Guy Carpenter & Company, LLC. John was responsible for the technical development behind the Guy Carpenter Catastrophe Index, which received the "1997 Innovation of the Year Award" from *The Review Worldwide Reinsurance* and "1997 Top Insurance Product of the Year Award" from *Risk & Insurance* magazine.

John is an Associate of the Society of Actuaries and a member of the Casualty Actuarial Society Committee on Theory of Risk. He earned a B.S. in mathematics from Worcester Polytechnic Institute and an M.A. in mathematics from Harvard University.

DONALD F. MANGO
Donald Mango is a Managing Director in the Instrat® unit at Guy Carpenter & Company, LLC, and focuses on analysis and advice for clients and prospects. Don has extensive experience and knowledge of Enterprise Risk Management.

Don is a Fellow and Board Member of the Casualty Actuarial Society and is a member of the American Academy of Actuaries. He has authored numerous actuarial papers and is a regular speaker at industry conferences. Don earned a B.S. from Rice University.

RICHARD SHAW
Richard Shaw is a Senior Vice President in the Instrat® unit at Guy Carpenter & Company, Ltd., and has more than 20 years of experience in the actuarial, insurance and financial modeling sector.

Richard is a Fellow of the Institute of Actuaries and is an active member of the Institute's Solvency II Committee. He has presented at several actuarial conferences in the UK. Richard earned a B.S. in mathematics from Durham University and a master's degree in finance from the London Business School.

GARY G. VENTER
Gary Venter is a Managing Director in the Instrat® unit at Guy Carpenter & Company, LLC. Gary has more than 30 years of experience as a practitioner in the insurance and reinsurance industry, is the author of a number of published research articles and frequently lectures on actuarial topics worldwide.

Gary is a Fellow of the Casualty Actuarial Society and a member of the American Academy of Actuaries and has served on numerous committees. He earned a B.S. in mathematics and philosophy from the University of California, Berkeley, and a Master's degree in mathematics from Stanford University.

Steven B. White
Steven White is a Managing Director and the Chairman of the Instrat® Actuarial Best Practices matrix group at Guy Carpenter & Company, LLC.

Steve is a Fellow of the Casualty Actuarial Society and has served on its Committee for Professionalism and Ethics. He is also a member of the American Academy of Actuaries. Steve earned a B.S. in mathematics and an M.A. in economics from Brigham Young University.

Susan E. Witcraft
Susan Witcraft is a Managing Director at Guy Carpenter & Company, LLC. Her responsibilities include actuarial services, MetaRisk® modeling and financial analysis. She is also chair of the Financial Integration Team and a member of the Agriculture Specialty Practice.

Susan is a Fellow of the Casualty Actuarial Society (CAS) and a former CAS Board Member. She is also a member of the Actuarial Advisory Committee at St. Thomas University and the Editorial Advisory Committee of the American Academy of Actuaries' *Contingencies* magazine. Susan earned a B.S. in statistics from Stanford University.